Study Guide

Prepared by
R. Wayne Mondy

Human Resource Management
Eleventh Edition

R. Wayne Mondy

Prentice Hall

New York Boston San Francisco
London Toronto Sydney Tokyo Singapore Madrid
Mexico City Munich Paris Cape Town Hong Kong Montreal

This work is protected by United States copyright laws and is provided solely for the use of instructors in teaching their courses and assessing student learning. Dissemination or sale of any part of this work (including on the World Wide Web) will destroy the integrity of the work and is not permitted. The work and materials from it should never be made available to students except by instructors using the accompanying text in their classes. All recipients of this work are expected to abide by these restrictions and to honor the intended pedagogical purposes and the needs of other instructors who rely on these materials.

Editorial Director: Sally Yagan
Acquisitions Editor: Jennifer M. Collins
Editorial Project Manager: Claudia Fernandes
Production Project Manager: Becca Richter
Senior Operations Specialist: Arnold Vila

Copyright © 2010 by Pearson Education, Inc., Upper Saddle River, New Jersey, 07458.
Pearson Prentice Hall. All rights reserved. Printed in the United States of America. This publication is protected by Copyright and permission should be obtained from the publisher prior to any prohibited reproduction, storage in a retrieval system, or transmission in any form or by any means, electronic, mechanical, photocopying, recording, or likewise. For information regarding permission(s), write to: Rights and Permissions Department.

Pearson Prentice Hall™ is a trademark of Pearson Education, Inc.
Pearson® is a registered trademark of Pearson plc
Prentice Hall® is a registered trademark of Pearson Education, Inc.

Pearson Education Ltd., London
Pearson Education Singapore, Pte. Ltd
Pearson Education, Canada, Inc.
Pearson Education–Japan
Pearson Education Australia PTY, Limited

Pearson Education North Asia, Ltd., Hong Kong
Pearson Educación de Mexico, S.A. de C.V.
Pearson Education Malaysia, Pte. Ltd
Pearson Education Upper Saddle River, New Jersey

Prentice Hall is an imprint of

www.pearsonhighered.com

10 9 8 7 6 5 4 3 2 1

ISBN-13: 978-0-13-607701-5
ISBN-10: 0-13-607701-3

PREFACE

The *Study Guide* for the eleventh edition of *Human Resource Management* was developed to assist students in learning human resource management. A brief overview of each section is described next:

Chapter Description

A brief description of the chapter is provided at the beginning of each chapter.

Key Terms

All key terms used in each chapter are listed. You can test your knowledge of the definitions when you use the key-term exercise.

Chapter Study Outline

A comprehensive chapter study outline is prepared for each chapter.

Exercises

Three exercises are provided for each chapter to give you additional insight into the contents of the chapter.

You and HR

Included in this section are memos that represent typical, day-to-day matters that a human resource manager might face. You should assume the role of the human resource manager and respond with your own memos. Each of your memos should be a response to the respective incoming memos and reflect your understanding of human resource concepts and practices based on related chapter material that you have read.

Discussion Questions

These questions are tied directly to the text. If your instructor gives Discussion Questions, these questions should be beneficial in studying for the test.

Study Quiz—Fill-in Questions

Ten fill-in-the-blank questions are provided in each chapter to test your knowledge of the chapter material. If your instructor gives fill-in questions, these will prove invaluable in studying for the test.

Study Quiz—True/False Questions

Ten true/false questions are provided in each chapter to test your knowledge of the chapter material. If your instructor gives true/false questions, these will prove invaluable in studying for the test.

Study Quiz—Multiple Choice Questions

Ten multiple choice questions tied directly to the text are provided. If your instructor gives multiple choice questions, these will prove invaluable in studying for the test.

Study Quiz—Matching Exercise

For each key term, there is a correct definition. Your task will be to match the key term with the proper definition.

Study Quiz—Answers to Chapter Study Quizzes

Answers to Chapter Study Quizzes to Study Quizzes are provided in this section.

Good luck in this course.

R. Wayne Mondy
SPHR

TABLE OF CONTENTS

PREFACE iii

TABLE OF CONTENTS v

CHAPTER 1: STRATEGIC HUMAN RESOURCE MANAGEMENT: AN OVERVIEW
    Chapter Description 1
    Key Terms 1
    Chapter Study Outline 1
    Exercises 6
    You and HR 6
    Discussion Questions 7
    Study Quiz—Fill-in 7
    Study Quiz—True/False 7
    Study Quiz—Multiple Choice 8
    Study Quiz—Matching Exercise 10
    Study Quiz—Answers to Chapter Study Quizzes 11

CHAPTER 2: BUSINESS ETHICS AND CORPORATE SOCIAL RESPONSIBILITY
    Chapter Description 12
    Key Terms 12
    Chapter Study Outline 12
    Exercises 15
    You and HR 16
    Discussion Questions 16
    Study Quiz—Fill-in 17
    Study Quiz—True/False 17
    Study Quiz—Multiple Choice 17
    Study Quiz—Matching Exercise 20
    Study Quiz—Answers to Chapter Study Quizzes 21

CHAPTER 3: WORK FORCE DIVERSITY, EQUAL EMPLOYMENT OPPORTUNITY, AND AFFIRMATIVE ACTION

- Chapter Description 22
- Key Terms 22
- Chapter Study Outline 22
- Exercises 28
- You and HR 28
- Discussion Questions 29
- Study Quiz—Fill-in 30
- Study Quiz—True/False 30
- Study Quiz—Multiple Choice 31
- Study Quiz—Matching Exercise 33
- Study Quiz—Answers to Chapter Study Quizzes 36

CHAPTER 4: JOB ANALYSIS, STRATEGIC PLANNING, AND HUMAN RESOURCE PLANNING

- Chapter Description 37
- Key Terms 37
- Chapter Study Outline 38
- Exercises 43
- You and HR 43
- Discussion Questions 44
- Study Quiz—Fill-in 45
- Study Quiz—True/False 45
- Study Quiz—Multiple Choice 46
- Study Quiz—Matching Exercise 48
- Study Quiz—Answers to Chapter Study Quizzes 50

CHAPTER 5: RECRUITMENT

- Chapter Description 51
- Key Terms 51
- Chapter Study Outline 52
- Exercises 55
- You and HR 56
- Discussion Questions 56
- Study Quiz—Fill-in 57
- Study Quiz—True/False 57
- Study Quiz—Multiple Choice 58
- Study Quiz—Matching Exercise 60
- Study Quiz—Answers to Chapter Study Quizzes 62

CHAPTER 6: SELECTION

    Chapter Description 63
    Key Terms 63
    Chapter Study Outline 64
    Exercises 70
    You and HR 71
    Discussion Questions 71
    Study Quiz—Fill-in 72
    Study Quiz—True/False 72
    Study Quiz—Multiple Choice 72
    Study Quiz—Matching Exercise 74
    Study Quiz—Answers to Chapter Study Quizzes 76

CHAPTER 7: TRAINING AND DEVELOPMENT

    Chapter Description 77
    Key Terms 77
    Chapter Study Outline 78
    Exercises 82
    You and HR 83
    Discussion Questions 83
    Study Quiz—Fill-in 84
    Study Quiz—True/False 84
    Study Quiz—Multiple Choice 85
    Study Quiz—Matching Exercise 87
    Study Quiz—Answers to Chapter Study Quizzes 89

CHAPTER 7 APPENDIX: CAREER PLANNING AND DEVELOPMENT

- Key Terms ... 90
- Appendix Study Outline ... 90
- Study Quiz—Fill-in ... 93
- Study Quiz—True/False ... 93
- Study Quiz—Multiple Choice ... 94
- Study Quiz—Matching Exercise ... 96
- Study Quiz—Answers to Appendix Study Quizzes ... 98

CHAPTER 8: PERFORMANCE MANAGEMENT AND APPRAISAL

- Chapter Description ... 99
- Key Terms ... 99
- Chapter Study Outline ... 100
- Exercises ... 104
- You and HR ... 105
- Discussion Questions ... 105
- Study Quiz—Fill-in ... 106
- Study Quiz—True/False ... 106
- Study Quiz—Multiple Choice ... 107
- Study Quiz—Matching Exercise ... 109
- Study Quiz—Answers to Chapter Study Quizzes ... 111

CHAPTER 9: COMPENSATION

- Chapter Description ... 112
- Key Terms ... 112
- Chapter Study Outline ... 113
- Exercises ... 118
- You and HR ... 119
- Discussion Questions ... 119
- Study Quiz—Fill-in ... 120
- Study Quiz—True/False ... 120
- Study Quiz—Multiple Choice ... 121
- Study Quiz—Matching Exercise ... 123
- Study Quiz—Answers to Chapter Study Quizzes ... 126

CHAPTER 10: BENEFITS, NONFINANCIAL COMPENSATION, AND OTHER COMPENSATION ISSUES

Chapter Description 127
Key Terms 127
Chapter Study Outline 128
Exercises 133
You and HR 134
Discussion Questions 134
Study Quiz—Fill-in 135
Study Quiz—True/False 135
Study Quiz—Multiple Choice 136
Study Quiz—Matching Exercise 138
Study Quiz—Answers to Chapter Study Quizzes 140

CHAPTER 11: A SAFE AND HEALTHY WORK ENVIRONMENT

Chapter Description 141
Key Terms 141
Chapter Study Outline 141
Exercises 145
You and HR 146
Discussion Questions 146
Study Quiz—Fill-in 147
Study Quiz—True/False 147
Study Quiz—Multiple Choice 148
Study Quiz—Matching Exercise 150
Study Quiz—Answers to Chapter Study Quizzes 151

CHAPTER 12: LABOR UNIONS AND COLECTIVE BARGAINING

Chapter Description 152
Key Terms 152
Chapter Study Outline 153
Exercises 158
You and HR 159
Discussion Questions 159
Study Quiz—Fill-in 160
Study Quiz—True/False 160
Study Quiz—Multiple Choice 161
Study Quiz—Matching Exercise 163
Study Quiz—Answers to Chapter Study Quizzes 165

CHAPTER 12: APPENDIX: HISTORY OF UNIONS IN THE UNITED STATES
    Key Terms 166
    Appendix Study Outline 166
    Study Quiz—Fill-in 167
    Study Quiz—True/False 167
    Study Quiz—Multiple Choice 168
    Study Quiz—Matching Exercise 170
    Study Quiz—Answers to Appendix Study Quizzes 171

CHAPTER 13: INTERNAL EMPLOYEE RELATIONS
    Chapter Description 172
    Key Terms 172
    Chapter Study Outline 173
    Exercises 175
    You and HR 176
    Discussion Questions 176
    Study Quiz—Fill-in 177
    Study Quiz—True/False 177
    Study Quiz—Multiple Choice 178
    Study Quiz—Matching Exercise 180
    Study Quiz—Answers to Chapter Study Quizzes 182

CHAPTER 14: GLOBAL HUMAN RESOURCE MANAGEMENT
    Chapter Description 183
    Key Terms 183
    Chapter Study Outline 183
    Exercises 186
    You and HR 187
    Discussion Questions 187
    Study Quiz—Fill-in 188
    Study Quiz—True/False 188
    Study Quiz—Multiple Choice 189
    Study Quiz—Matching Exercise 191
    Study Quiz—Answers to Chapter Study Quizzes 193

CHAPTER 1

HUMAN RESOURCE MANAGEMENT: AN OVERVIEW

CHAPTER DESCRIPTION

In the first part of this chapter, employer branding is discussed. Next, human resource management and the human resource management functions are described. Then the dynamic human resource management environment is presented. Next, the changing role of HR and the development of the human resource manager into a strategic partner with upper management are addressed. Implementation of a strategic HR audit is then discussed. Measuring quality of hire in today's environment and measuring strategic HR effectiveness through the use of HR capital metrics is then described and human resource designations are discussed. The evolution of HRM and the evolving HR organization are described, and a description of the scope of this book is provided. The chapter concludes with a global perspective entitled "Cultural Differences in Global HR."

KEY TERMS

Branding: Firm's corporate image or culture.
Human resource management: Utilization of individuals to achieve organizational objectives.
Staffing: Process through which an organization ensures that it always has the proper number of employees with the appropriate skills in the right jobs, at the right time, to achieve organizational objectives.
Human resource development: Major HRM function consisting not only of training and development but also of individual career planning and development activities, organization development, and performance management and appraisal.
External environment: Factors outside an organization's boundaries that affect a firm's human resources make-up.
Union: Comprised of employees who have joined together for the purpose of dealing with their employer.
Shareholders: Owners of a corporation.
Cyberwork: Possibility of a never-ending workday.
Human resource managers: Individuals who normally act in an advisory (or staff) capacity when working with other (line) managers regarding human resource matters.
Outsourcing: Process of hiring an external provider to do the work that was previously done internally.
Shared service center: A center that takes routine, transaction-based activities dispersed throughout the organization and consolidates them in one place.
Professional employer organization: Company that leases employees to other businesses.
Line managers: Individuals directly involved in accomplishing the primary purpose of the organization.
Human capital metrics: Measures of HR performance.
Executive: Top-level manager who reports directly to a corporation's chief executive officer or to the head of a major division.
Generalist: Person who may be an executive and performs tasks in a variety of HR-related areas.
Specialist: Individual who may be a HR executive, a human resource manager, or a nonmanager, and who is typically concerned with only one of the five functional areas of human resource management.
Country's culture: Set of values, symbols, beliefs, languages, and norms that guide human behavior within the country.

CHAPTER STUDY OUTLINE

NOT HR BRANDING, EMPLOYER BRANDING
Branding refers to the firm's corporate image or culture. Today, branding has become a major recruitment strategy. With employer branding, it is not just HR that is involved; it is the business of everyone in the company to work to establish the chosen brand.

HUMAN RESOURCE MANAGEMENT
Utilization of individuals to achieve organizational objectives.

HUMAN RESOURCE MANAGEMENT FUNCTIONS
Five functional areas are associated with effective human resource management: staffing, human resource development, compensation, safety and health, and employee and labor relations.

MEASURING QUALITY OF HIRE IN TODAY'S ENVIRONMENT
How do you measure quality of hire? The answer is it depends on the system, the company, and the implementation.

> **STAFFING**—Process through which an organization ensures that it always has the proper number of employees with the appropriate skills in the right jobs, at the right time, to achieve organizational objectives.
>
>> **Job analysis**: Systematic process of determining the skills, duties, and knowledge required for performing specific jobs in an organization.
>>
>> **Human resource planning**: Systematic process of matching the internal and external supply of people with job openings anticipated in the organization over a specified period of time.
>>
>> **Recruitment**: Process of attracting qualified individuals and encouraging them to apply for work with the organization.
>>
>> **Selection**: Process through which the organization chooses, from a group of applicants, those individuals best suited both for open positions and the company.
>
> **HUMAN RESOURCE DEVELOPMENT**—Major HRM function consisting not only of training and development but also of career planning and development activities, organization development, and performance management and appraisal.
>
>> **Training**: Activities designed to provide learners with the knowledge and skills needed for their present jobs.
>>
>> **Development**: Process that involves learning that goes beyond today's job; it has a more long-term focus.
>>
>> **Career planning**: Ongoing process whereby an individual sets career goals and identifies the means to achieve them.
>>
>> **Career development**: Formal approach used by the organization to ensure that people with the proper qualifications and experiences are available when needed.
>>
>> **Organization development**: Planned and systematic attempts to change the organization, typically to a more behavioral environment.
>>
>> **Performance management**: Goal-oriented process that is directed toward ensuring that organizational processes are in place to maximize the productivity of employees, teams, and ultimately, the organization.
>>
>> **Performance appraisal**: Formal system of review and evaluation of individual or team task performance.
>
> **COMPENSATION**—All rewards that individuals receive as a result of their employment.
>
>> **Direct Financial Compensation**—Pay that a person receives in the form of wages, salaries, bonuses, and commissions.

Indirect Financial Compensation (Benefits): All financial rewards that are not included in direct compensation such as paid vacations, sick leave, holidays, and medical insurance.

Nonfinancial Compensation: Satisfaction that a person receives from the job itself or from the psychological and/or physical environment in which the person works.

SAFETY AND HEALTH—Employees who work in a safe environment and enjoy good health are more likely to be productive and yield long-term benefits to the organization.

Safety: Activities involved in protecting employees from injuries caused by work-related accidents.

Health: Activities involved in securing an employees' freedom from illness and their general physical and mental well being.

EMPLOYEE AND LABOR RELATIONS—The number of workers belonging to a union rose by 311,000 to 15.7 million in 2007. The union membership rate for public sector workers (35.9 percent) was substantially higher than for private industry workers (7.5 percent). A business firm is required by law to recognize a union and bargain with it in good faith if the firm's employees want the union to represent them.

HUMAN RESOURCE RESEARCH—Pervades all HRM functional areas and the researcher's laboratory is the entire work environment.

INTERRELATIONSHIPS OF HRM FUNCTIONS—All HRM functional areas are highly interrelated.

DYNAMIC HUMAN RESOURCE MANAGEMENT ENVIRONMENT
Many interrelated factors affect the five HRM functions. Factors outside an organization's boundaries that affect a firm's human resources make up the *external environment*.

LEGAL CONSIDERATIONS—Federal, state, and local legislation, and the many court decisions interpreting this legislation, in addition to, many presidential executive orders have had a major impact on human resource management.

LABOR MARKET—Potential employees located within the geographic area from which employees are normally recruited.

SOCIETY—Society may also exert pressure on human resource management.

Ethics: Discipline dealing with what is good and bad, or right and wrong, or with moral duty and obligation.

Corporate social responsibility: Implied, enforced, or felt obligation of managers, acting in their official capacity, to serve or protect the interests of groups other than themselves.

UNIONS—Employees who have joined together for the purpose of dealing collectively with their employer. Treated as an environmental factor because they become a third party when dealing with the company.

SHAREHOLDERS—Owners of a corporation. Because shareholders have invested money in a firm, they may at times challenge programs considered by management to be beneficial to the organization.

COMPETITION—Firms may face intense competition in both their product or service and labor markets.

CUSTOMERS—People who actually use a firm's goods and services. Management has the task of ensuring that its employment practices do not antagonize the members of the market it serves.

TECHNOLOGY—The world has never before seen the rapid rate of technological change that is occurring today. The development of HR technology has created new roles for HR professionals but also places additional pressures on them to keep abreast of the technology.

ECONOMY—As a generalization, when the economy is booming, it is often more difficult to recruit qualified workers.

UNANTICIPATED EVENTS—Many of the human resource functions require modification when unanticipated events occur.

HR'S CHANGING STRATEGIC ROLE: WHO PERFORMS THE HUMAN RESOURCE MANAGEMENT TASKS?
The person or units who perform human resource management tasks has changed dramatically in recent years.

HUMAN RESOURCE MANAGER—Individuals who normally act in an advisory (or staff) capacity when working with other (line) managers regarding human resource matters. Today, many HR departments continue to get smaller because others are now accomplishing certain functions.

HR OUTSOURCING—Process of hiring an external provider to do the work that was previously done internally. The market for human resource outsourcing is growing dramatically.

HR SHARED SERVICE CENTERS—Take routine, transaction-based activities that are dispersed throughout the organization and consolidate them in one place.

PROFESSIONAL EMPLOYER ORGANIZATION (EMPLOYEE LEASING)—Company that leases employees to other businesses. When a decision is made to use a PEO, the company releases its employees who are then hired by the PEO.

LINE MANAGERS—Individuals directly involved in accomplishing the primary purpose of the organization. As the traditional work of HR managers diminishes, line managers are stepping up and performing some duties typically done by human resource professionals.

HR AS A STRATEGIC PARTNER
HR professionals must assume a strategic role when it comes to the management of human resources. Tasks that CEOs want from HR include: make workforce strategies integral to company strategies and goals, leverage HR's role in major change initiatives such as strategic planning, mergers and acquisitions, systems implementation, and reorganizing/downsizing.

A STRATEGIC HR AUDIT
If HR professionals are to achieve the level of respect they desire, they must also be subjected to the audit process.

HUMAN CAPITAL METRICS: MEASURING HR'S EFFECTIVENESS
Measures of HR performance.

HUMAN RESOURCE DESIGNATIONS

EXECUTIVE—Top-level manager who reports directly to a corporation's chief executive officer or to the head of a major division.

GENERALIST—Person who may be an executive and performs tasks in a variety of HR-related areas.

SPECIALIST—Individual who may be a HR executive, a human resource manager, or a nonmanager, and who is typically concerned with only one of the five functional areas of human resource management.

EVOLUTION OF HUMAN RESOURCE MANAGEMENT
Today, the person or persons who perform HR tasks is certainly different than it was even a decade ago. As more and more companies use alternative means to accomplish HR tasks, the role of the traditional HR manager is diminishing. HR must now enter into the business of strategic HR, focus more on the bottom line of the organization and leave the more administrative tasks to technology or others.

EVOLVING HR ORGANIZATIONS
Line managers, HR outsourcing, HR shared service centers, and professional employer organizations are now handling many more of the traditional HR tasks.

CULTURAL DIFFERENCES IN GLOBAL HR
Culture differences are often the biggest barrier to doing business in the world market. A country's culture is the set of values, symbols, beliefs, languages, and norms that guide human behavior within the country. It is a learned behavior that develops as individuals grow from childhood to adulthood. Companies operating in the global environment recognize that national cultures differ and that such differences cannot be ignored.

EXERCISES

1. Interview three human resource managers from different types of organizations (for example, talk to human resource managers in a bank, manufacturing firm, or college/university). Have a list of prepared questions including, but not limited to, the following:
    a. Why did you get into human resource management?
    b. What does your job as a human resource manager entail? Describe your major functions.
    c. What skills are necessary for success as a human resource manager?
    d. What advice would you give a person interested in a career in human resource management?

2. Review the employment classified ads in the *Wall Street Journal*, *HR Magazine*, and a Sunday edition of a large city newspaper. Make a list of the types of human resource management jobs, the companies offering employment, and the qualifications needed to obtain the positions. What is your basic conclusion after this review in terms of the availability of human resource management positions and the necessary qualifications for obtaining a position?

3. There are numerous Internet sites that pertain to information covered in this chapter. Identify two sites that apply to information contained in the chapter.

YOU AND HR

Directions: The following memos represent typical, day-to-day matters that a human resource manager might face. You should assume the role of the human resource manager and respond with your own memos. Each of your memos should be a response to the respective incoming memos and reflect your understanding of human resource concepts and practices based on related chapter material that you have read.

Memo One
To: (You) Human Resource Manager
From: Manager of Manufacturing
Subject: Openings for Five New Assemblers

Please recruit and hire five new assemblers for the entry-grade assembly positions. You'll recall headquarters approved these positions last month. You have recruited for us before. Why don't you go ahead and recruit and select five for us? We've been so busy down here that we don't have time to do the interviewing. We trust your judgment.

Memo One Response
To: Manager of Manufacturing
From: (You) Human Resource Manager
Subject: Recruiting and Selecting Responsibilities

(Your memo goes here in 50 to 75 words.)

Memo Two
To: (You) Human Resource Manager
From: President, CEO
Subject: Strategic HR

When I go to professional meetings and talk to other executives, they are all talking about how their HR department has become strategically involved in the company. You have assisted with CEO matters in the past. What can you do strategically to help me now?

Memo Two Response
To: President, CEO
From: (You) Human Resource Manager
Subject: Strategic HR

(Your memo goes here in 75 to 100 words.)

DISCUSSION QUESTIONS
1. What are the functions of human resource management?
2. Define *shared service centers*.
3. Describe the role of HR as a strategic partner.
4. What are human capital metrics? Give some examples.
5. Distinguish among human resource generalists, specialists, and executives.

CHAPTER STUDY QUIZZES
Fill-in
1. _____ is an ongoing process whereby an individual sets career goals and identifies the means to achieve them.
2. _____ affords employees the opportunity to capitalize on their strengths and overcome identified deficiencies, thereby helping them to become more satisfied and productive employees.
3. Union members accounted for _____ percent of employed wage and salary workers.
4. One executive in your text said "We have seen more technological changes in the last 36 months than we have seen over the last _____ years."
5. _____ take routine, transaction-based activities that are dispersed throughout the organization and consolidate them in one place.
6. The HR professional must now integrate the goals of HR to the goals of the _____.
7. Human capital metrics are measures of HR _____.
8. The HR _____ is involved in several, or all, of the five human resource management functions.
9. Managers are being assisted by _____, the use of software and the corporate network to automate paper-based human resource-related processes that require a manager's approval, record-keeping or input, and processes that support the manager's job.
10. _____ is the discipline dealing with what is good and bad, or right and wrong, or with moral duty and obligation.

True/False
1. Selection is the process of attracting individuals in sufficient numbers and encouraging them to apply for jobs with the organization.
2. Health involves protecting employees from injuries caused by work-related accidents.
3. Direct financial compensation includes the satisfaction that a person receives from the job itself or from the psychological and/or physical environment in which the person works.
4. As a shift is made in determining who will perform the human resource functions, many HR departments continue to get smaller because others are now accomplishing certain functions.
5. The wireless industry, whose market has already surpassed that of personal computers, has created the potential for cyberwork, a possibility of a never-ending workday.
6. Approximately twenty-five percent of the Fortune 500 companies use shared service centers for some of their HR tasks.
7. Because leasing companies provide workers for many companies, they often enjoy economies of scale that permit them to offer a wider selection of benefits at considerably lower cost, due to the large numbers of employees in their pools.
8. The one-size-fits-all approach that employers can adopt will achieve greater hiring efficiency.
9. A survey conducted by NYU's School of Continuing and Professional Studies showed that on average, individuals will change careers (not merely "jobs") five times in their life.
10. Although human resource research is not a distinct HRM function, it pervades all functional areas, and the researcher's laboratory is the entire work environment.

Multiple Choice

1. What is the definition of *human resource management*?
    A. The utilization of individuals to achieve organizational objectives
    B. The process through which an organization ensures that it always has the proper number of employees with the appropriate skills in the right jobs, at the right time, to achieve organizational objectives
    C. The systematic process of determining the skills, duties, and knowledge required for performing jobs in an organization
    D. The process of choosing from a group of applicants the individual best suited for a particular position and the organization

2. What is the definition of *human resource planning*?
    A. The systematic process of matching the internal and external supply of people with job openings anticipated in the organization over a specified period of time.
    B. The process of attracting individuals on a timely basis, in sufficient numbers, and with appropriate qualifications, to apply for jobs with an organization
    C. The process of choosing from a group of applicants the individual best suited for a particular position and the organization
    D. The systematic process of determining the skills, duties, and knowledge required for performing jobs in an organization

3. What is the definition of *selection*?
    A. The systematic process of determining the skills, duties, and knowledge required for performing jobs in an organization
    B. The process through which the organization chooses, from a group of applicants, those individuals best suited both for the open position and for the company
    C. The process of choosing from a group of applicants the individual best suited for a particular position and the organization
    D. An ongoing process whereby an individual sets career goals and identifies the means to achieve them

4. What is the definition of *shared service centers*?
    A. Process of hiring an external provider to do the work that was previously done internally
    B. Centers that take routine, transaction-based activities dispersed throughout the organization and consolidate them in one place
    C. Centers that act as dispersion organizations
    D. A center that leases employees to other businesses

5. According to your text, what is the total of all rewards provided employees in return for their services referred to as?
    A. compensation
    B. direct financial compensation
    C. indirect financial compensation
    D. nonfinancial compensation

6. In 2007, union members account for approximately what percent of the private sector workforce?
    A. 37.5
    B. 27.5
    C. 7.5
    D. 17.5

7. What is the definition of *staffing*?
   A. The process called through which an organization ensures that it always has the proper number of employees with the appropriate skills in the right jobs, at the right time, to achieve organizational objectives
   B. The systematic process of determining the skills, duties, and knowledge required for performing jobs in an organization
   C. The process through which the organization chooses, from a group of applicants, those individuals best suited both for the open position and for the company
   D. An ongoing process whereby an individual sets career goals and identifies the means to achieve them

8. According to your text, what type of tasks does a human resource specialist performs?
   A. highly specialized in nature
   B. a wide variety of human resource-related activities
   C. one of the five functional areas of human resource management
   D. very repetitive

9. Which of the following is one of the tasks that a HR manager would perform in their new strategic role?
   A. strategic planning
   B. advise managers on affirmative action
   C. job posting
   D. job descriptions

10. What is the definition of *human resource managers?*
    A. Individuals directly involved in accomplishing the primary purpose of the organization
    B. Top level line managers
    C. Individuals who are responsible for the production of goods and services
    D. Individual who normally acts in an advisory or staff capacity, working with other managers to help them deal with human resource matters

Matching Exercise
Directions: On the line provided, place the letter of the statement beside the key term.

1. _____ Branding
2. _____ Cyberwork
3. _____ Executive
4. _____ External environment
5. _____ Generalist
6. _____ Human capital metrics
7. _____ Human resource development
8. _____ Human resource management
9. _____ Human resource manager
10. _____ Line manager
11. _____ Outsourcing
12. _____ Professional employer organization
13. _____ Shared service centers
14. _____ Shareholders
15. _____ Specialist
16. _____ Staffing
17. _____ Union
18. _____ Country's Culture

a. Firm's corporate image or culture.
b. Utilization of individuals to achieve organizational objectives.
c. Process through which an organization ensures that it always has the proper number of employees with the appropriate skills in the right jobs at the right time to achieve organizational objectives.
d. Major HRM function consisting not only of training and development but also of individual career planning and development activities, organization development, and performance management and appraisal.
e. Factors outside an organization's boundaries that affect a firm's human resources make up.
f. Comprised of employees who have joined together for the purpose of dealing with their employer.
g. Owners of a corporation.
h. Possibility of a never-ending workday.
i. Individual who normally acts in an *advisory* or *staff* capacity, working with other managers to help them deal with human resource matters.
j. Process of hiring an external provider to do the work that was previously done internally.
k. Centers that take routine, transaction-based activities dispersed throughout the organization and consolidate them in one place.
l. Company that leases employees to other businesses.
m. Individuals directly involved in accomplishing the primary purpose of the organization.
n. Measures of HR performance.
o. Top-level manager who reports directly to a corporation's chief executive officer or to the head of a major division.
p. Person who performs tasks in a variety of human resource-related areas.
q. Individual who may be a human resource executive, a human resource manager, or a nonmanager, and who is typically concerned with only one of the five functional areas of human resource management.
r. Set of values, symbols, beliefs, languages, and norms that guide human behavior within the country.

ANSWERS TO CHAPTER STUDY QUIZZES

Fill-in
1. Career planning
2. Performance appraisal
3. 12.1
4. 18
5. Shared service centers
6. Organization
7. Performance
8. Generalist
9. Manager self-service
10. Ethics

True/False
1. False (recruitment)
2. False (safety)
3. False (Nonfinancial compensation)
4. True
5. True
6. False (fifty)
7. True
8. False (no)
9. False (three)
10. True

Multiple Choice
1. A
2. A
3. B
4. B
5. A
6. C
7. A
8. C
9. A
10. D

Matching Exercise
1. A
2. H
3. O
4. E
5. P
6. N
7. D
8. B
9. I
10. M
11. J
12. L
13. K
14. G
15. Q
16. C
17. F
18. R

CHAPTER 2

BUSINESS ETHICS AND CORPORATE SOCIAL RESPONSIBILITY

CHAPTER DESCRIPTION

This chapter begins by discussing how HR is going strategic with corporate social responsibility followed by a discussion of ethics and the presentation of a model of ethics. Next, attempts that have been made to legislate ethics are presented. Then, the importance of a code of ethics, human resource ethics, and ethics training is discussed. The professionalization of human resource management is then described. This is followed by a discussion of the concept of corporate social responsibility and why Bayer Corporation provides an excellent example of corporate social responsibility. Then stakeholder analysis and the social contract is discussed. Next, we examine how a corporate social responsibility program is implemented, and the chapter concludes with a global perspective feature entitled "Whistle-blowing in a Multinational Environment."

KEY TERMS

Ethics: Discipline dealing with what is good and bad, or right and wrong, or with moral duty and obligation.
Type I ethics: Strength of the relationship between what an individual or an organization believes to be moral and correct and what available sources of guidance suggest is morally correct.
Type II ethics: Strength of the relationship between what one believes and how one behaves.
Human resource ethics: Application of ethical principles to human resource relationships and activities.
Profession: Vocation characterized by the existence of a common body of knowledge and a procedure for certifying members.
Corporate social responsibility: Implied, enforced, or felt obligation of managers, acting in their official capacity, to serve or protect the interests of groups other than themselves.
Organizational stakeholder: Individual or group whose interests are affected by organizational activities.
Social contract: Set of written and unwritten rules and assumptions about acceptable interrelationships among the various elements of society.
Social audit: Systematic assessment of a company's activities in terms of its social impact.

LECTURE OUTLINE

GOING STRATEGIC WITH CORPORATE SOCIAL RESPONSIBILITY
Some HR professionals have helped their careers by doing work that impacts the bottom line and focusing their efforts on corporate social responsibility. *Corporate social responsibility* (CSR) is the implied, enforced, or felt obligation of managers, acting in their official capacity, to serve or protect the interests of groups other than themselves. Many corporations are becoming CSR advocates. HR professionals that are leaders of CSR activities place themselves in the spotlight for top management to see.

ETHICS
Discipline dealing with what is good and bad, or right and wrong, or with moral duty and obligation.

A MODEL OF ETHICS

> **SOURCES OF ETHICAL GUIDANCE**—One might use a number of sources to determine what is right or wrong, good or bad, moral or immoral. These sources include the Bible and other holy books. They also include the still, small voice that many refer to as conscience. Another source of ethical guidance is the behavior and advice of the people psychologists call significant others—our parents, friends, and role models, and members of our churches, clubs, and associations. For most professionals, there are codes of ethics that prescribe certain behavior.

TYPE I ETHICS—Strength of the relationship between what an individual or an organization believes to be moral and correct and what available sources of guidance suggest is morally correct.

TYPE II ETHICS—Strength of the relationship between what one believes and how one behaves.

LEGISLATING ETHICS

PROCUREMENT INTEGRITY ACT of 1988—Prohibits the release of source selection and contractor bid or proposal information. Passed after reports of military contracts for $500 toilet seats.

FEDERAL SENTENCING GUIDELINES FOR ORGANIZATIONS of 1992—Outlined an effective ethics program.

CORPORATE AND AUDITING ACCOUNTABILITY, RESPONSIBILITY AND TRANSPARENCY ACT of 2002—Known as the Sarbanes Oxley Act, the primary focus of the Act is to redress accounting and financial reporting abuses in light of recent corporate scandals. The Act has teeth, because in the 2003 *Bechtel v Competitive Technologies Inc.* Supreme Court case involving wrongful termination under Sarbanes–Oxley's whistle-blower-protection rule, the Court ruled that the company violated the Act by firing two employees and ordered them reinstated.

CODE OF ETHICS
Most companies have codes of ethics.

HUMAN RESOURCE ETHICS
Application of ethical principles to human resource relationships and activities.

ETHICS TRAINING
The Federal Sentencing Guidelines for Organizations Act outlined an effective ethics training program and explained the seven minimum requirements for an effective program to prevent and detect violations. Ethics training is not merely for top level managers; it should be for everyone from the bottom to the top.

PROFESSIONALIZATION OF HUMAN RESOURCE MANAGEMENT
Profession is a vocation characterized by the existence of a common body of knowledge and a procedure for certifying members.

SOCIETY FOR HUMAN RESOURCE MANAGEMENT—Largest national professional organization for individuals involved in all areas of human resource management.

HUMAN RESOURCE CERTIFICATION INSTITUTE—Goal is to recognize human resource professionals through a certification program.

AMERICAN SOCIETY FOR TRAINING AND DEVELOPMENT—Grown to become the largest specialized professional organization in human resources.

WORLDATWORK—Managerial and human resource professionals who are responsible for the establishment, execution, administration, or application of compensation practices and policies in their organizations.

CORPORATE SOCIAL RESPONSIBILITY
Implied, enforced, or felt obligation of managers, acting in their official capacity, to serve or protect the interests of groups other than themselves.

BAYER CORPORATION: A QUALITY EXAMPLE OF CORPORATE SOCIAL RESPONSIBILITY
United States Bayer Corporation continues the world recognized tradition of social responsibility its parent company, Bayer AG, began many years ago. Its slogan "Science for a Better Life," lays the foundation "demonstrating a distinct kind of corporate citizenship that benefits humankind and society at large. The company has more than 300 corporate social responsibility programs worldwide.

STAKEHOLDER ANALYSIS AND THE SOCIAL CONTRACT
Most organizations have a large number of stakeholders.

> **ORGANIZATIONAL STAKEHOLDER**—Individual or group whose interests are affected by organizational activities.
>
> **SOCIAL CONTRACT**—Set of written and unwritten rules and assumptions about acceptable interrelationships among the various elements of society.
>
> **OBLIGATIONS TO INDIVIDUALS**—Organizations have certain obligations to their employees.
>
> **OBLIGATIONS TO OTHER ORGANIZATIONS**—Managers must be concerned with relationships involving other organizations--both organizations that are like their own, such as competitors, and very different ones.
>
> **OBLIGATIONS TO GOVERNMENT**—Government is an important party to the social contract for every kind of organization.
>
> **OBLIGATIONS TO SOCIETY IN GENERAL**—Businesses operate by public consent with the basic purpose of satisfying the needs of society.

IMPLEMENTING A CORPORATE SOCIAL RESPONSIBILITY PROGRAM
Social audit is a systematic assessment of a company's activities in terms of its social impact.

> **A PERSON SHOULD BE ASSIGNED THE RESPONSIBILITY FOR THE PROGRAM AND A STRUCTURE SHOULD BE DEVELOPED**
>
> **A REVIEW OF WHAT THE COMPANY IS PRESENTLY DOING WITH REGARD TO CSR SHOULD BE DETERMINED**
>
> **SHAREHOLDERS' EXPECTATIONS AND PERSPECTIVES ARE DETERMINED**
>
> **A POLICY STATEMENT IS WRITTEN COVERING CSR AREAS SUCH ENVIRONMENTAL, SOCIAL AND COMMUNITY ISSUES**
>
> **A SET OF CORPORATE OBJECTIVES AND AN ACTION PLAN TO IMPLEMENT THE POLICIES SHOULD BE DEVELOPED**
>
> **COMPANY-WIDE QUANTITATIVE AND QUALITATIVE TARGETS AND KEY PERFORMANCE INDICATORS OVER A TWO- TO FIVE-YEAR PERIOD, TOGETHER WITH THE NECESSARY MEASUREMENT, MONITORING AND AUDITING MECHANISMS SHOULD BE CREATED**
>
> **COMMUNICATE TO STAKEHOLDERS AND FUND MANAGERS THE DIRECTION OF CSR FOR THE COMPANY**
>
> **THE PROGRESS OF THE CSR PROGRAM SHOULD BE DETERMINED**

THE PROGRESS OF THE CSR PROGRAM SHOULD BE REPORTED

MULTINATIONAL WHISTLE BLOWING

Multinational companies face significant challenges when they try to encourage whistle-blowing across a wide variety of cultures. There are a number of cultural factors that discourage international employees from reporting misconduct. In parts of East Asia, members of the corporation are a family; if you view them as family members, it is wrong to report them. In Japan, lifetime employment and a strict seniority system can discourage workers from questioning management decisions, dictating, instead, that employees show unbounded loyalty to their co-workers.

EXERCISES

1. Contact an HR professional with an organization within your area. Ask whether or not the organization has a code of ethics. What are the major topics included in their code of ethics?

2. Visit three businesses in your area. Ask the owner or manager what type ethical decision they are most often confronted with.

3. There are numerous Internet sites that pertain to information covered in this chapter. Identify two sites that apply to information contained in the chapter.

YOU AND HR

Memo One

To: (You) Human Resource Manager
From: Sales Manager
Subject: Inflated Sales Expense Reports

Some of my sales representatives have asked me to sign and verify their annual out-of-pocket sales expenses so they can deduct their expenses when they do their income tax preparation.

Frankly, I know some of their expense reports are inflated as much as 25 percent, but they seem to have receipts to verify these false expenses. I'm willing to sign. No harm seeing them get a little more back from Uncle Sam. What do you think?

Memo One Response

To: Sales Manager
From: (You) Human Resource Manager
Subject: Verification of Apparently Inflated Sales Expense Records

(Your memo goes here in 75 to 100 words.)

Memo Two

To: (You) Human Resource Manager
From: Production Supervisor
Subject: Hiring Advice

A well-qualified minority applicant applied for a job in my department. I don't think my workers would want to work with this individual. How do I get out of this problem?

Memo Two Response

To: Production Supervisor
From: (You) Human Resource Manager
Subject: Hiring Advice

(Your memo goes here in 50 to 75 words.)

DISCUSSION QUESTIONS

1. Describe the model of ethics presented in your text. Distinguish between Type I and Type II ethics.
2. What laws have been passed in an attempt to legislate ethics?
3. Why is it important to have a code of ethics?
4. What are the areas where HR professionals can have a major impact on ethics?
5. How might being socially responsible behavior pay off on the bottom line?

CHAPTER STUDY QUIZZES

Fill-in
1. _____ is a philosophical discipline that describes and directs moral conduct.
2. Known as the _____, the primary focus of the Corporate and Auditing Accountability, Responsibility and Transparency Act (CAART) is to redress accounting and financial reporting abuses in light of recent corporate scandals.
3. A (An) _____ is an individual or group whose interests are affected by organizational activities.
4. The _____ is the set of written and unwritten rules and assumptions about acceptable interrelationships among the various elements of society.
5. The traditional view of business responsibility has been that businesses should produce and distribute goods and services in return for a _____.
6. In the sixteenth century, _____ said, "If virtue were profitable, common sense would make us good and greed would make us saintly."
7. _____ is a philosophical discipline that describes and directs moral conduct.
8. _____ is the strength of the relationship between what one believes and how one behaves.
9. _____ is the application of ethical principles to human resource relationships and activities.
10. The largest national professional organization for individuals involved in all areas of human resource management is the _____.

True/False
1. Ethics is the implied, enforced, or felt obligation of managers, acting in their official capacity, to serve or protect the interests of groups other than themselves.
2. An organization's top executives usually determine a corporation's approach to social responsibility.
3. The Procurement Integrity Act of 1988 outlined an effective ethics training program.
4. An organizational stakeholder is an individual or group whose interests are affected by organizational activities.
5. To overcome the negative publicity of corporate misdeeds and to restore their trust, businesses are now conducting more audits of their social responsibility activities, not just financial ones.
6. Social responsibility is about deciding whether an action is good or bad and what to do about it if it is "bad."
7. Suppose an HR manager believes it is acceptable to not hire minorities, despite the fact that almost everyone condemns this practice. This person is unethical, but perhaps only in a Type II sense.
8. A code of ethics establishes the rules that the organization lives by.
9. Ethics training is not merely for top level managers; it should be for everyone from the bottom to the top.
10. The largest national professional organization for individuals involved in all areas of human resource management is the Human Resource Certification Institute (HRCI).

Multiple Choice

1. What is the definition of *ethics*?
    A. The implied, enforced, or felt obligation of managers, acting in their official capacity, to serve or protect the interests of groups other than themselves
    B. The set of written and unwritten rules and assumptions about acceptable interrelationships among the various elements of society
    C. A systematic assessment of a company's activities in terms of its social impact
    D. The discipline dealing with what is good and bad or right and wrong or with moral duty and obligation

2. Which of the following would provide an example of Type I ethics?
    A. A board of directors considers it wrong to pay excessive salaries to the CEO, yet pays salaries that are shameful
    B. An HR executive manager knows that it is wrong to recommend outrageous compensation for executives, but does so anyway
    C. A manager knows that it is wrong to discriminate, but does so anyway
    D. A manager believes it is acceptable to not hire minorities, despite the fact that almost everyone condemns this practice

3. Which of the following would provide an example of Type II ethics?
    A. A manager believes it is acceptable to not hire minorities, despite the fact that almost everyone condemns this practice
    B. A manager knows that it is wrong to discriminate, but does so anyway
    C. An HR executive manager believes it is proper to recommend outrageous compensation for executives, despite the fact that most condemn the practice
    D. A board of directors believes it is proper to pay inappropriately high salaries to executives despite the fact that most condemn the practice

4. Which act bars for one year a former employee who served in certain positions on a procurement action or contract in excess of $10 million from receiving compensation as an employee or consultant from that contractor?
    A. Procurement Integrity Act
    B. Federal Sentencing Guidelines for Organizations
    C. Corporate and Auditing Accountability, Responsibility and Transparency Act
    D. Integrity Sentencing Guidelines

5. According to your text, what is the definition of *Type I ethics*?
    A. The strength of the relationship between what an individual or an organization believes to be moral and correct and what available sources of guidance suggest is morally correct
    B. The relationship between bottom line profitability and social guidance
    C. The strength of the relationship between what one believes and how one behaves
    D. The strength of the relationship between the Procurement Integrity Act and corporate guidance

6. According to your text, what is the definition of *Type II ethics*?
    A. The relationship between bottom line profitability and social guidance
    B. The strength of the relationship between the Federal Sentencing Guidelines for Organizations Act and organizational strength
    C. The strength of the relationship between what one believes and how one behaves
    D. The strength of the relationship between what an individual or an organization believes to be moral and correct and what available sources of guidance suggest is morally correct

7. What is a code of ethics?
   A. The strength of the relationship between what an individual or an organization believes to be moral and correct and what available sources of guidance suggest is morally correct
   B. The relationship between bottom line profitability and social guidance
   C. The strength of the relationship between what an individual or an organization believes to be moral and correct and what available sources of guidance suggest is morally correct
   D. A statement of the values adopted by the company, its employees and its directors and sets the official tone of top management regarding expected behavior

8. What is the definition of *corporate social responsibility*?
   A. Individuals or groups whose interests are affected by organizational activities
   B. The implied, enforced, or felt obligation of managers, acting in their official capacity, to serve or protect the interests of groups other than themselves
   C. The set of written and unwritten rules and assumptions about acceptable interrelationships among the various elements of society
   D. A systematic assessment of a company's activities in terms of its social impact

9. What is the definition of a *social audit*?
   A. The set of written and unwritten rules and assumptions about acceptable interrelationships among the various elements of society
   B. The implied, enforced, or felt obligation of managers, acting in their official capacity, to serve or protect the interests of groups other than themselves
   C. A systematic assessment of a company's activities in terms of its social impact
   D. Individuals or groups who analyze organizational activities

10. What is the definition of *organizational stakeholder*?
    A. Individual who normally acts in an advisory or staff capacity, working with other managers to help them deal with human resource matters
    B. An individual or group whose interests are affected by organizational activities
    C. Individuals directly involved in accomplishing the primary purpose of the organization
    D. Individual who normally acts in an advisory or staff capacity, working with other managers to help them deal with human resource matters

Matching Exercise

Directions: On the line provided, place the letter of the statement beside the key term.

1. _____ Corporate social responsibility
2. _____ Ethics
3. _____ Human resource ethics
4. _____ Organizational stakeholder
5. _____ Profession
6. _____ Social audit
7. _____ Social contract
8. _____ Type I ethics
9. _____ Type II ethics

a. Implied, enforced, or felt obligation of managers, acting in their official capacity, to serve or protect the interests of groups other than themselves.
b. Individual or group whose interests are affected by organizational activities.
c. Set of written and unwritten rules and assumptions about acceptable interrelationships among the various elements of society.
d. Systematic assessment of a company's activities in terms of its social impact.
e. Discipline dealing with what is good and bad, or right and wrong, or with moral duty and obligation.
f. Strength of the relationship between what an individual or an organization believes to be moral and correct and what available sources of guidance suggest is morally correct.
g. Strength of the relationship between what one believes and how one behaves.
h. Application of ethical principles to human resource relationships and activities.
i. Vocation characterized by the existence of a common body of knowledge and a procedure for certifying members.

ANSWERS TO CHAPTER STUDY QUIZZES

Fill-in
1. Ethics
2. Sarbanes-Oxley Act
3. Organizational stakeholder
4. Social contract
5. Profit
6. Sir Thomas More
7. Ethics
8. Type II ethics
9. Human resource ethics
10. Society for Human Resource Management

True/False
1. False (corporate social responsibility)
2. True
3. False (Federal Sentencing Guidelines for Organizations)
4. True
5. True
6. False (ethics)
7. False (Type I)
8. True
9. True
10. False (Society for Human Resource Management)

Multiple Choice
1. D
2. D
3. B
4. A
5. A
6. C
7. D
8. B
9. C
10. B

Matching Exercise
1. A
2. E
3. H
4. B
5. I
6. D
7. C
8. F
9. G

CHAPTER 3

WORKFORCE DIVERSITY, EQUAL EMPLOYMENT OPPORTUNITY

AND AFFIRMATIVE ACTION

CHAPTER DESCRIPTION

In this chapter, we first describe paternity leave for dads. Then the projected future diverse workforce is explained, followed by a discussion of diversity and diversity management and the various components of the diverse workforce. The development of this diverse workforce did not just happen; laws, executive orders, and Supreme Court decisions have had a major impact in formulating this new work environment. Therefore, the second part of this chapter provides an overview of the major Equal Employment Opportunity legislation that impacted human resource management and helped to create this diverse workforce. Toward this end, significant equal employment opportunity laws affecting human resource management are discussed; significant Supreme Court decisions affecting equal employment opportunity and affirmative action are presented, and the Equal Employment Opportunity Commission is described. The *Uniform Guidelines on Employee Selection Procedures* are then explained, and the issues of disparate treatment and adverse impact are addressed. Additional guidelines on employee selection procedures are also explained in addition to family responsibilities discrimination. The importance of presidential Executive Orders 11246 and 11375 and affirmative action programs is also discussed. This chapter concludes with a Global Perspective feature entitled "Global Equal Employment Opportunity."

KEY TERMS

Diversity: Any perceived difference among people: age, race, religion, functional specialty, profession, sexual orientation, geographic origin, lifestyle, tenure with the organization or position, and any other perceived difference.
Diversity management: Ensuring factors are in place to provide for and encourage the continued development of a diverse workforce by melding these actual and perceived differences among workers to achieve maximum productivity.
Dual-career family: Situation in which both husband and wife have jobs and family responsibilities.
Glass ceiling: Invisible barrier in organizations that prevents many women and minorities from achieving top-level management positions.
Disparate treatment: Occurs when an employer treats some people less favorably than others because of race, religion, sex, national origin, or age.
Adverse impact: This concept established by the *Uniform Guidelines* occurs if women and minorities are not hired at the rate of at least 80 percent of the best-achieving group.
Family responsibilities discrimination: Discrimination against employees based on their obligations to care for family members.
Executive order: Directive issued by the president that has the force and effect of law enacted by Congress as it applies to federal agencies and federal contractors.
Affirmative action: Stipulated by Executive Order 11246, it requires employers to take positive steps to ensure employment of applicants and treatment of employees during employment without regard to race, creed, color, or national origin.
Affirmative action program: Approach developed by organizations with government contracts to demonstrate that workers are employed in proportion to their representation in the firm's relevant labor market.

CHAPTER STUDY OUTLINE

PATERNITY LEAVE FOR DAD
There is much to learn about making the workplace more family friendly. Companies that provide paternity leave to working dads are taking a small step to a more compatible environment.

PROJECTED FUTURE DIVERSE WORKFORCE
The U.S. labor force in 2007 was 146 million. By 2010, the civilian labor force is projected to increase to 158 million. Even though the labor force in the United States is expanding, evidently it is not doing so at a fast enough pace. The U.S. Department of Labor projects that by 2013, available jobs will outnumber workers by 6.7 million and by 2030, available jobs will outnumber workers by 30 million.

DIVERSITY AND DIVERSITY MANAGEMENT

> **DIVERSITY**—Any perceived difference among people: age, race, religion, functional specialty, profession, sexual orientation, geographic origin, lifestyle, tenure with the organization or position, and any other perceived difference.
>
> **DIVERSITY MANAGEMENT**—Ensuring factors are in place to provide for and encourage the continued development of a diverse workforce by melding these actual and perceived differences among workers to achieve maximum productivity.
>
> **SINGLE PARENTS AND WORKING MOTHERS**—Number of nontraditional, single-parent households in the United States is growing.
>
> **WOMEN IN BUSINESS**—Base of building a diverse workforce rests on an employer's ability to attract and retain females.
>
> **MOTHERS RETURNING TO THE WORKFORCE**—Today, more new mothers are leaving the labor force only to return later. To get them to return, many companies are going beyond federal law and giving mothers a year or more for maternity leave.
>
> **DUAL-CAREER FAMILIES**—Situation in which both husband and wife have jobs and family responsibilities.
>
> **WORKERS OF COLOR**—Workers of color often experience stereotypes about their group (Hispanics, African Americans, Asians, etc.).
>
> **OLDER WORKERS**—Population of the United States is growing older and will have a tremendous impact on workplace issues, because of increasing life longevity and delaying of retirement
>
> **PERSONS WITH DISABILITIES**—A handicap, or disability, limits the amount or kind of work a person can do or makes achievement unusually difficult.
>
> **IMMIGRANTS**—Large numbers of immigrants have settled in many parts of the United States.
>
> **YOUNG PERSONS WITH LIMITED EDUCATION OR SKILLS**—Each year thousands of young, unskilled workers are hired, especially during peak periods, such as holiday buying seasons. These workers generally have limited education, sometimes even less than a high school diploma. Those who have completed high school often find that their education hardly fits the work they are expected to do.

EQUAL EMPLOYMENT OPPORTUNITY: AN OVERVIEW
The concept of equal employment opportunity has undergone much modification and fine-tuning since the passage of the Equal Pay Act of 1963, the Civil Rights Act of 1964, and the Age Discrimination in Employment Act of 1967.

LAWS AFFECTING EQUAL EMPLOYMENT OPPORTUNITY
Numerous national laws have been passed that have had an impact on equal employment opportunity.

CIVIL RIGHTS ACT OF 1866—Oldest federal legislation affecting staffing.

EQUAL PAY ACT OF 1963—Prohibits an employer from paying an employee of one gender less money than an employee of the opposite gender, if both employees do work that is substantially the same.

TITLE VII OF THE CIVIL RIGHTS ACT OF 1964—AMENDED 1972—Prohibits discrimination based on race, color, sex, religion, or national origin.

AGE DISCRIMINATION IN EMPLOYMENT ACT OF 1967—AMENDED IN 1978 AND 1986—Prohibits discrimination against anyone who is age forty and older.

AGE CAN ACTUALLY BE A BONA FIDE OCCUPATIONAL QUALIFICATION—Age can actually be a bona fide occupational qualification where it is reasonably necessary to the essence of the business, and the employer has a rational or factual basis for believing that all, or substantially all, people within the age class would not be able to perform satisfactorily.

REHABILITATION ACT OF 1973—Prohibits discrimination against disabled workers who are employed by certain government contractors and subcontractors and organizations that receive federal grants in excess of $2,500.

PREGNANCY DISCRIMINATION ACT OF 1978—Passed as an amendment to Title VII of the Civil Rights Act, the Pregnancy Discrimination Act prohibits discrimination in employment based on pregnancy, childbirth, or related medical conditions.

IMMIGRATION REFORM AND CONTROL ACT OF 1986—Granted amnesty to approximately 1.7 million long-term unauthorized workers in an effort to bring them out of the shadows and improve their labor market opportunities. It also established criminal and civil sanctions against employers who knowingly hire unauthorized aliens.

ILLEGAL IMMIGRATION REFORM AND IMMIGRANT RESPONSIBILITY ACT OF 1996—Placed severe limitations on persons who have come to the United States and remain in the country longer than permitted by their visas and/or persons who have violated their non-immigrant status.

AMERICANS WITH DISABILITIES ACT OF 1990—Prohibits discrimination against qualified individuals with disabilities.

CIVIL RIGHTS ACT OF 1991—Amended the Civil Rights Act of 1964 and had the following purposes:

1. To provide appropriate remedies for intentional discrimination and unlawful harassment in the workplace.

2. To codify the concepts of *business necessity* and *job related* pronounced by the Supreme Court in *Griggs v Duke Power Company*.

3. To confirm statutory authority and provide statutory guidelines for the adjudication of disparate impacts under Title VII of the Civil Rights Act of 1964.

4. To respond to recent decisions of the Supreme Court by expanding the scope of relevant civil rights statutes in order to provide adequate protection to victims of discrimination.

GLASS CEILING—Invisible barrier in organizations that prevents many women and minorities from achieving top-level management positions.

UNIFORMED SERVICES EMPLOYMENT AND REEMPLOYMENT RIGHTS ACT OF 1994—Provides protections to Reservists and National Guard members. Under this act those workers are entitled to return to their civilian employment after completing their military service.

VETERANS' BENEFITS IMPROVEMENT ACT OF 2004—Enhances housing, education, and other benefits for veterans.

STATE AND LOCAL LAWS—When EEOC regulations conflict with state or local civil rights regulations, the legislation more favorable to women and minorities applies.

SIGNIFICANT U.S. SUPREME COURT DECISIONS AFFECTING EQUAL EMPLOYMENT OPPORTUNITY

Knowledge of the law is obviously important. However, much more than the words in the law itself must be understood. There are significant U.S. Supreme Court decisions affecting equal employment.

GRIGGS v DUKE POWER COMPANY—When human resource management practices eliminate a higher percentage of minority or women applicants, the burden of proof is on the employer to show that the practice is job related.

ALBERMARLE PAPER COMPANY v MOODY—Reaffirmed the idea that any test used in the selection process or in promotion decisions must be validated if it is found that its use has had an adverse impact on women and minorities.

PHILLIPS v MARTIN MARIETTA CORPORATION—Ruled that the company had discriminated against a woman because she had young children. A major implication of this decision is that a firm cannot impose standards for employment only on women.

ESPINOZA v FARAH MANUFACTURING COMPANY—Ruled that Title VII does not prohibit discrimination on the basis of lack of citizenship.

DOTHARD v RAWLINGSON—Impact of the decision is that height and weight requirements must be job related.

AMERICAN TOBACCO COMPANY v PATTERSON—Allows seniority and promotion systems established since Title VII to stand, although they unintentionally hurt minority workers.

O'CONNOR v CONSOLIDATED COIN CATERERS CORPORATION—Discrimination is illegal even when all the employees are members of the protected age group.

SIGNIFICANT U.S. SUPREME COURT DECISIONS AFFECTING AFFIRMATIVE ACTION

Discussed below are some of the more significant U.S. Supreme Court decisions affecting affirmative action.

UNIVERSITY OF CALIFORNIA REGENTS v BAKKE—Reaffirmed that race may be taken into account in admission decisions.

ADARAND CONSTRUCTORS v PENA—In a 5-4 decision, the U.S. Supreme Court criticized the moral justification for affirmative action, saying that race-conscious programs can amount to unconstitutional reverse discrimination and even harm those they seek to advance.

GRUTTER V BOLLINGER—Supreme Court appeared to support the Bakke decision. Court ruled in a 5-4 decision that colleges and universities have a "compelling interest" in achieving diverse campuses.

GRATZ V BOLLINGER—Court, in a 6-3 decision, said that in trying to achieve diversity, colleges and universities cannot use point systems that blindly give extra credit to minority applicants.

EQUAL EMPLOYMENT OPORTUNITY COMMISSION
Title VII of the Civil Rights Act, as amended, created the Equal Employment Opportunity Commission. Under Title VII, filing a discrimination charge initiates EEOC action.

UNIFORM GUIDELINES ON EMPLOYEE SELECTION PROCEDURES
The *Uniform Guidelines* provide a single set of principles that were designed to assist employers, labor organizations, employment agencies, and licensing and certification boards in complying with federal prohibitions against employment practices that discriminate on the basis of race, color, religion, gender, and national origin.

CONCEPT OF DISPARATE TREATMENT
Occurs when an employer treats some people less favorably than others because of race, religion, sex, national origin, or age.

CONCEPT OF ADVERSE IMPACT
Concept established by the *Uniform Guidelines* occurs if women and minorities are not hired at the rate of at least 80 percent of the best-achieving group.

ADDITIONAL GUIDELINES ON EMPLOYEE SELECTION PROCEDURES
Three major changes—*Interpretative Guidelines on Sexual Harassment, Guidelines on Discrimination Because of National Origin,* and *Guidelines on Discrimination Because of Religion*—merit additional discussion.

GUIDELINES ON SEXUAL HARASSMENT—EEOC has issued interpretative guidelines that state employers have an affirmative duty to maintain a workplace free from sexual harassment.

Faragher v City of Boca Raton **and** *Burlington Industries, Inc. v Ellerth*: Supreme Court held that an employer is strictly liable, meaning that it has absolutely no defense, when sexual harassment by a supervisor involves a tangible employment action.

Meritor Savings Bank v Vinson: First sexual harassment case to reach the U.S. Supreme Court. The Court recognized for the first time that Title VII could be used for offensive environment claims.

Harris v Forklift Systems, Inc: Expanded the hostile workplace concept and made it easier to win sexual harassment claims.

Oncale v Sundowner Offshore Services: Supreme Court held that same-sex sexual harassment *may* be unlawful under Title VII.

GUIDELINES ON DISCRIMINATION BECAUSE OF NATIONAL ORIGIN—EEOC broadly defined discrimination on the basis of national origin as the denial of equal employment opportunity because of an individual's ancestors or place of birth; or because an individual has the physical, cultural, or linguistic characteristics of a national origin group.

GUIDELINES ON DISCRIMINATION BECAUSE OF RELIGION—Employers have an obligation to accommodate religious practices unless they can demonstrate a resulting hardship.

FAMILY RESPONSIBILITIES DISCRIMINATION
Family responsibilities discrimination is discrimination against employees based on their obligations to care for family members. The increase in bias claims involving caregivers led to the Equal Employment Opportunity Commission's 2007 enforcement guidance entitled, "Unlawful Disparate Treatment of Workers with Caregiving Responsibilities." According to the EEOC, the guidance "is not intended to create a new protected category but rather to illustrate circumstances in which stereotyping or other forms of disparate treatment may violate Title VII or the prohibition under the ADA against discrimination based on a worker's association with an individual with a disability."

AFFIRMATIVE ACTION: EXECUTIVE ORDER 11246, AS AMENDED BY EXECUTIVE ORDER 11375

EXECUTIVE ORDER—Directive issued by the president and has the force and effect of laws enacted by Congress.

AFFIRMATIVE ACTION—Stipulated by EO 11246, requires employers to take positive steps to ensure employment of applicants and treatment of employees during employment without regard to race, creed, color, or national origin. EO 11375, which changed the word *creed* to *religion* and added sex discrimination to the other prohibited items, amended EO 11246.

AFFIRMATIVE ACTION PROGRAMS
An approach that an organization with government contracts develops to demonstrate that workers are employed in proportion to their representation in the firm's relevant labor market. An acceptable AAP must include an analysis of deficiencies in the utilization of minority groups and women. The first step in conducting a utilization analysis is to make a workforce analysis. The second step involves an analysis of all major job groups. An explanation of the situation is required if minorities or women are currently being underutilized. A job group is defined as one or more jobs having similar content, wage rates, and opportunities. Underutilization is defined as having fewer minorities or women in a particular job group than would reasonably be expected by their availability.

GLOBAL EQUAL EMPLOYMENT OPPORTUNITY
The global assignment of women and members of racial/ethnic minorities can involve legal issues, as these individuals may be protected by EEO regulations. American workers employed by American-controlled businesses operating overseas are still protected under the American employment laws. Women presently makeup nearly 25 percent of expatriates which is up from 14 percent a decade ago.

EXERCISES

1. You are a human resource manager with a large manufacturing firm that does a large portion of its business with the federal government with sales over $1,000,000. Your application form asks the following questions:

    *Marital Status
    *Height and Weight
    *Age
    *Sex
    *Occupation of Spouse
    *Education
    *Have you ever been convicted?
    *If you are a female, do you plan to have children?
    *Are you handicapped?
    *Work experience

    Are any of these factors employment standards to avoid? Why? Discuss as appropriate.

2. During 2009, 300 people were hired for a particular job. Of the total, 200 were white and 100 were black. There were 1000 applicants for these jobs, of whom 500 were white and 500 were black. Does adverse impact exist? What does the answer mean?

3. There are numerous Internet sites that pertain to information covered in this chapter. Identify two sites that apply to information contained in the chapter.

YOU AND HR

Memo One

To:	(You) Human Resource Manager
From:	Manager of Manufacturing
Subject:	English Only Speaking Requirement

I have a lot of complaints about some of the workers not speaking English on their break. The workers think that these employees are "bad mouthing" them and laughing behind their back in their native language.

Can I force everyone to speak English on his or her break? Please advise.

Memo One Response

To:	Manager of Manufacturing
From:	(You) Human Resource Manager
Subject:	English Only Speaking Requirement

(Your memo goes here in 50-75 words.)

Memo Two
To: (You) Human Resource Manager
From: Receptionist, Jane Smith
Subject: Request for Help

John Hart is sort of becoming a nuisance. He has asked me out for a date for the fourth time in the last four days. When I'm receiving outsiders, I find it awkward to see John waiting in the hall to get his chance to talk to me again when I'm not with a customer or on the phone. It looks kind of silly seeing him in the hall with his sheepish grin.

My first response to his date request was a distinct, polite "no thanks." After the fourth date request I said "no, and don't bother me again." However, I have the feeling he is going to come back. John is a nice guy, but I'm not interested in a social relationship with him! What should I do?

Memo Two Response
To: Receptionist, Jane Smith
From: (You) Human Resource Manager
Subject: John's Advances

(Your memo goes here in 50 to 75 words.)

DISCUSSION QUESTIONS
1. Distinguish between adverse impact and affirmative action programs.
2. What is the purpose of the Office of Federal Contract Compliance Programs?
3. What is the purpose of the *Uniform Guidelines on Employee Selection Procedures*?
4. How does the Equal Employment Opportunity Commission (EEOC) define sexual harassment?
5. What is a presidential executive order?

CHAPTER STUDY QUIZZES
Fill-in
1. The _____ prohibits discrimination based on race, color, sex, religion, or national origin.
2. A 1986 amendment to the Age Discrimination in Employment Act made employer discrimination against anyone age _____ and older.
3. Passed as an amendment to _____, the Pregnancy Discrimination Act prohibits discrimination in employment based on pregnancy, childbirth, or related medical conditions.
4. According to the _____ anyone unlawfully present in the United States for one year or more are subject to a 10-year ban for admission to the United States.
5. The _____ is the invisible barrier in organizations that prevents many women and minorities from achieving top-level management positions.
6. In 1965, President Lyndon B. Johnson signed EO _____ which establishes the policy of the U.S. government as providing equal opportunity in federal employment for all qualified people.
7. In 1968, EO 11246 was amended by EO 11375, which changed the word *creed* to *religion* and added _____ to the other prohibited items.
8. In _____, the Supreme Court ruled the company had discriminated against a woman because she had young children.
9. The _____ provide a framework for making legal employment decisions about hiring, promotion, demotion, referral, retention, licensing and certification, the proper use of tests, and other selection procedures.
10. The _____ defense means that only one group is capable of performing the job successfully.

True/False
1. Title VII covers employers with twenty or more employees for at least twenty calendar weeks in the year in which a charge is filed, or the year preceding the filing of a charge engaged in an industry affecting interstate commerce.
2. The Age Discrimination in Employment Act differs from Title VII of the Civil Rights Act in that it provides for a trial by jury.
3. The Immigration Act established criminal and civil sanctions against employers who knowingly hire an unauthorized alien.
4. Under the Age Discrimination in Employment Act, a complaining party may recover punitive damages if the complaining party demonstrates that the company engaged in a discriminatory practice with malice or with reckless indifference to the law.
5. When EEOC regulations conflict with state or local civil rights regulations, the legislation more favorable to women and minorities applies.
6. A major provision of EO 11375 requires adherence to a policy of nondiscrimination in employment as a condition for the approval of a grant, contract, loan, insurance, or guarantee.
7. In 1975, the Supreme Court, in *Albermarle Paper Company v Moody*, reaffirmed the idea that any test used in the selection process, or in promotion decisions, must be validated if it is found its use has had an adverse impact on women and minorities.
8. The *American Tobacco Company v Patterson* Supreme Court decision allows seniority and promotion systems established since Title VII to stand, although they unintentionally hurt minority workers.
9. Adverse impact, a concept established by the *Uniform Guidelines*, occurs if women and minorities are not hired at the rate of at least 90 percent of the best achieving group.
10. In *Miller v Bank of America*, a U.S. Circuit Court of Appeals held an employer liable for the sexually harassing acts of its supervisors, even though the company had a policy prohibiting such conduct, and even though the victim did not formally notify the employer of the problem.

Multiple Choice

1. What was the major impact of the Supreme Court decision in *Griggs v Duke Power*?
    A. When human resource management practices eliminate substantial numbers of minority or women applicants (prima facie evidence), the burden of proof is on the employer to show that the practice is job related
    B. Reaffirmed the idea that any test used in the selection process or in promotion decisions must be validated if it has an adverse impact on women and minorities
    C. A firm cannot impose standards for employment only on women
    D. Argument does not rebut *prima facie* evidence showing these requirements have a discriminatory impact on women, whereas no evidence was produced correlating these requirements with a requisite amount of strength thought essential to good performance

2. What act prohibits discrimination based on race, national origin, sex, religion, or color?
    A. Civil Rights Act of 1991
    B. Civil Rights Act of 1964
    C. Civil Rights Act of 1866
    D. Pregnancy Discrimination Act of 1978

3. What was the major impact of the Supreme Court decision in *Phillips v Martin Marietta Corporation*?
    A. Reaffirmed the idea that any test used in the selection process or in promotion decisions must be validated if it has an adverse impact on women and minorities
    B. When human resource management practices eliminate substantial numbers of minority or women applicants (prima facie evidence), the burden of proof is on the employer to show that the practice is job related
    C. A firm cannot impose standards for employment only on women
    D. Reaffirmed that race may be taken into account in admission decisions

4. What equal employment opportunity act had a threshold coverage of 15 employees?
    A. Age Discrimination in Employment Act of 1967
    B. Equal Pay Act of 1963
    C. Civil Rights Act of 1964
    D. Rehabilitation Act of 1963

5. What is the purpose of the Equal Pay Act?
    A. Prohibits discrimination against disabled workers who are employed by certain government contractors and subcontractors and organizations that receive federal grants in excess of $2,500
    B. Prohibited employers from discriminating against individuals age 40 or older
    C. Illegal for an employer to discriminate in hiring, firing, promoting, compensating, or in terms, conditions, or privileges of employment on the basis of race, color, sex, religion, or national origin
    D. Prohibits an employer from paying an employee of one gender less money than an employee of the opposite gender, if both employees do work that is substantially the same

6. What was the major impact of the U.S. Supreme Court decision in *Harris v Forklift Systems, Inc.*?
    A. Expanded the hostile workplace concept and made it easier to win sexual harassment claims
    B. Recognized for the first time that Title VII could be used for offensive environment claims
    C. An employer is liable for the sexually harassing acts of its supervisors, even though the company had a policy prohibiting such conduct, and even though the victim did not formally notify the employer of the problem
    D. An employer is strictly liable, meaning that it has absolutely no defense, when sexual harassment by a supervisor involves a tangible employment action

7. What was the major impact of the Supreme Court decision in *Dothard v Rawlingson*?
   A. When human resource management practices eliminate substantial numbers of minority or women applicants (prima facie evidence), the burden of proof is on the employer to show that the practice is job related
   B. Defense argument does not rebut *prima facie* evidence showing that height and weight requirements have a discriminatory impact on women, whereas no evidence was produced correlating these requirements with a requisite amount of strength thought essential to good performance
   C. Allows seniority and promotion systems established since Title VII to stand, although they unintentionally hurt minority workers
   D. Discrimination is illegal even when all the employees are members of the protected age group

8. What is the purpose of the Uniformed Services Employment and Reemployment Rights Act?
   A. Enhances housing, education, and other benefits for veterans
   B. Prohibits discrimination against disabled workers who are employed by certain government contractors and subcontractors and organizations that receive federal grants in excess of $2,500
   C. Codified the concepts of *business necessity* and *job related* pronounced by the Supreme Court in *Griggs v Duke Power Co.*
   D. Workers are entitled to return to their civilian employment after completing their military service

9. What was the major impact of the Supreme Court decision in *Espinoza v Farah Manufacturing Company*?
   A. Discrimination is illegal even when all the employees are members of the protected age group
   B. Prohibits discrimination against disabled workers who are employed by certain government contractors and subcontractors and organizations that receive federal grants in excess of $2,500
   C. Title VII does not prohibit discrimination on the basis of lack of citizenship
   D. Allows seniority and promotion systems established since Title VII to stand, although they unintentionally hurt minority workers

10. What was the major provision of Executive Order 11246?
    A. Allows seniority and promotion systems established since Title VII to stand, although they unintentionally hurt minority workers
    B. Prohibits discrimination in employment because of race, creed, color, or national origin
    C. Prohibits discrimination against disabled workers who are employed by certain government contractors and subcontractors and organizations that receive federal grants in excess of $2,500
    D. Reaffirmed the idea that any test used in the selection process or in promotion decisions must be validated if it has an adverse impact on women and minorities

Matching Exercise

Directions: On the line provided, place the letter of the statement beside the key term.

1. _____ Adverse impact
2. _____ Affirmative action
3. _____ Affirmative action program
4. _____ Age Discrimination in Employment Act of 1967, Amended in 1978 and 1986
5. _____ *Albermarle Paper Company v Moody*
6. _____ *American Tobacco Company v Patterson*
7. _____ Americans with Disabilities Act
8. _____ Civil Rights Act of 1866
9. _____ Civil Rights Act of 1991
10. _____ Disparate treatment
11. _____ Diversity
12. _____ Diversity management
13. _____ *Dothard v Rawlingson*
14. _____ Dual-career family
15. _____ Equal Pay Act of 1963
16. _____ *Espinoza v Farah Manufacturing Company*
17. _____ Executive order
18. _____ Glass ceiling
19. _____ *Gratz v Bollinger*
20. _____ *Griggs v Duke Power Company*
21. _____ *Grutter v Bollinger*
22. _____ Illegal Immigration Reform and Immigrant Responsibility Act
23. _____ Immigration Reform and Control Act
24. _____ *O'Connor v Consolidated Coin Caterers Corp.*
25. _____ *Phillips v Martin Marietta Corporation*
26. _____ Pregnancy Discrimination Act of 1978
27. _____ Rehabilitation Act of 1973
28. _____ Family responsibilities discrimination
29. _____ Title VII of the Civil Rights Act of 1964, Amended 1972
30. _____ Uniformed Services Employment and Reemployment Rights Act of 1994
31. _____ *University of California Regents v Bakke*

a. Discrimination against employees based on their obligations to care for family members.
b. Any perceived difference among people: age, race, religion, functional specialty, profession, sexual orientation, geographic origin, lifestyle, tenure with the organization or position, and any other perceived difference.
c. Ensuring factors are in place to provide for and encourage the continued development of a diverse workforce by melding these actual and perceived differences among workers to achieve maximum productivity.
d. Situation in which both husband and wife have jobs and family responsibilities.
e. Oldest federal legislation affecting staffing is based on the Thirteenth Amendment to the U.S. Constitution.
f. Prohibits an employer from paying an employee of one gender less money than an employee of the opposite gender, if both employees do work that is substantially the same.
g. Act that made it illegal for an employer to discriminate in hiring, firing, promoting, compensating, or in terms, conditions, or privileges of employment on the basis of race, color, sex, religion, or national origin.
h. Act that differs from Title VII of the Civil Rights Act in that it provided for a trial by jury and carries possible criminal penalty for violation of the act.
i. Prohibits discrimination against disabled workers who are employed by certain government contractors and subcontractors and organizations that receive federal grants in excess of $2,500.
j. Prohibits discrimination in employment based on pregnancy, childbirth, or related medical conditions.
k. Established criminal and civil sanctions against employers who knowingly hire unauthorized aliens. The act also makes unlawful the hiring of anyone unless the person's employment authorization and identity are verified.
l. Law places severe limitations on persons who come to the United States and remain in the country longer than permitted by their visas and/or persons who violate their nonimmigrant status.
m. Prohibits discrimination against *qualified individuals with disabilities.*
n. Codified the concepts of *business necessity* and *job related* pronounced by the Supreme Court in *Griggs v Duke Power Co.*
o. Invisible barrier in organizations that impedes women and minorities from career advancement.
p. Act is intended to eliminate or minimize employment disadvantages to civilian careers that can result from service in the uniformed services.
q. A major implication of this Supreme Court decision is that when human resource management practices eliminate substantial numbers of minority or women applicants (prima facie evidence), the burden of proof is on the employer to show that the practice is job related.
r. Reaffirmed the idea that any test used in the selection process or in promotion decisions must be validated if it is found its use has had an adverse impact on women and minorities.
s. Supreme Court ruled that the company had discriminated against a woman because she had young children.
t. Supreme Court ruled that Title VII does not prohibit discrimination on the basis of lack of citizenship.
u. Supreme Court upheld the U.S. District Court's decision that Alabama's statutory minimum height requirement of five feet two inches and minimum weight requirement of 120 pounds for the position of correctional counselor had a discriminatory impact on women applicants.
v. First major test involving reverse discrimination.
w. Supreme Court decision allows seniority and promotion systems established since Title VII to stand, although they unintentionally hurt minority workers.
x. Court declared that discrimination is illegal even when all the employees are members of the protected age group.
y. Directive issued by the president that has the force and effect of law enacted by Congress as it applies to federal agencies and federal contractors.
z. Requires employers to take positive steps to ensure employment of applicants and treatment of employees during employment without regard to race, creed, color, or national origin.
aa. Supreme Court ruled in a 5-4 decision that colleges and universities have a "compelling interest" in achieving diverse campuses.
bb. Supreme Court, in a 6-3 decision, said that in trying to achieve diversity, colleges and universities could not use point systems that blindly give extra credit to minority applicants.

cc. Employer treats some people less favorably than others because of race, religion, sex, national origin, or age.
dd. Concept established by the *Uniform Guidelines*, occurs if women and minorities are not hired at the rate of at least 80 percent of the best-achieving group.
ee. Approach developed by organizations with government contracts to demonstrate that workers are employed in proportion to their representation in the firm's relevant labor market.

ANSWERS TO CHAPTER STUDY QUIZZES
Fill-in
1. Civil Rights Act of 1964
2. 40
3. Title VII of the Civil Rights Act
4. Illegal Immigration Reform and Immigration Act
5. Glass ceiling
6. 11246
7. Sex discrimination
8. *Phillips v Martin Marietta Corporation*
9. *Uniform Guidelines*
10. BFOQ

True/False
1. False (fifteen)
2. True
3. False (Immigration Reform and Control Act)
4. False (Civil Rights Act of 1991)
5. True
6. False (11246)
7. True
8. True
9. False (80)
10. True

Multiple Choice
1. A
2. B
3. C
4. C
5. D
6. A
7. B
8. D
9. C
10. B

Matching Exercise
1. DD
2. Z
3. EE
4. H
5. R
6. W
7. M
8. E
9. N
10. CC
11. B
12. C
13. U
14. D
15. F
16. T
17. Y
18. O
19. BB
20. Q
21. AA
22. L
23. K
24. X
25. S
26. J
27. I
28. A
29. G
30. P
31. V

CHAPTER 4

JOB ANALYSIS, STRATEGIC PLANNING, AND HUMAN RESOURCE PLANNING

CHAPTER DESCRIPTION

This chapter begins by describing social networking as a way of getting to know each other. Next, the reason why job analysis is a basic human resource management tool is shown and the reasons for conducting job analysis are explained. Then, the types of job analysis information required are reviewed and the job analysis methods are discussed. Conducting job analysis is then presented, and the components of a job description are explained. The timeliness of job analysis, job analysis for team members, and the way job analysis helps to satisfy various legal requirements are then discussed. Then talent management, along with the strategic planning process and the human resource planning process is explained. Next, the forecasting of human resource requirements and availability is shown, and how HR databases can assist matching internal employees to positions is explained. Then, actions that can be taken should either a shortage or a surplus of workers exist are presented. Downsizing, succession planning, and disaster planning are then described. Sections devoted to human resource information systems (HRIS), manager and employee self-service, and some job design concepts are then described. The chapter concludes with a Global Perspective entitled "India Getting the Job Done, but Differently."

KEY TERMS

Job analysis: Systematic process of determining the skills, duties, and knowledge required for performing specific jobs in an organization.
Job: Group of tasks that must be performed if an organization is to achieve its goals.
Position: Collection of tasks and responsibilities performed by one person.
Job description: Document that provides information regarding the essential tasks, duties, and responsibilities of a job.
Job specification: Document that outlines the minimum acceptable qualifications a person should possess to perform a particular job.
Talent management: Process of anticipating workforce needs, managing current workers, and attracting highly skilled workers and integrating and developing them to achieve maximum workforce productivity.
Strategic planning: Process by which top management determines overall organizational purposes and objectives and how they are to be achieved.
Mission: Unit's continuing purpose, or reason for being.
Human resource planning: Systematic process of matching the internal and external supply of people with job openings anticipated in the organization over a specified period of time.
Requirements forecast: Determining the number, skill, and location of employees the organization will need at future dates in order to meet its goals.
Availability forecast: Determination of whether the firm will be able to secure employees with the necessary skills, and from what sources.
Zero-base forecasting: Forecasting method that uses the organization's current level of employment as the starting point for determining future staffing needs.
Bottom-up approach: Forecasting method in which each successive level in the organization, starting with the lowest, forecasts its requirements, ultimately providing an aggregate forecast of employees needed.
Simulation: Forecasting technique for experimenting with a real-world situation through a mathematical model.
Downsizing: Reverse of a company growing; suggests a one-time change in the organization and the number of people employed (also known as *restructuring* or *rightsizing*).
Outplacement: Procedure whereby laid-off employees are given assistance in finding employment elsewhere.
Succession planning: Process of ensuring that qualified persons are available to assume key managerial positions once the positions are vacant.
Human resource information system: Any organized approach for obtaining relevant and timely information on which to base human resource decisions.
Manager self-service: Use of software and the corporate network to automate paper-based human resource processes that require a manager's approval, record-keeping or input, and processes that support the manager's job.

Employee self-service: Processes that automate transactions that previously were labor-intensive for both employees and HR professionals.
Job design: Process of determining the specific tasks to be performed, the methods used in performing these tasks, and how the job relates to other work in an organization.
Job enrichment: Changes in the content and level of responsibility of a job so as to provide greater challenges to the worker.
Job enlargement: Increasing the number of tasks a worker performs, with all of the tasks at the same level of responsibility.
Reengineering: Fundamental rethinking and radical redesign of business processes to achieve dramatic improvements in critical, contemporary measures of performance such as cost, quality, service, and speed.

CHAPTER STUDY OUTLINE

SOCIAL NETWORKING: GETTING TO KNOW EACH OTHER
A social networking site is a Website that serves as a virtual community, where a group of people use the Internet to communicate with each other about anything and everything. Hundred of millions of people were using these sites. Because of the rapid growth of these sites, companies are having to determine if they should permit employees to use public sites at work such as MySpace and Facebook to communicate with co-workers or does the company want control access.

JOB ANALYSIS: A BASIC HUMAN RESOURCE TOOL

JOB—Group of tasks that must be performed for an organization to achieve its goals.

POSITION—Collection of tasks and responsibilities performed by one person.

JOB ANALYSIS—Systematic process of determining the skills, duties, and knowledge required for performing specific jobs in an organization..

JOB DESCRIPTION—Document that provides information regarding the essential tasks, duties, and responsibilities of a job.

JOB SPECIFICATION—Document that outlines the minimum acceptable qualifications a person should possess to perform a particular job.

REASONS FOR CONDUCTING JOB ANALYSIS
A sound job analysis system is extremely critical and is needed for numerous reasons.

STAFFING—All areas of staffing would be haphazard if the recruiter did not know the qualifications needed to perform the job.

TRAINING AND DEVELOPMENT—If the specification suggests that the job requires a particular knowledge, skill, or ability, and the person filling the position does not possess all the qualifications required, training and/or development is probably in order.

COMPENSATION—Relative value of a particular job to the company must be known before a dollar value can be placed on it. From an internal perspective the more significant its duties and responsibilities, the more the job is worth.

SAFETY AND HEALTH—Information derived from job analysis is also valuable in identifying safety and health considerations.

EMPLOYEE AND LABOR RELATIONS—Regardless of whether the firm is unionized, information obtained through job analysis can often lead to more objective human resource decisions.

LEGAL CONSIDERATIONS—Having properly accomplished a job analysis is particularly important for supporting the legality of employment practices.

TYPES OF JOB ANALYSIS INFORMATION
Considerable information is needed if job analysis is to be accomplished successfully.

JOB ANALYSIS METHODS
Job analysis traditionally has been conducted in a number of different ways.

QUESTIONNAIRES—Job analyst administers a structured questionnaire to employees who identify the tasks they perform in accomplishing the job.

OBSERVATION—Job analyst usually inspects the work being performed and records his or her observations.

INTERVIEWS—Job analyst interviews both the employee and the supervisor.

EMPLOYEE RECORDING—Gathered by having the employees describe their daily work activities in a diary or log.

COMBINATION OF METHODS—Likely, no one job analysis method will be used exclusively. A combination is often more appropriate.

CONDUCTING JOB ANALYSIS
People who participate in job analysis should include, at a minimum, the employee and the employee's immediate supervisor.

JOB DESCRIPTION
Document that provides information regarding the essential tasks, duties, and responsibilities of a job.

JOB IDENTIFICATION—Includes the job title, department, reporting relationship, and a job number or code.

DATE OF THE JOB ANALYSIS—Job analysis date is placed on the job description to aid in identifying job changes that would make the description obsolete.

JOB SUMMARY—Provides a concise overview of the job.

DUTIES PERFORMED—Body of the job description delineates the major duties to be performed.

JOB SPECIFICATION—Document that outlines the minimum acceptable qualifications a person should possess to perform a particular job.

TIMELINESS OF JOB ANALYSIS
Rapid pace of technological change makes the need for accurate job analysis even more important now and in the future.

JOB ANALYSIS FOR TEAM MEMBERS
In many firms today, people are being hired as team members. Whenever someone asks a team member, "What is your job description?" the reply might well be "Whatever." What this means is that if a project has to be completed, individuals do what has to be done to complete the task.

JOB ANALYSIS AND THE LAW
Legislation requiring thorough job analysis includes the following acts.

FAIR LABOR STANDARDS ACT—Employees are categorized as exempt or nonexempt, and job analysis is basic to this determination.

EQUAL PAY ACT—If jobs are not substantially different, similar pay must be provided. When pay differences exist, job descriptions can be used to show whether jobs are substantially equal in terms of skill, effort, responsibility, or working conditions.

CIVIL RIGHTS ACT—Job descriptions may provide the basis for adequate defenses against unfair discrimination charges in initial selection, promotion, and all other areas of human resource administration.

OCCUPATIONAL SAFETY AND HEALTH ACT—Job descriptions are required to specify elements of the job that endanger health or are considered unsatisfactory or distasteful by the majority of the population.

AMERICANS WITH DISABILITIES ACT—Employers are required to make reasonable accommodations for workers with disabilities.

TALENT MANAGEMENT
Process of anticipating workforce needs, managing current workers, and attracting highly skilled workers and integrating and developing them to achieve maximum workforce productivity.

STRATEGIC PLANNING PROCESS
Process by which top management determines overall organizational purposes and objectives and how they are to be achieved.

MISSION DETERMINATION—Unit's continuing purpose, or reason for being.

ENVIRONMENTAL ASSESSMENT—Organization must be assessed for strengths and weaknesses, and the threats and opportunities (often referred as a SWOT analysis) in the external environment must be evaluated.

OBJECTIVE SETTING—Desired end results of any activity.

STRATEGY SETTING—Strategies should be developed to take advantage of the company's strengths and minimize its weaknesses in order to grasp opportunities and avoid threats.

STRATEGY IMPLEMENTATION—Strategy implementation requires changes in the organization's behavior, which can be brought about by changing one or more organizational dimensions, including management's leadership ability, organizational structure, information and control systems, production technology, and human resources.

STRATEGIC HUMAN RESOURCE PLANNING
Systematic process of matching the internal and external supply of people with job openings anticipated in the organization over a specified period of time.

HUMAN RESOURCE PLANNING PROCESS

STRATEGIC PLANNING

HUMAN RESOURCE PLANNING

FORECAST HUMAN RESOURCE REQUIREMENTS

FORECAST HUMAN RESOURCE AVAILABILITY

COMPARE REQUIREMENTS AND AVAILABILITY

DEMAND = SUPPLY—NO ACTION

SURPLUS OF WORKERS—RESTRICTED HIRING, REDUCED HOURS, EARLY RETIREMENT, LAYOFFS, DOWNSIZING

SHORTAGE OF WORKERS—EXTERNAL RECRUITMENT AND SELECTION

FORECASTING HUMAN RESOURCE REQUIREMENTS
Determining the number, skill, and location of employees the organization will need at future dates in order to meet its goals.

ZERO-BASE FORECASTING—Forecasting method that uses the organization's current level of employment as the starting point for determining future staffing needs.

BOTTOM-UP APPROACH—Forecasting method in which each successive level in the organization, starting with the lowest, forecasts its requirements, ultimately providing an aggregate forecast of employees needed.

RELATIONSHIP BETWEEN VOLUME OF SALES AND NUMBER OF WORKERS REQUIRED—One of the most useful predictors of employment levels is sales volume. The relationship between demand and the number of employees needed is a positive one.

SIMULATION MODELS—Forecasting technique for experimenting with a real-world situation through a mathematical model.

FORECASTING HUMAN RESOURCE AVAILABILITY
Determination of whether the firm will be able to secure employees with the necessary skills, and from what sources.

USE OF HR DATABASES
Many of the workers needed for future positions may already work for the firm.

SHORTAGE OF WORKERS FORECASTED
There are several actions that companies can take.

CREATIVE RECRUITING—New approaches to recruiting must be used.

COMPENSATION INCENTIVES—Firms competing for workers in a high-demand situation may have to rely on compensation incentives. Premium pay is one obvious method.

TRAINING PROGRAMS—Special training programs may be needed to prepare previously unemployable individuals for positions with a firm. Remedial education and skills training are two types of programs that may help attract individuals to a particular company.

DIFFERENT SELECTION STANDARDS—Selection criteria that screen out certain workers may have to be altered to ensure that enough people are available to fill jobs.

SURPLUS OF EMPLOYEES FORECASTED
When a comparison of requirements and availability indicates a worker surplus will result, restricted hiring, reduced hours, early retirements, or downsizing may be required to correct the situation.

RESTRICTED HIRING—reduces the workforce by not replacing employees who leave.

REDUCED HOURS—Reduces the total number of hours worked.

EARLY RETIREMENT

DOWNSIZING
Reverse of a company growing; suggests a one-time change in the organization and the number of people employed (also known as *restructuring* or *rightsizing*).

NEGATIVE ASPECTS OF DOWNSIZING—There may also be a negative side to downsizing. First, there is the cost associated with low morale of those that remain. Second, often layers are pulled out of a firm, making advancement in the organization more difficult. Third, workers begin seeking better opportunities because they believe they may be the next in line. Fourth, employee loyalty is often significantly reduced. Fifth, institutional memory (how the organization comes across to customers in all their dealings) or corporate culture is lost. Sixth, remaining workers are being required to do more. Finally, when demand for the products or services returns, the company often realizes that it has cut too deep.

OUTPLACEMENT—Procedure whereby laid-off employees are given assistance in finding employment elsewhere.

SUCCESSION PLANNING
Process of ensuring that qualified persons are available to assume key managerial positions once the positions are vacant.

DISASTER PLANNING
Disaster plans should focus on catastrophes that range from natural calamities such as hurricanes, earthquakes, and floods to man-made crises such as 9/11. The events of 9/11 reinforced the uncertainty of today's business world and the need for disaster planning. Merrill Lynch, Morgan Stanley, Bank of New York, and Deutsche Bank, among others, activated their comprehensive disaster plans and were back up and running almost immediately after the World Trade Center tragedy.

HUMAN RESOURCE INFORMATION SYSTEMS
Any organized approach for obtaining relevant and timely information on which to base human resource decisions.

MANAGER SELF-SERVICE
Use of software and the corporate network to automate paper-based human resource processes that require a manager's approval, record-keeping or input, and processes that support the manager's job.

EMPLOYEE SELF-SERVICE
Processes that automate transactions that used to be labor-intensive for both employees and HR professionals.

JOB DESIGN
Process of determining the specific tasks to be performed, the methods used in performing these tasks, and how the job relates to other work in the organization.

JOB ENRICHMENT—Basic changes in the content and level of responsibility of a job so as to provide greater challenges to the worker.

JOB ENLARGEMENT—Increasing the number of tasks a worker performs, with all of the tasks at the same level of responsibility.

REENGINEERING—Fundamental rethinking and radical redesign of business processes to achieve dramatic improvements in critical, contemporary measures of performance such as cost, quality, service, and speed.

INDIA GETTING THE JOB DONE, BUT DIFFERENTLY
Today, India firms are not just receiving business from other countries; they are investing in countries throughout the world and creating jobs in other countries.

EXERCISES
1. Prepare a job description for each of the following jobs:
    a. data-entry clerk
    b. automobile mechanic for General Motors
    c. safety engineer

2. Visit an HR manager in your area. Ask what human resource planning process is used.

3. There are numerous Internet sites that pertain to information covered in this chapter. Identify two sites that apply to information contained in the chapter.

YOU AND HR
Memo One
To: (You) Human Resource Manager
From: Production Manager
Subject: Best Job Analysis Method to Use

As you know, it has been eight years since we conducted a formal job analysis in our assembly plant, and we've had a lot of changes. There are more than 50 different kinds of jobs being done here and several hundred people involved. With this size group, what do you suggest as the appropriate job analysis method?

Memo One Response
To: Production Manager
From: (You) Human Resource Manager
Subject: Job Analysis

(Your memo goes here in 50-75 words.)

Memo Two
To: (You) Human Resource Manager
From: Store Manager, Retail Department Store Chain
Subject: Surplus of Supervisors

Anticipated sales growth that we forecasted earlier in the year is not nearly as great as expected. We are temporarily "top heavy" in terms of first-level supervisors. I hate to terminate these newly-recruited college graduates who we trained extensively. What do you suggest?

Memo Two Response
To: Store Manager
From: (You) Human Resource Manager
Subject: Alternative (Creative) Ways to Handle Employee Surpluses
(Your memo goes here in 50-75 words.)

DISCUSSION QUESTIONS
1. Distinguish between a job and a position.
2. What are the most common methods used to conduct job analysis?
3. What are the items typically included in a job description?
4. Describe the human resource planning process.
5. Distinguish between forecasting human resource requirements and availability.

CHAPTER STUDY QUIZZES
Fill-in
1. A (An) _____ consists of a group of tasks that must be performed for an organization to achieve its goals.
2. The _____ is a document that provides information regarding the tasks, duties, and responsibilities of the job.
3. The _____ job analysis method is used primarily to gather information on jobs emphasizing manual skills, such as those of a machine operator.
4. The _____ section of the job description includes the job title, the department, the reporting relationship, and a job number or code.
5. In practice, job specifications are often included as a major section of _____.
6. The first step of the strategic planning process is to determine the corporate _____.
7. _____ is the systematic process of matching the internal and external supply of people with job openings anticipated in the organization over a specified period of time.
8. Essentially the same procedure is used for human resource planning as for _____, whereby each budget must be justified each year.
9. A (An) _____ forecast involves determining the number, skill, and location of employees the organization will need at future dates in order to meet its goals.
10. _____ planning is the process of ensuring that qualified persons are available to assume key managerial positions once the positions are vacant.

True/False
1. A position consists of a group of tasks that must be performed for an organization to achieve its goals.
2. Job analysis is the systematic process of determining the skills, duties, and knowledge required for performing jobs in an organization.
3. The job specification is a document that provides information regarding the essential tasks, duties, and responsibilities of the job.
4. The questionnaire method is used primarily to gather information on jobs emphasizing manual skills, such as those of a machine operator.
5. The people who participate in job analysis should include, at a minimum, the employee and the employee's immediate supervisor.
6. Job analysis is the systematic process of matching the internal and external supply of people with job openings anticipated in the organization over a specified period of time.
7. Job descriptions are required to specify elements of the job that endanger health, or are considered unsatisfactory or distasteful by the majority of the population.
8. The bottom-up forecasting approach uses the organization's current level of employment as the starting point for determining future staffing needs.
9. Determining whether the firm will be able to secure employees with the necessary skills and from what sources is called a requirement forecast.
10. Job enlargement consists of basic changes in the content and level of responsibility of a job so as to provide greater challenge to the worker.

Multiple Choice

1. How many jobs and positions are involved in a work group consisting of a supervisor, three machine operators, and two maintenance workers?
   A. 3; 6
   B. 6; 1
   C. 7; 3
   D. 1; 6

2. What is the definition of *job analysis*?
   A. Minimum acceptable qualifications a person should possess in order to perform a particular job
   B. Collection of tasks and responsibilities performed by *one* person; there is a position for every individual in an organization
   C. Group of tasks that must be performed for an organization to achieve its goals
   D. Systematic process of determining the skills, duties, and knowledge required for performing jobs in an organization

3. According to your text, what is the definition of a *job*?
   A. A group of tasks that must be performed for an organization to achieve its goals
   B. Collection of tasks and responsibilities performed by *one* person
   C. Minimum acceptable qualifications a person should possess in order to perform a particular job
   D. Document that provides information regarding the essential tasks, duties, and responsibilities of the job

4. Job analysis is most often performed because of
   A. new jobs.
   B. obsolescence in jobs.
   C. changes in the nature of jobs.
   D. implementation of a job analysis program within a firm.

5. What is the definition of a *job specification*?
   A. A document that outlines the minimum acceptable qualifications a person should possess to perform a particular job
   B. A document that includes the job title, the department, the reporting relationship, and a job number or code
   C. Collection of tasks and responsibilities performed by *one* person; there is a position for every individual in an organization
   D. Duties, skills and responsibilities required of a job

6. What is the definition of a *job description*?
   A. A document that outlines the minimum acceptable qualifications a person should possess to perform a particular job
   B. A document that provides information regarding the essential tasks, duties, and responsibilities of the job
   C. Collection of tasks and responsibilities performed by *one* person in an organization
   D. job specifications of HR tasks

7. How may employment be reduced in a firm when a surplus of workers is projected?
   A. restricted hiring
   B. early retirements
   C. layoffs
   D. all of the above

8. What is the definition of the *bottom-up approach* to forecasting?
   A. Uses the organization's current level of employment as the starting point for determining future staffing needs
   B. Forecasts progress upward in the organization from small units to ultimately provide an aggregate forecast of employment needs
   C. Relationship between demand and the number of employees needed is a positive one
   D. Forecasting technique for experimenting with a real-world situation through a mathematical model

9. What is the definition of an *availability forecast*?
   A. Uses the organization's current level of employment as the starting point for determining future staffing needs
   B. Determining the number, skill, and location of employees the organization will need at future dates in order to meet its goals
   C. Determination of whether the firm will be able to secure employees with the necessary skills, and from what sources
   D. Each successive level in the organization, starting with the lowest, forecasts its requirements, ultimately providing an aggregate forecast of employees needed

10. What is the definition of *job enrichment*?
    A. Consists of basic changes in the content and level of responsibility of a job so as to provide greater challenge to the worker
    B. Increasing the number of tasks a worker performs, with all of the tasks at the same level of responsibility
    C. Process of determining the specific tasks to be performed, the methods used in performing these tasks, and how the job relates to other work in the organization
    D. Fundamental rethinking and radical redesign of business processes to achieve dramatic improvements in critical contemporary measures of performance, such as cost, quality, service, and speed

Matching Exercise
Directions: On the line provided, place the letter of the statement beside the key term.

1. _____ **Availability forecast**
2. _____ **Bottom-up approach**
3. _____ **Downsizing**
4. _____ **Employee self-service**
5. _____ **Human resource information system**
6. _____ **Human resource planning**
7. _____ **Job**
8. _____ **Job analysis**
9. _____ **Job description**
10. _____ **Job design**
11. _____ **Job enlargement**
12. _____ **Job enrichment**
13. _____ **Job specification**
14. _____ **Manager self-service**
15. _____ **Mission**
16. _____ **Outplacement**
17. _____ **Position**
18. _____ **Reengineering**
19. _____ **Requirement forecast**
20. _____ **Simulation**
21. _____ **Strategic planning**
22. _____ **Succession planning**
23. _____ **Zero-base forecasting**
24. _____ **Talent management**

a. Systematic process of determining the skills, duties, and knowledge required for performing specific jobs in an organization.
b. Consists of a group of tasks that must be performed for an organization to achieve its goals.
c. Tasks and responsibilities performed by one person; there is one for every individual in an organization.
d. Document that provides information regarding the essential tasks, duties, and responsibilities of a job.
e. Document that outlines the minimum acceptable qualifications a person should possess to perform a particular job.
f. Process by which top management determines overall organizational purposes and objectives and how they are to be achieved.
g. Unit's continuing purpose or reason for being.
h. Systematic process of matching the internal and external supply of people with job openings anticipated in the organization over a specified period of time.
i. Forecasting method which uses the organization's current level of employment as the starting point for determining future staffing needs.
j. Forecasting method in which each successive level in the organization, starting with the lowest, forecasts its requirements, ultimately providing an aggregate forecast of employees needed.
k. Forecasting technique for experimenting with a real-world situation through a mathematical model.
l. Determining the number, skill, and location of employees the organization will need at future dates in order to meet its goals.
m. Determination of whether the firm will be able to secure employees with the necessary skills, and from what sources.
n. Reverse of a company growing; suggests a one-time change in the organization and the number of people employed (also known as *restructuring* or *rightsizing*).
o. Procedure whereby laid-off employees are given assistance in finding employment elsewhere.
p. Process of ensuring that qualified persons are available to assume key managerial positions once the positions are vacant.
q. Any organized approach for obtaining relevant and timely information on which to base human resource decisions.
r. Use of software and the corporate network to automate paper-based human resource processes that require a manager's approval, record-keeping or input, and processes that support the manager's job.
s. Consist of processes that automate transactions that used to be labor-intensive for both employees and HR professionals.
t. Process of determining the specific tasks to be performed, the methods used in performing these tasks, and how the job relates to other work in an organization.
u. Consists of basic changes in the content and level of responsibility of a job so as to provide greater challenge to the worker.
v. Increasing the number of tasks a worker performs, with all of the tasks at the same level of responsibility.
w. Fundamental rethinking and radical redesign of business processes to achieve dramatic improvements in critical, contemporary measures of performance such as cost, quality, service, and speed.
x. Process of anticipating workforce needs, managing the keeping current workers, attracting highly skilled workers and integrating and developing them to achieve maximum workforce productivity.

ANSWERS TO CHAPTER STUDY QUIZZES

Fill-in
1. Job
2. Job description
3. Observation
4. Job identification
5. Job descriptions
6. Mission
7. Human resource planning
8. Zero-base budgeting
9. Requirements
10. Succession

True/False
1. False (job)
2. True
3. False (job description)
4. False (observation)
5. True
6. False (human resource planning)
7. True
8. False (zero-base)
9. False (availability forecast)
10. False (job enrichment)

Multiple Choice
1. A
2. D
3. A
4. C
5. A
6. B
7. D
8. B
9. C
10. A

Matching Exercise
1. M
2. J
3. N
4. S
5. Q
6. H
7. B
8. A
9. D
10. T
11. V
12. U
13. E
14. R
15. G
16. O
17. C
18. W
19. L
20. K
21. F
22. P
23. I
24. X

CHAPTER 5

RECRUITMENT

CHAPTER DESCRIPTION

This chapter begins by discussing the trend to use CEOs in the recruitment process. Next, recruitment is defined and alternatives to recruitment are explained. This is followed by a discussion of the external environments of recruitment and promotion policies. A description of the recruitment process precedes a discussion of internal recruitment methods. Then, how twittering can be a useful tool in the selection process, external sources of recruitment, and online recruitment methods are examined. Traditional external recruiting methods are presented next, and applicant-tracking systems are described. Then the importance of tailoring recruitment methods and sources and recruitment for diversity are discussed. The chapter concludes with a Global Perspective entitled "U.S. Firms in Vietnam."

KEY TERMS

Recruitment: Process of attracting individuals on a timely basis, in sufficient numbers, and with appropriate qualifications, to apply for jobs with an organization.
Contingent workers: Described as the "disposable American workforce" by a former secretary of labor, have a nontraditional relationship with the worksite employer and work as part-timers, temporaries, or independent contractors.
Promotion from within: Policy of filling vacancies above entry-level positions with current employees.
Employee requisition: Document that specifies job title, department, the date the employee is needed for work, and other details.
Recruitment sources: Where qualified candidates are located.
Recruitment methods: Specific means used to attract potential employees to the firm.
Job posting: Procedure for informing employees that job openings exist.
Job bidding: Procedure that permits employees who believe that they possess the required qualifications to apply for a posted position.
Internet recruiter: Person whose primary responsibility is to use the Internet in the recruitment process (also called cyber recruiter).
Virtual job fair: Online recruiting method engaged in by a single employer or group of employers to attract a large number of applicants to the company.
Corporate career Websites: Job sites accessible from a company homepage that list available company positions and provide a way for applicants to apply for specific jobs.
Niche sites: Websites that cater to a specific profession.
Employment agency: Organization that helps firms recruit employees and at the same time aids individuals in their attempt to locate jobs.
Job fair: Recruiting method engaged in by a single employer or group of employers to attract a large number of applicants for interviews.
Internship: Special form of recruitment that involves placing students in temporary jobs with no obligation either by the company to hire the student permanently or by the student to accept a permanent position with the firm following graduation.
Contingency search firms: Executive search firm that receives fees only upon successful placement of a candidate in a job opening.
Retained search firms: Executive search firm considered as consultants to their client organizations, serving on an exclusive contractual basis; typically recruit top business executives.
Event recruiting: Recruiters going to events being attended by individuals the company is seeking.

CHAPTER STUDY OUTLINE

USING THE CEO IN THE RECRUITMENT PROCESS
The CEO can often be valuable in attracting the brightest and best applicants to join the firm. They have to be used at the right time, however.

RECRUITMENT DEFINED
Process of attracting individuals on a timely basis, in sufficient numbers, and with appropriate qualifications, to apply for jobs with an organization.

ALTERNATIVES TO RECRUITMENT
Firm should consider its alternatives before engaging in recruitment.

> **OUTSOURCING**—Process of hiring an external provider to do the work that was previously done internally.

> **CONTINGENT WORKERS**—Described as the "disposable American workforce" by a former Secretary of Labor, work as part-timers, temporaries, or independent contractors.

> **PROFESSIONAL EMPLOYER ORGANIZATION (EMPLOYEE LEASING)**—Company that leases employees to other businesses.

> **OVERTIME**—Most commonly used method of meeting short-term fluctuations in work volume.

EXTERNAL ENVIRONMENT OF RECRUITMENT

> **LABOR MARKET CONDITIONS**—Of particular importance is the demand for and supply of specific skills in the labor market.

> **LEGAL CONSIDERATIONS**—Nondiscriminatory practices in recruitment are absolutely essential.

PROMOTION POLICIES
Organization can stress a policy of promotion from within its own ranks or a policy of filling positions from outside the organization. Promotion from within is the policy of filling vacancies above entry-level positions with current employees.

RECRUITMENT PROCESS

> **EMPLOYEE REQUISITION**—Document that specifies job title, department, date the employee is needed for work, and other details.

> **DETERMINE WHETHER QUALIFIED EMPLOYEES ARE AVAILABLE WITHIN THE FIRM OR MUST BE RECRUITED FROM EXTERNAL SOURCES**

>> **Recruitment sources**: Places where qualified candidates can be found.

>> **Recruitment methods**: Specific means used to attract potential employees to the firm.

INTERNAL RECRUITMENT METHODS
Management should be able to identify current employees who are capable of filling positions as they become available.

JOB POSTING AND JOB BIDDING

Job posting: Procedure for informing employees that job openings exist.

Job bidding: Procedure that permits employees who believe that they possess the required qualifications to apply for a posted position.

EMPLOYEE REFERRALS—Employees can serve an important role in the recruitment process by actively soliciting applications from their friends and associates.

TWITTERING FOR THE BEST RECRUIT

Twitter is a free social networking and micro-blogging service that allows users to send updates commonly known as tweets which are text-based posts, ranging up to 140 characters long. The Twitter "achieves hyper-connectivity by filling in the gaps between e-mails and blog posts with short snippets chronicling users' up-to-the-minute thoughts, feelings and activities."

EXTERNAL RECRUITMENT SOURCES

HIGH SCHOOLS AND VOCATIONAL SCHOOLS—Organizations concerned with recruiting clerical and entry-level employees often depend on high schools and vocational schools.

COMMUNITY COLLEGES—Number of community colleges are sensitive to the specific employment needs in their local labor market and graduate highly sought-after students with marketable skills.

COLLEGES AND UNIVERSITIES—Potential professional, technical, and management employees are typically found in these institutions.

COMPETITORS IN THE LABOR MARKET—When recent experience is required, competitors and other firms in the same industry or geographic area may be the most important source of recruits.

FORMER EMPLOYEES—Smart employers try to get their best ex-employees to come back.

UNEMPLOYED—Individuals who are unemployed, regardless of the reason, often provide a valuable source of recruitment.

MILITARY PERSONNEL—Typically has a proven work history, are flexible, motivated, and drug free.

SELF-EMPLOYED WORKERS—May provide a source of applicants to fill any number of jobs requiring technical, professional, administrative, or entrepreneurial expertise.

EX-OFFENDERS—Some organizations have discovered it beneficial to hire ex-offenders.

ONLINE RECRUITMENT METHODS

Online recruiting revolutionized the way companies recruit employees and job seekers search and apply for jobs.

INTERNET RECRUITER—Person whose primary responsibility is to use the Internet in the recruitment process (also called cyber recruiter).

VIRTUAL JOB FAIRS—Online recruiting method engaged in by a single employer or group of employers to attract a large number of applicants to the company.

CORPORATE CAREER WEBSITE—Job sites accessible from a company homepage that list available company positions and provide a way for applicants to apply for specific jobs.

.JOBS DOMAIN—A company registers part of its corporate name online and job candidates can access it more quickly than they could if they had to go directly to the organization's Website and then look for the jobs page.

WEBLOGS (BLOGS FOR SHORT)—Weblogs, or *blogs*, have changed the ways in which individuals access information. Google or a blog search engine such as Technorati.com can be used.

General-Purpose Job Boards—Firms utilize employment Websites by typing in key job criteria, skills, and experience and indicating their geographic location.

> **Monster.com**
>
> **HotJobs.com**
>
> **CareerBuilder.com**

NACElink Network—The alliance among the National Association of Colleges and Employers, DirectEmployers Association, and Symplicity Corporation is a national recruiting network and suite of web based recruiting and career services automation tools serving the needs of colleges, employers and job candidates.

NICHE SITES—Websites that cater to a specific profession.

CONTRACT WORKERS' SITES—Sites are now available to assist this segment of the workforce. Professionals searching for freelance work are increasingly turning to Websites that let them market themselves globally.

HOURLY WORKERS' JOB SITES—After years of focusing primarily on professionals and their prospective employers, the big general employment job sites are trying to attract blue-collar and service workers.

TRADITIONAL EXTERNAL RECRUITMENT METHODS
Recruitment methods are the specific means through which potential employees are attracted to the firm.

MEDIA ADVERTISING—Way of communicating the employment needs within the firm to the public through media such as newspaper, radio, television, trade journals, and billboards.

EMPLOYMENT AGENCIES—Organization that helps firms recruit employees and, at the same time, aid individuals in their attempt to locate jobs.

> **Private employment agencies**: Best known for recruiting white-collar employees and offer an important service in bringing qualified applicants and open positions together.
>
> **Public employment agencies**: Operated by each state, receive overall policy direction from the U.S. Employment Service.

RECRUITERS—Most common use of recruiters is with technical and vocational schools, community colleges, colleges, and universities.

JOB FAIRS—recruiting method engaged in by a single employer or group of employers to attract a large number of applicants for interviews.

INTERNSHIPS—Special form of recruitment that involves placing students in temporary jobs with no obligation either by the company to hire the student permanently or by the student to accept a permanent position with the firm following graduation.

EXECUTIVE SEARCH FIRMS

Contingency search firms: Executive search firm that receives fees only upon successful placement of a candidate in a job opening.

Retained search firms: Executive search firm considered as consultants to their client organizations, serving on an exclusive contractual basis; typically recruit top business executives.

PROFESSIONAL ASSOCIATIONS—Associations in many business professions such as finance, marketing, information technology, and human resources provide recruitment and placement services for their members.

UNSOLICITED APPLICANTS—If an organization has the reputation of being a good place to work, it may be able to attract good prospective employees without extensive recruitment efforts.

OPEN HOUSES—Firms pair potential hires and managers in a warm, causal environment that encourages on-the-spot job offers.

EVENT RECRUITING—Recruiters going to events being attended by individuals the company is seeking.

SIGN-ON BONUSES—Some firms are offering sign-on bonuses to high-demand prospects.

COMPETITIVE GAMES—Unique way to get individuals interested in applying for positions.

TAILORING RECRUITMENT METHODS TO SOURCES
For recruitment efforts to be successful, they must be tailored to meet the needs of each firm.

U.S. FIRMS IN VIETNAM
At one time the United States was at war with Vietnam. Now U.S. multinational firms are locating in this country largely because of lower labor costs.

EXERCISES
1. We discussed the process of matching sources and methods of recruitment. For the following positions, match sources and methods. Assume that in all cases you must use external recruitment to fill the position. Justify your statements.
    a. Entry-level machine operator
    b. Vice-president of marketing for a top 500 company
    c. CPA with five years of experience to be an auditor for a major firm

2. You see the following ad in your local newspaper:
Telephone sales: Woman, age 25-40, needed for telephone sales. Must have high school diploma and good credit rating. Call Mr. Smith at Acme Manufacturing Co., Inc.
Is there anything wrong with this ad?

3. There are numerous Internet sites that pertain to information covered in this chapter. Identify two sites that apply to information contained in the chapter.

YOU AND HR

Memo One

To: (You) Human Resource Manager
From: Manager of Accounting
Subject: Shortage of Accountants

The end-of-year accounting crunch is coming up soon, and I have sent you a requisition to recruit and select three new accountants. I think we can keep them busy even after the end-of-year crunch. If the Marketing Department's predictions hold up, we'll have plenty of work for these new accountants.

Memo One Response

To: Manager of Accounting
From: (You) Human Resource Manager
Subject: Some Alternatives to Hiring New Employees to Help Handle Your Work Overload

(Your memo goes here in 75 to 100 words.)

Memo Two

To: (You) Human Resource Manager
From: Marketing Manager
Subject: New Market Research Function

As you know, the Marketing Department has been given the go ahead by top management as well as by the board to set up our own market research function.

This entails setting up a three-person operation now, with the addition of two more people later. Since the success of this new function is crucial to our future success, I would like to hand pick people from within the organization. I want people known in terms of their knowledge, skills and motivation. It is very important that we start up as a real working team.

Memo Two Response

To: Manager of Marketing
From: (You) Human Resource Manager
Subject: Suggestions Regarding Your Request to Recruit Internally

(Your memo goes here in 75 to 100 words.)

DISCUSSION QUESTIONS

1. What might you attempt to do prior to engaging in recruitment?
2. What are the basic components of the recruitment process?
3. What is meant by the term internal recruitment?
4. What are the possible external recruitment sources?
5. What are the possible external recruitment methods?

CHAPTER STUDY QUIZZES
Fill-in
1. _____ is the process of attracting individuals on a timely basis, in sufficient numbers, and with appropriate qualifications, to apply for jobs with an organization.
2. _____ is the process of hiring an external provider to do the work that was previously done internally.
3. Perhaps the most commonly used method of meeting short-term fluctuations in work volume is through the use of _____.
4. The _____ is a document that specifies job title, department, the date the employee is needed for work, and other details.
5. _____ is the policy of filling vacancies above entry-level positions with current employees.
6. _____ is a procedure for informing employees that job openings exist.
7. _____ are best known for recruiting white-collar employees and offer an important service in bringing qualified applicants and open positions together.
8. A _____ is a recruiting method engaged in by a single employer or group of employers to attract a large number of applicants to one location for interviews.
9. An _____ is a special form of recruitment that involves placing a student in a temporary job with no obligation either by the company to hire the student permanently or by the student to accept a permanent position with the firm following graduation.
10. Recruitment _____ are the specific means used to attract potential employees to the firm, such as online recruiting.

True/False
1. Contingent workers are the human equivalents of just-in-time inventory.
2. The reasons that organizations choose to use leased workers are numerous and include seasonal fluctuations, project-based work, the desire to acquire skill sets that are not available in the employee population, hiring freezes, and rapid growth.
3. Recruitment methods are where qualified individuals are located.
4. It is likely that a firm can adhere rigidly to a practice of promotion from within.
5. Job bidding is a technique that permits employees who believe that they possess the required qualifications to apply for a posted position.
6. When recent experience is required, competitors and other firms in the same industry or geographic area may be the most important source of recruits.
7. The process of actively recruiting employees from competitors is called poaching.
8. An internship is a special form of recruitment that involves placing a student in a temporary job with no obligation either by the company to hire the student permanently or by the student to accept a permanent position with the firm following graduation.
9. Many companies have found that their employees can serve an important role in the recruitment process by actively soliciting applications from their friends and associates.
10. Recruiters most commonly focus on technical and vocational schools, community colleges, colleges, and universities.

Multiple Choice

1. A firm that is recruiting for an experienced professional would likely use what source?
    A. competitors and other firms
    B. community colleges
    C. universities
    D. military

2. The policy of filling vacancies above entry-level positions with current employees is
    A. external recruitment.
    B. regional recruitment.
    C. promotion from within.
    D. promotion based on seniority.

3. What is the definition of a *professional employer organization*?
    A. Individuals who work as part-timers, temporaries, or independent contractors
    B. Take routine, transaction-based activities dispersed throughout the organization and consolidate them in one place
    C. Company that leases employees to other businesses
    D. Process of transferring responsibility for an area of service and its objectives to an external provider

4. What is the definition of *job posting*?
    A. Procedure that permits employees who believe that they possess the required qualifications to apply for a posted job
    B. Procedure for informing employees that job openings exist
    C. Unique form of employee referral where every employee becomes a company recruiter
    D. An online recruiting method engaged in by a single employer or group of employers to attract a large number of applicants

5. What is the definition of a *virtual job fair*?
    A. Online recruiting method engaged in by a single employer or group of employers to attract a large number of applicants
    B. Job sites accessible from a company homepage that list the company positions available, providing a way for applicants to apply for specific jobs
    C. National, web-based system for recruiting college students for all types of employment, such as full-time, part-time, internship, co-op, work-study, and alumni
    D. Websites that cater to a specific profession

6. What is the definition of an *internship*?
    A. Online recruiting method engaged in by a single employer or group of employers to attract a large number of applicants
    B. Job sites accessible from a company homepage that list the company positions available, providing a way for applicants to apply for specific jobs
    C. A special form of recruiting that involves placing students in temporary jobs with no obligation either by the company to permanently hire the student or by the students to accept a permanent position with the firm
    D. A national, web-based system for recruiting college students for all types of employment, such as full-time, part-time, internship, co-op, work-study, and alumni

7. What is the definition of a *retained search firm*?
   A. An organization that helps firms recruit employees and at the same time aids individuals in their attempt to locate jobs
   B. Often called *head hunters*, are best known for recruiting white-collar employees and offer an important service in bringing qualified applicants and open positions together
   C. Executive search firm that receive fees only upon successful placement of a candidate in a job opening
   D. Executive search firm that is considered as a consultant to their client organizations, serving on an exclusive contractual basis, and typically recruits top business executives

8. What is the definition of *event recruiting*?
   A. Firms pair potential hires and recruiters in a warm, casual environment that encourages on-the-spot job offers
   B. Organizations used by some firms to locate experienced professionals and executives when other sources prove inadequate
   C. Having recruiters going to events where individuals that the company is seeking attend
   D. Recruiting method engaged in by a single employer or group of employers to attract a large number of applicants to one location for interviews

9. What is the typical signing bonus for middle managers and professionals?
   A. 5 percent to 10 percent of base salary
   B. 10 percent to 15 percent of base salary
   C. 15 percent to 20 percent of base salary
   D. 20 percent to 25 percent of base salary

10. What is the definition of a corporate career Website?
    A. An online recruiting method engaged in by a single employer or group of employers to attract a large number of applicants.
    B. A Website that permits a company registers part of its corporate name online and job candidates can access it more quickly than they could if they had to go directly to the organization's Website and then look for the jobs page.
    C. Job sites accessible from a company homepage that list the company positions available and provide a way for applicants to apply for specific jobs.
    D. A person whose primary responsibility is to use the Internet in the recruitment process.

Matching Exercise
Directions: On the line provided, place the letter of the statement beside the key term.

1. _____ Poaching
2. _____ Contingency search firm
3. _____ Contingent workers
4. _____ Corporate career Websites
5. _____ Employee requisition
6. _____ Employment agency
7. _____ Event recruiting
8. _____ Internet recruiter
9. _____ Virtual job fair
10. _____ Internship
11. _____ Job bidding
12. _____ Job fair
13. _____ Job posting
14. _____ NACElink Network
15. _____ Niche sites
16. _____ Promotion from within
17. _____ Recruitment
18. _____ Recruitment methods
19. _____ Recruitment sources
20. _____ Retained search firms

a. Process of attracting individuals on a timely basis, in sufficient numbers, and with appropriate qualifications, to apply for jobs with an organization.
b. Described as the *disposable American workforce* by a former Secretary of Labor, work as part-timers, temporaries, or independent contractors.
c. Policy of filling vacancies above entry-level positions with current employees.
d. Document that specifies job title, department, the date the employee is needed for work, and other details.
e. Where qualified candidates are located.
f. Specific means used to attract potential employees to the firm.
g. Procedure for communicating to company employees the fact that a job opening exists.
h. Procedure that permits employees who believe that they possess the required qualifications to apply for a posted position.
i. Person whose primary responsibility is to use the Internet in the recruitment process (also called cyber recruiter).
j. Online recruiting method engaged in by a single employer or group of employers to attract a large number of applicants.
k. Job sites accessible from a company homepage that list available company positions and provide a way for applicants to apply for specific jobs.
l. An alliance among the National Association of Colleges and Employers, DirectEmployers Association, and Symplicity Corporation; a national recruiting network and suite of web based recruiting and career services automation tools serving the needs of colleges, employers and job candidates.
m. Websites that cater to a specific profession.
n. Organization that helps firms recruit employees and at the same time aids individuals in their attempt to locate jobs.
o. Recruiting method engaged in by a single employer or group of employers to attract a large number of applicants to one location for interviews.
p. Special form of recruitment that involves placing a student in a temporary job with no obligation either by the company to hire the student permanently or by the student to accept a permanent position with the firm following graduation.
q. Executive search firm that receives fees only upon successful placement of a candidate in a job opening.
r. Executive search firm considered as consultants to their client organizations, serving on an exclusive contractual basis; typically recruit top business executives.
s. Recruiters going to events where individuals the company is seeking attend.
t. Process of actively recruiting employees from competitors.

ANSWERS TO CHAPTER STUDY QUIZZES
Fill-in

1.	Recruitment	6.	Job posting
2.	Outsourcing	7.	Private employee agencies
3.	Overtime	8.	Job fairs
4.	Employee requisition	9.	Internship
5.	Promotion from within	10.	Methods

True/False

1.	True	6.	True
2.	False (contingent)	7.	True
3.	False (sources)	8.	True
4.	False (unlikely)	9.	True
5.	True	10.	True

Multiple Choice

1.	A	6.	C
2.	C	7.	D
3.	C	8.	C
4.	B	9.	A
5.	A	10.	C

Matching Exercise

1.	T	11.	H
2.	Q	12.	O
3.	B	13.	G
4.	K	14.	L
5.	D	15.	M
6.	N	16.	C
7.	S	17.	A
8.	I	18.	F
9.	J	19.	E
10.	P	20.	R

CHAPTER 6

SELECTION

CHAPTER DESCRIPTION

This chapter begins with a discussion of the stress interview, followed by a discussion of the significance of employee selection and identification of environmental factors that affect the selection process. Next, the general selection process is described. The next two sections involve the preliminary interview and review of applications and résumés. A section on sending résumés via the Internet follows, and the advantages and potential problems and characteristics of properly designed selection tests are explained. The types of validation studies and types of employment tests are then discussed, and topics related to genetic testing, graphoanalysis, and polygraph tests are described. Aspects of online testing and the use of assessment centers are then presented, and the importance of the employment interview and the general types of interviewing is discussed. Then we examine the various methods of interviewing, realistic job previews, potential interviewing problems, and concluding the interview. Next, the use of pre-employment screening, including background investigations, reference checks, and continuous background checking is presented, followed by a discussion of negligent hiring and negligent referral. Topics related to the selection decision, hiring temporary executives, the medical examination, and notification of candidates is discussed, and metrics for evaluating recruitment/selection effectiveness are explained. The chapter concludes with a Global Perspective entitled "Changing of the Guard: Will the New Expatriates Step Forward?"

KEY TERMS

Stress interview: Form of interview in which the interviewer intentionally creates anxiety.
Selection: Process of choosing from a group of applicants the individual best suited for a particular position and the organization.
Applicant pool: Number of qualified applicants recruited for a particular job.
Selection ratio: Number of people hired for a particular job compared to the total number of individuals in the applicant pool.
Résumé: Goal-directed summary of a person's experience, education, and training developed for use in the selection process.
Keywords: Words or phrases that are used to search databases for résumés that match.
Keyword résumé: Résumé that contains an adequate description of the job seeker's characteristics and industry-specific experience presented in keyword terms in order to accommodate the computer search process.
Standardization: Uniformity of the procedures and conditions related to administering tests.
Objectivity: Condition that is achieved when everyone scoring a given test obtains the same results.
Norm: Frame of reference for comparing an applicant's performance with that of others.
Reliability: Extent to which a selection test provides consistent results.
Validity: Extent to which a test measures what it claims to measure.
Criterion-related validity: Test validation method that compares the scores on selection tests to some aspect of job performance determined, for example, by performance appraisal.
Content validity: Test validation method whereby a person performs certain tasks that are actual samples of the kind of work a job requires or completes a paper-and-pencil test that measures relevant job knowledge.
Construct validity: Test validation method that determines whether a test measures certain constructs, or traits, that job analysis finds to be important in performing a job.
Cognitive aptitude tests: Tests that determine general reasoning ability, memory, vocabulary, verbal fluency, and numerical ability.
Psychomotor abilities tests: Tests that measure strength, coordination, and dexterity.
Job-knowledge tests: Tests designed to measure a candidate's knowledge of the duties of the job for which he or she is applying.
Work-sample tests: Tests that require an applicant to perform a task or set of tasks representative of the job.

Vocational interest tests: Tests that indicate the occupation a person is most interested in and the one likely to provide satisfaction.
Personality tests: Self-reported measures of traits, temperaments, or dispositions.
Genetic testing: Tests given to identify predisposition to inherited diseases, including cancer, heart disease, neurological disorders, and congenital diseases.
Graphoanalysis: Use of handwriting analysis as a selection factor.
Assessment center: selection approach that requires individuals to perform activities similar to those they might encounter in an actual job.
Employment interview: Goal-oriented conversation in which the interviewer and applicant exchange information.
Organizational fit: Management's perception of the degree to which the prospective employee will fit in with the firm's culture or value system.
Unstructured interview: Interview in which the job applicant is asked probing, open-ended questions.
Structured interview: Interview in which the interviewer asks each applicant for a particular job the same series of job-related questions.
Behavioral interview: Structured interview in which applicants are asked to relate actual incidents from their past relevant to the target job.
Group interview: Meeting in which several job applicants interact in the presence of one or more company representatives.
Board interview: Interview approach in which several of the firm's representatives interview a candidate at the same time.
Realistic job preview: Method of conveying both positive and negative job information to an applicant in an unbiased manner.
Reference checks: Information from individuals who know the applicant that provide additional insight into the information furnished by the applicant and verification of its accuracy.
Negligent hiring: Liability a company incurs when it fails to conduct a reasonable investigation of an applicant's background, and then assigns a potentially dangerous person to a position in which he or she can inflict harm.
Negligent referral: Liability former employers may incur when they fail to offer a warning about a particularly severe problem with a past employee.
Applicant tracking system: Software application designed to help an enterprise select employees more efficiently.

CHAPTER STUDY OUTLINE

PUTTING THE INTERVIEWEE UNDER PRESSURE: THE STRESS INTERVIEW
In the stress interview, the interviewer intentionally creates anxiety. Most interviewers strive to minimize stress for the candidate. However, in the stress interview, the interviewer deliberately makes the candidate uncomfortable by asking blunt and often discourteous questions.

SIGNIFICANCE OF EMPLOYEE SELECTION
Selection is the process of choosing from a group of applicants the individual best suited for a particular position and the organization. Properly matching people with jobs and the organization is the goal of the selection process. If individuals are overqualified, underqualified, or for any reason do not *fit* either the job or the organization's culture, they will be ineffective and probably leave the firm, voluntarily or otherwise.

ENVIRONMENTAL FACTORS AFFECTING THE SELECTION PROCESS
Numerous environmental factors affect the selection process.

> **OTHER HR FUNCTIONS**—Selection process affects, and is affected by, virtually every other HR function.

> **LEGAL CONSIDERATIONS**—Legislation, executive orders, and court decisions have a major impact on human resource management.

> **SPEED OF DECISION MAKING**—Time available to make the selection decision can have a major effect on the selection process.

ORGANIZATIONAL HIERARCHY—Different approaches to selection are generally taken for filling positions at different levels in the organization.

APPLICANT POOL—Number of qualified applicants recruited for a particular job.

TYPE OF ORGANIZATION—Sector of the economy in which individuals are to be employed—private, governmental, or not-for-profit—can also affect the selection process.

PROBATIONARY PERIOD—Many firms use a probationary period that permits evaluating an employee's ability based on performance.

SELECTION PROCESS

RECRUITED INDIVIDUAL

PRELIMINARY INTERVIEW

REVIEW OF APPLICATIONS AND RÉSUMÉS

SELECTION TESTS

EMPLOYMENT INTERVIEWS

REFERENCE AND BACKGROUND CHECKS

SELECTION DECISION

PHYSICAL EXAMINATION

NEW EMPLOYEE

PRELIMINARY INTERVIEW
Selection process often begins with an initial screening of applicants to remove individuals who obviously do not meet the position requirements.

REVIEW OF APPLICATIONS
Application form must reflect not only the firm's informational needs but also EEO requirements.

REVIEW OF RÉSUMÉS
Practice has evolved into a more advanced procedure, with résumés automatically evaluated.

SENDING RÉSUMÉS VIA THE INTERNET
E-mail has become a popular method of providing résumés to organizations.

SELECTION TESTS: ADVANTAGES AND POTENTIAL PROBLEMS
Evidence suggests that the use of tests is becoming more prevalent for assessing an applicant's qualifications and potential for success.

ADVANTAGES OF SELECTION TESTS—Selection testing can be a reliable and accurate means of selecting qualified candidates from a pool of applicants if they are job related.

POTENTIAL PROBLEMS USING SELECTION TESTS—Selection tests may accurately predict an applicant's ability to perform the job, the *can do*, but they are less successful in indicating the extent to which the individual will be motivated to perform it, the *will do*.

CHARACTERISTICS OF PROPERLY DESIGNED SELECTION TESTS—Properly designed selection tests are standardized, objective, based on sound norms, reliable and—of utmost importance—valid.

STANDARDIZATION—Uniformity of the procedures and conditions related to administering tests.

OBJECTIVITY—Condition that is achieved when everyone scoring a given test obtains the same results.

NORM—Frame of reference for comparing an applicant's performance with that of others.

RELIABILITY—Extent to which a selection test provides consistent results.

VALIDITY—Extent to which a test measures what it claims to measure. If a test cannot indicate ability to perform the job, it has no value as a predictor.

TYPES OF VALIDATION STUDIES
Uniform Guidelines established three approaches that may be followed to validate selection tests: criterion-related validity, content validity, and construct validity.

CRITERION-RELATED VALIDITY—Test validation method that compares the scores on selection tests to some aspect of job performance determined, for example, by performance appraisal.

CONTENT VALIDITY—Test validation method whereby a person performs certain tasks that are actual samples of the kind of work a job requires or completes a paper-and-pencil test that measures relevant job knowledge.

CONSTRUCT VALIDITY—Test validation method that determines whether a test measures certain constructs, or traits, that job analysis finds to be important in performing a job.

TYPES OF EMPLOYMENT TESTS
Individuals differ in characteristics related to job performance. Various tests measure these differences.

COGNITIVE APTITUDE TESTS—Tests that determine general reasoning ability, memory, vocabulary, verbal fluency, and numerical ability.

PSYCHOMOTOR ABILITIES TESTS—Measure strength, coordination, and dexterity.

JOB KNOWLEDGE TESTS—Tests designed to measure a candidate's knowledge of the duties of the job for which he or she is applying.

WORK-SAMPLE TESTS—Tests that require an applicant to perform a task or set of tasks representative of the job.

VOCATIONAL INTEREST TESTS—Tests that indicate the occupation a person is most interested in and the one likely to provide satisfaction.

PERSONALITY TESTS—Self-reported measures of traits, temperaments, or dispositions.

UNIQUE FORMS OF TESTING

GENETIC TESTING—Tests given to identify predisposition to inherited diseases, including cancer, heart disease, neurological disorders, and congenital diseases.

GRAPHOANALYSIS (HANDWRITING ANALYSIS)—Use of handwriting analysis as a selection factor.

POLYGRAPH TESTS—Employee Polygraph Protection Act of 1988 severely limited the use of polygraph tests in the private sector.

ONLINE TESTING
Organizations are increasingly using the Internet to test various skills required by applicants.

ASSESSMENT CENTERS—Selection approach that requires individuals to perform activities similar to those they might encounter in an actual job.

EMPLOYMENT INTERVIEW
Goal-oriented conversation in which the interviewer and applicant exchange information.

> **INTERVIEW PLANNING**—Essential to effective employment interviews.
>
> **CONTENT OF THE INTERVIEW**—Specific content of employment interviews varies greatly by organization and the level of the job concerned.
>
>> **Occupational experience**: Exploring an individual's occupational experience requires determining the applicant's skills, abilities, and willingness to handle responsibility.
>>
>> **Academic achievement**: In the absence of significant work experience, a person's academic background takes on greater importance.
>>
>> **Interpersonal skills**: If an individual cannot work well with other employees, chances for success are slim.
>>
>> **Personal qualities**: Personal qualities normally observed during the interview include physical appearance, speaking ability, vocabulary, poise, adaptability, and assertiveness.
>>
>> **Organizational fit**: Management's perception of the degree to which the prospective employee will fit in with, for example, the firm's culture or value system.
>
> **CANDIDATE'S ROLE AND EXPECTATIONS**—While the interviewer will provide information about the company, it is still important that candidates do their homework.

GENERAL TYPES OF INTERVIEWS

> **UNSTRUCTURED INTERVIEW**— Interview in which the interviewer asks each applicant for a particular job the same series of job-related questions.
>
> **STRUCTURED INTERVIEW**—Interviewer asks each applicant for a particular job the same series of job-related questions. A structured interview typically contains four types of questions.
>
>> **Situational questions**: Pose a hypothetical job situation to determine what the applicant would do in that situation.
>>
>> **Job knowledge questions**: Probe the applicant's job-related knowledge.
>>
>> **Job-sample simulation questions**: Involve situations in which an applicant may be actually required to perform a sample task from the job.
>>
>> **Worker requirements questions**: Seek to determine the applicant's willingness to conform to the requirements of the job.

BEHAVIORAL INTERVIEWS—Structured interview in which applicants are asked to relate actual incidents from their past relevant to the target job.

METHODS OF INTERVIEWING
Interviews may be conducted in several ways.

ONE-ON-ONE INTERVIEW—Applicant meets one-on-one with an interviewer.

GROUP INTERVIEW—Meeting in which several job applicants interact in the presence of one or more company representatives.

BOARD (OR PANEL) INTERVIEW—Interview approach in which several of the firm's representatives interview a candidate at the same time.

MULTIPLE INTERVIEWS—At times the applicants are interviewed by peers, subordinates, and supervisors.

REALISTIC JOB PREVIEWS
Method of conveying both positive and negative job information to an applicant in an unbiased manner.

POTENTIAL INTERVIEWING PROBLEMS
Interviewing problems that can threaten the success of employment interviews.

INAPPROPRIATE QUESTIONS—Although no questions are illegal, many are clearly inappropriate. When they are asked, the responses generated create a legal liability for the employer. The most basic interviewing rule is this: "Ask only job-related questions."

PREMATURE JUDGMENTS—Research suggests that interviewers often make judgments about candidates in the first few minutes of the interview. When this occurs, a great deal of potentially valuable information is not considered.

INTERVIEWER DOMINATION—In successful interviews, relevant information must flow both ways.

PERMITTING NON-JOB RELATED INFORMATION—If a candidate begins volunteering personal information that is not job related, the interviewer should steer the conversation back on course.

CONTRAST EFFECT—An error in judgment may occur when, for example, in interviewer meets with several poorly qualified applicants and then confronts a mediocre candidate.

LACK OF TRAINING—Anyone who has ever conducted an interview realizes that it is much more than carrying on a conversation with another person.

NONVERBAL COMMUNICATION—*Body language* is the nonverbal communication method in which physical actions such as motions, gestures, and facial expressions convey thoughts and emotions. The interviewer is attempting to view the nonverbal signals from the applicant. Applicants are also reading the nonverbal signals of the interviewer.

CONCLUDING THE INTERVIEW
When the interviewer has obtained the necessary information and answered the applicant's questions, he or she should conclude the interview. Management must then determine whether the candidate is suitable for the open position and organization. If the conclusion is positive, the process continues; if there appears to be no match, the candidate is no longer considered. Also, in concluding the interview, the interviewer should tell the applicant that he or she will be notified of the selection decision shortly.

PRE-EMPLOYMENT SCREENING: BACKGROUND INVESTIGATIONS
It is now time to determine the accuracy of the information submitted or to determine if vital information was not submitted. Background investigations involve obtaining data from various sources, including previous employers, business associates, credit bureaus, government agencies, and academic institutions and have become increasingly more important.

PRE-EMPLOYMENT SCREENING: REFERENCE CHECKS
Information from individuals who know the applicant that provide additional insight into the information furnished by the applicant and verification of its accuracy.

CONTINUOUS BACKGROUND CHECKS
Employee background checks are not just for pre-employment any more. The techniques and attitudes companies employ to maintain a law-abiding workforce is being upgraded to meet real-world requirements. In certain industries such as banking and health care, employers are required by regulation to routinely research the criminal records of employees.

NEGLIGENT HIRING
Liability a company incurs when it fails to conduct a reasonable investigation of an applicant's background, and then assigns a potentially dangerous person to a position where he or she can inflict harm.

NEGLIGENT REFERRAL
Liability former employers may incur when they fail to offer a warning about a particularly severe problem with a past employee.

SELECTION DECISION
Person whose qualifications most closely conform to the requirements of the open position should be selected.

HIRING TEMPORARY EXECUTIVES
Recruiting and hiring executives on a temporary basis has increasingly become a popular practice with some companies. Individuals who have proven their ability as a top-level manager are entering this new arena. Bringing in an interim executive is a tactical approach that is sometimes used to run a department, a division, or even the whole company.

MEDICAL EXAMINATION
Typically, a job offer is contingent on successful passing this examination.

NOTIFICATION TO CANDIDATES
Selection process results should be made known to candidates—successful and unsuccessful—as soon as possible.

APPLICANT TRACKING SYSTEM
A software application designed to help an enterprise select employees more efficiently. Current applicant tracking systems permit human resource and line managers to oversee the entire selection process. They often involve screening résumés and spotting qualified candidates, conducting personality and skills tests, and handling background checks.

METRICS FOR EVALUATING RECRUITMENT/SELECTION EFFECTIVENESS
Metrics that can be collected in order to assess HR efficiency are numerous and a comprehensive set of metrics can be produced to evaluate recruitment and selection.

> **TURNOVER RATE**—The number of times on average employees have to be replaced during a year.

> **RECRUITING COSTS**—In determining the recruiting cost per hire, the total recruiting expense must first be calculated.

SELECTION RATE—Number of applicants hired from a group of candidates expressed as a percentage is the selection rate.

ACCEPTANCE RATE—Number of applicants who accepted the job divided by the number who were offered the job.

YIELD RATE—Percentage of applicants from a particular source and method that makes it to the next stage of the selection process.

COST/BENEFIT OF RECRUITMENT SOURCES AND METHODS—Although not an easy process, companies are beginning to establish metrics to help them assess both quantitative and qualitative aspects of the recruitment and selection process.

TIME REQUIRED TO HIRE—Time required to fill an opening is critical.

CHANGING OF THE GUARD: WILL THE NEW EXPATRIATES STEP FORWARD?
A new generation of expats is evolving for the ever increasing markets of China and India. These global executives are busy searching for local talent and adapting to a very different culture. The market they are in is growing by leaps and bounds which is vital to their firm's future. When they return to the U.S., opportunities abound for them, perhaps even the corner office.

EXERCISES
1. Contact a HR professional in your area. Ask the following questions:
    a. How important is the interview in the selection process?
    b. What type interview does he or she normally use (structured or unstructured)?
    c. How valid is the interview in the selection process?

2. What do you believe would be the most important elements of the selection process for the following jobs?
    a. word processing operator
    b. experienced salesperson
    c. company president
    d. student desiring a college internship

3. There are numerous Internet sites that pertain to information covered in this chapter. Identify two sites that apply to information contained in the chapter.

YOU AND HR
Memo One
To: (You) Human Resource Manager
From: General Manager
Subject: Behavioral Interview

As you know, the supervisors we have been hiring lately have just not been working out. They seem to do great in the interview but we must not be asking the right questions. Someone suggested that the behavioral interview might improve our selection rate. What is this thing called a behavioral interview? Do you believe it would benefit us?

Memo One Response
To: General Manager
From: (You) Human Resource Manager
Subject: Behavioral Interview

(Your memo goes here in 50 to 75 words.)

Memo Two
To: (You) Human Resource Manager
From: Newly-promoted Supervisor
Subject: Possible Change in the Application Blank

A friend of mind with another company about our size showed me their application blank the other day. They asked a lot more questions than we do and I wonder if we could also ask them. Listed below are some of items that were being asked:

*Marital Status
*Height and Weight
*Age
*Sex
*Occupation of Spouse
*Have you ever been convicted?
*If you are a female, do you plan to have children any time soon?
*Are you handicapped?

Could we add these questions to our application blank?

Memo Two Response
To: Newly-promoted Supervisor
From: (You) Human Resource Manager
Subject: Request for Change to Application Blank

(Your memo goes here in 75 to 100 words.)

DISCUSSION QUESTIONS
1. What basic steps normally are followed in the selection process?
2. What would be the selection ratio if there were ten applicants to choose from and only one position to fill?
3. What is the purpose of the preliminary interview?
4. What basic conditions should be met if selection tests are to be used in the screening process?
5. What are the types of validation studies that the *Uniform Guidelines* say should be used?

CHAPTER STUDY QUIZZES
Fill-in
1. It costs an average of _____ times an individual's salary to replace an employee who does not work out.
2. A selection ratio of _____ indicates that there was only one qualified applicant for an open position.
3. _____ typically begins with the preliminary interview.
4. Selection tests may accurately predict an applicant's ability to perform the job, but they are less successful in indicating the extent to which the individual will _____ to perform it.
5. _____ refers to the uniformity of the procedures and conditions related to administering tests.
6. _____ is determined by comparing the scores on selection tests to some aspect of job performance.
7. _____ tests measure strength, coordination, and dexterity.
8. In the _____ interview, the interviewer asks probing, open-ended questions.
9. In a (an) _____ interview, several of the firm's representatives interview a candidate at the same time.
10. A (An) _____ conveys job information to the applicant in an unbiased manner, including both positive and negative factors.

True/False
1. Organizations usually take different approaches to filling positions at varying levels.
2. A selection ratio of .10 indicates that there is only one qualified applicant for each position.
3. The specific information requested on an application for employment may vary from firm to firm, and even by job type within an organization.
4. Standardization in testing is achieved when everyone scoring a test obtains the same results.
5. The basic requirement for a selection test is that it be objective.
6. Construct validity is a test validation method whereby a person performs certain tasks that are actually required by the job or completes a paper-and-pencil test that measures relevant job knowledge.
7. Vocational interest tests indicate the occupation a person is most interested in and the one likely to provide satisfaction.
8. The unstructured interview is a series of job-related questions asked of each applicant for a particular job.
9. Behavioral interviews ask applicants about specific events as opposed to just having them tell about themselves.
10. Because the interview is a test, if adverse impact is shown, it is subject to the same validity requirements as any other step in the selection process.

Multiple Choice
1. What is the definition of a *stress interview*?
    A. Interviewer asks each applicant for a particular job the same series of job-related questions.
    B. Form of interview in which the interviewer intentionally creates anxiety
    C. Interview in which the job applicant is asked probing, open-ended questions
    D. Meeting in which several job applicants interact in the presence of one or more company representatives

2. What is a goal-directed summary of a person's experience, education, and training developed for use in the selection process called?
    A. résumé
    B. application form
    C. vita
    D. application blank

3. Which Act limited the use of polygraph tests in the private sector?
    A. Lie Detector Protection Act
    B. Federal Polygraph Protection Act
    C. Polygraph Confirmation Act
    D. Employee Polygraph Protection Act

4. In terms of employee testing, what is the definition of *standardization*?
   A. Condition that is achieved when everyone scoring a given test obtains the same results
   B. Frame of reference for comparing an applicant's performance with that of others
   C. Uniformity of the procedures and conditions related to administering tests
   D. Extent to which a selection test provides consistent results

5. In terms of employee testing, what is the definition of *objective*?
   A. The uniformity of the procedures and conditions related to administering tests.
   B. Occurs when everyone scoring a test obtains the same results.
   C. A frame of reference for comparing an applicant's performance with that of others.
   D. The extent to which a selection test provides consistent results.

6. A selection ratio of .1 would indicate how many applicants for the job?
   A. 1
   B. 5
   C. 10
   D. 20

7. What is the definition of a *structured interview*?
   A. Several applicants interact in the presence of one or more company representatives
   B. Interview in which the job applicant is asked probing, open-ended questions
   C. Interviewer asks each applicant for a particular job the same series of job-related questions
   D. Form of interview in which the interviewer intentionally creates anxiety

8. What is the definition of *negligent hiring*?
   A. Liability former employers may occur when they fail to offer a warning about a particularly severe problem with a past employee
   B. Liability former employers may occur when they fail to supervise properly
   C. Liability an employer incurs when it fails to conduct a reasonable investigation of an applicant's background, and then assigns a potentially dangerous person to a position where he or she can inflict harm
   D. Liability former employers may occur when they fail to conduct a successful interview

9. Who is the individual who typically makes the final selection on a new employee?
   A. HR manager
   B. President
   C. manager of that employee
   D. group decision

10. What is the definition of *selection*?
    A. Process of choosing from a group of applicants the individual best suited for a particular position and the organization
    B. Process of attracting individuals on a timely basis, in sufficient numbers, and with appropriate qualifications, to apply for jobs with an organization
    C. Systematic process of matching the internal and external supply of people with job openings anticipated in the organization over a specified period of time
    D. Systematic process of determining the skills, duties, and knowledge required for performing jobs in an organization

Matching Exercise

Directions: On the line provided, place the letter of the statement beside the key term.

1.	_____	Applicant pool	19.	_____	Objectivity
2.	_____	Assessment center	20.	_____	Organizational fit
3.	_____	Behavioral interview	21.	_____	Personality tests
4.	_____	Board interview	22.	_____	Psychomotor abilities tests
5.	_____	Cognitive aptitude tests	23.	_____	Realistic job preview
6.	_____	Construct validity	24.	_____	Reference checks
7.	_____	Content validity	25.	_____	Reliability
8.	_____	Criterion-related validity	26.	_____	Résumé
9.	_____	Employment interview	27.	_____	Selection
10.	_____	Genetic testing	28.	_____	Selection ratio
11.	_____	Graphoanalysis	29.	_____	Standardization
12.	_____	Group interview	30.	_____	Stress interview
13.	_____	Job knowledge tests	31.	_____	Structured interview
14.	_____	Keywords	32.	_____	Unstructured interview
15.	_____	Keyword résumé	33.	_____	Validity
16.	_____	Negligent hiring	34.	_____	Vocational interest tests
17.	_____	Negligent referral	35.	_____	Work-sample tests
18.	_____	Norm	36.	_____	Applicant tracking system

a. Process of choosing from a group of applicants the individual best suited for a particular position and organization.
b. Number of qualified applicants recruited for a particular job.
c. Number of people hired for a particular job compared to the individuals in the applicant pool.
d. Goal directed summary of a person's experience, education, and training developed for use in the selection process.
e. Words or phrases that are used to search databases for résumés that match.
f. Résumé that contains an adequate description of the job seeker's characteristics and industry-specific experience presented in keyword terms in order to accommodate the computer search process.
g. Uniformity of the procedures and conditions related to administering tests.
h. Condition that is achieved when everyone scoring a given test obtain the same results.
i. Frame of reference for comparing an applicant's performance with that of others.
j. Extent to which a selection test provides consistent results.
k. The extent to which a test measures what it claims to measure.
l. Test validation method that compares the scores on selection tests to some aspect of job performance determined, for example, by performance appraisal.
m. Test validation method whereby a person performs certain tasks that are actual samples of the kind of work a job requires or completes a paper-and-pencil test that measures relevant job knowledge.
n. Test validation method that determines whether a test measures certain constructs, or traits, that job analysis finds to be important in performing a job.
o. Tests that determine general reasoning ability, memory, vocabulary, verbal fluency, and numerical ability.
p. Tests that measure strength, coordination, and dexterity.
q. Tests designed to measure a candidate's knowledge of the duties of the job for which he or she is applying.
r. Tests that require an applicant to perform a task or set of tasks representative of the job.
s. Tests that indicate the occupation a person is most interested in and the one likely to provide satisfaction.
t. Self-reported measures of traits, temperaments, or dispositions.
u. Tests given to identify predisposition to inherited diseases, including cancer, heart disease, neurological disorders, and congenital diseases.
v. Use of handwriting analysis as a selection factor
w. Selection technique that requires individuals to perform activities similar to those they might encounter in an actual job.
x. Goal-oriented conversation in which an interviewer and an applicant exchange information.
y. Management's perception of the degree to which the prospective employee will fit in with the firm's culture or value system.
z. Interview in which the job applicant is asked probing, open-ended questions.
aa. Interviewer asks each applicant for a particular job the same series of job-related questions.
bb. Structured interview where applicants are asked to relate actual incidents from their past relevant to the target job.
cc. Meeting in which several job applicants interact in the presence of one or more company representatives.
dd. Interview approach in which several of the firm's representatives interview a candidate at the same time.
ee. Form of interview in which the interviewer intentionally creates anxiety.
ff. Conveying both positive and negative job information to the applicant in an unbiased manner
gg. Information from individuals who know the applicant that provide additional insight into the information furnished by the applicant and verification of its accuracy.
hh. Liability a company incurs when it fails to conduct a reasonable investigation of an applicant's background, and then assigns a potentially dangerous person to a position where he or she can inflict harm.
ii. Liability former employers may incur when they fail to offer a warning about a particularly severe problem with a past employee.
jj. Software application designed to help an enterprise select employees more efficiently.

ANSWERS TO CHAPTER STUDY QUIZZES

Fill-in
1. 2.5
2. 1.00
3. The selection process
4. Be motivated
5. Standardization
6. Criterion-related validity
7. Psychomotor abilities
8. Unstructured
9. Board
10. Realistic job preview

True/False
1. True
2. False (1.00)
3. True
4. False (objectivity)
5. False (valid)
6. False (content)
7. True
8. False (structured)
9. True
10. True

Multiple Choice
1. B
2. A
3. D
4. C
5. B
6. C
7. C
8. C
9. C
10. A

Matching Exercise
1. B
2. W
3. BB
4. DD
5. O
6. N
7. M
8. L
9. X
10. U
11. V
12. CC
13. Q
14. E
15. F
16. HH
17. II
18. I
19. H
20. Y
21. T
22. P
23. FF
24. GG
25. J
26. D
27. A
28. C
29. G
30. EE
31. AA
32. Z
33. K
34. S
35. R
36. JJ

CHAPTER 7

TRAINING AND DEVELOPMENT

CHAPTER DESCRIPTION

The first portion of this chapter is devoted to high-tech videoconferencing. Next, strategic training and development (T&D) and the factors influencing T&D will be explained. Following this, we examine the T&D process and how T&D needs are determined and objectives established. Then, the numerous T&D methods are discussed and T&D delivery systems are described. Management development, orientation, and the executive orientation concept of onboarding are then discussed. The means by which T&D programs are implemented are then explained, followed by a discussion of the metrics for evaluating training and development. After that, the Workforce Investment Act is explained, organization development is described and the chapter concludes with a Global Perspective entitled "Learning to Deal with Cultural Differences."

KEY TERMS

Training and development (T&D): Heart of a continuous effort designed to improve employee competency and organizational performance.
Training: Activities designed to provide learners with the knowledge and skills needed for their present jobs.
Development: Learning that goes beyond today's job and has a more long-term focus.
Learning organization: Firm that recognizes the critical importance of continuous performance-related T&D and takes appropriate action.
Just-in-time training: Training provided anytime, anywhere in the world when it is needed.
Case study: T&D method in which trainees are expected to study the information provided in the case and make decisions based on it.
Behavior modeling: T&D method that permits a person to learn by copying or replicating behaviors of others to show managers how to handle various situations
Role playing: T&D method in which participants are required to respond to specific problems they may encounter in their jobs by acting out real-world situations.
Business games: T&D method that permits participants to assume roles such as president, controller, or marketing vice president of two or more similar hypothetical organizations and compete against each other by manipulating selected factors in a particular business situation.
In-basket training: T&D method in which the participant is asked to establish priorities for and then handle a number of business papers, e-mail messages, memoranda, reports, and telephone messages that would typically cross a manager's desk.
On-the-job training (OJT): Informal T&D method that permits an employee to learn job tasks by actually performing them.
Job rotation: T&D method in which employees move from one job to another to broaden their experience.
Apprenticeship training: Training method that combines classroom instruction with on-the-job training.
Corporate university: T&D delivery system provided under the umbrella of the organization.
Online higher education: Educational opportunities including degree and training programs that are delivered, either entirely or partially, via the Internet.
Vestibule system: T&D delivery system that takes place away from the production area on equipment that closely resembles equipment actually used on the job.
E-learning: T&D delivery system for online instruction.
Virtual reality: Unique extension of e-learning that permits trainees to view objects from a perspective that is otherwise impractical or impossible.
Simulators: T&D delivery system comprised of devices or programs that replicate actual job demands.
Management development: Consists of all learning experiences provided by an organization resulting in upgrading skills and knowledge required in current and future managerial positions.
Mentoring: Approach to advising, coaching, and nurturing, for creating a practical relationship to enhance individual career, personal, and professional growth and development.
Coaching: Often considered a responsibility of the immediate boss, who provides assistance, much as a mentor.
Reverse mentoring: A process in which older employees learn from younger ones.

Orientation: Initial T&D effort for new employees that informs them about the company, the job, and the workgroup.
Onboarding: Process companies use to help new executives quickly learn an organization's structure, culture and politics so that they can start making contributions to the organization as soon as possible.
Benchmarking: Process of monitoring and measuring a firm's internal processes, such as operations, and then comparing the data with information from companies that excel in those areas.
Organization development: Planned and systematic attempts to change the organization, typically to a more behavioral environment.
Survey feedback: Process of collecting data from an organizational unit through the use of questionnaires, interviews, and objective data from other sources, such as records of productivity, turnover, and absenteeism.
Quality circles: Groups of employees who voluntarily meet regularly with their supervisors to discuss problems, investigate causes, recommend solutions, and take corrective action when authorized to do so.
Team building: Conscious effort to develop effective workgroups and cooperative skills throughout the organization.
Sensitivity training: An organization development technique that is designed to help individuals learn how others perceive their behavior.

CHAPTER STUDY OUTLINE

HIGH-TECH VIDEOCONFERENCING
HP's Halo and Cisco's TelePresence technologies cost up to $300,000 a unit but are said to usually pay for themselves in as little as nine months.

STRATEGIC TRAINING AND DEVELOPMENT

    TRAINING AND DEVELOPMENT—Heart of a continuous effort designed to improve employee competency and organizational performance.

    TRAINING—Designed to permit learners to acquire knowledge and skills needed for their present jobs.

    DEVELOPMENT—Learning that goes beyond today's job and has a more long-term focus.

    LEARNING ORGANIZATION—Firm that recognizes the critical importance of continuous performance-related T&D and takes appropriate action.

FACTORS INFLUENCING TRAINING AND DEVELOPMENT

    TOP MANAGEMENT SUPPORT

    TECHNOLOGICAL ADVANCES

    WORLD COMPLEXITY

    ORGANIZATIONAL COMPLEXITY

    LEARNING STYLES

    OTHER HUMAN RESOURCE FUNCTIONS

TRAINING AND DEVELOPMENT PROCESS

    DETERMINE SPECIFIC T&D NEEDS

    ESTABLISH SPECIFIC TRAINING AND DEVELOPMENT OBJECTIVES

SELECT T&D METHOD(S)

SELECT T&D DELIVERY SYSTEM(S)

IMPLEMENT T&D PROGRAMS

EVALUATE T&D PROGRAMS

DETERMINE SPECIFIC T&D NEEDS
First step in the T&D process. In today's highly competitive business environment, undertaking a program because other firms are doing it is asking for trouble.

ESTABLISH SPECIFIC T&D OBJECTIVES
T&D must have clear and concise objectives and be developed to achieve organizational goals. Without them, designing meaningful T&D programs would not be possible.

TRAINING AND DEVELOPMENT METHODS
A number of methods are utilized in imparting knowledge and skills to employees.

    INSTRUCTOR-LED—Continue to be effective for many types of T&D.

    CASE STUDY—T&D method in which trainees are expected to study the information provided in the case and make decisions based on it.

    BEHAVIOR MODELING—T&D method that permits a person to learn by copying or replicating behaviors of others to show managers how to handle various situations.

    ROLE PLAYING—T&D method in which participants are required to respond to specific problems they may encounter in their jobs by acting out real-world situations.

    BUSINESS GAMES—T&D method that permits participants to assume roles such as president, controller, or marketing vice president of two or more similar hypothetical organizations and compete against each other by manipulating selected factors in a particular business situation.

    IN-BASKET TRAINING—T&D method in which the participant is asked to establish priorities for and then handle a number of business papers, e-mail messages, memoranda, reports, and telephone messages that would typically cross a manager's desk.

    ON-THE-JOB TRAINING—Informal T&D method that permits an employee to learn job tasks by actually performing them.

    JOB ROTATION—T&D method in which employees move from one job to another to broaden their experience.

    INTERNSHIPS—Training method whereby university students divide their time between attending classes and working for an organization.

    APPRENTICESHIP TRAINING—Training method that combines classroom instruction with on-the-job training.

TRAINING & DEVELOPMENT DELIVERY SYSTEMS

    CORPORATE UNIVERSITIES—T&D delivery system provided under the umbrella of the organization.

COLLEGES AND UNIVERSITIES—For decades, colleges and universities have been the primary means for training professional, technical, and management employees.

COMMUNITY COLLEGES—Publicly-funded higher education establishments that provide vocational training and associate degree programs.

ONLINE HIGHER EDUCATION—Educational opportunities including degree and training programs that are delivered, either entirely or partially, via the Internet.

VIDEOCONFERENCING—Approach to training is interactive and appears to offer the flexibility and spontaneity of a traditional classroom.

VESTIBULE SYSTEM—T&D delivery system that takes place away from the production area on equipment that closely resembles equipment actually used on the job.

VIDEO MEDIA—Use of video media such as DVDs, videotapes, and film clips continues to be popular training delivery systems.

E-LEARNING—T&D delivery system for online instruction.

SIMULATORS—T&D delivery system comprised of devices or programs that replicate actual job demands.

MANAGEMENT DEVELOPMENT
Consists of all learning experiences provided by an organization resulting in upgrading skills and knowledge required in current and future managerial positions.

MENTORING—Approach to advising, coaching, and nurturing, for creating a practical relationship to enhance individual career, personal, and professional growth and development.

COACHING—Often considered a responsibility of the immediate boss, who provides assistance, much as a mentor.

REVERSE MENTORING—A process in which older employees learn from younger ones.

ORIENTATION
Initial T&D effort for new employees that informs them about the company, the job, and the workgroup.

PURPOSES OF ORIENTATION—Some basic purposes include explaining the employment situation (the job, department, and company), company policies and rules, compensation, corporate culture, team membership, employee development, dealing with change, and socialization.

RESPONSIBILITY FOR AND SCHEDULING OF ORIENTATION—Although orientation is often the joint responsibility of the training staff and the line supervisor, peers often serve as excellent information agents.

ADDITIONAL BENEFITS OF ORIENTATION—Formal orientation programs are effective in retaining and motivating personnel.

ONBOARDING (EXECUTIVE ORIENTATION)
Process companies use to help new executives quickly learn an organization's structure, culture and politics so that they can start making contributions to the organization as soon as possible.

IMPLEMENTING HUMAN RESOURCE DEVELOPMENT PROGRAMS
Implementation of T&D programs is often difficult.

METRICS FOR EVALUATING TRAINING AND DEVELOPMENT
In evaluating T&D programs, managers should strive for metrics that they are effective because such information can smooth the way to budget approval and executive buy-in.

> **PARTICIPANTS' OPINIONS**—Evaluating a T&D program by asking the participants' opinions of it is an inexpensive approach that provides an immediate response and suggestions for improvements.

> **EXTENT OF LEARNING**—Some organizations administer tests to determine what the participants in T&D program have learned.

> **BEHAVIORAL CHANGE**—Tests may indicate fairly accurately what has been learned, but they give little insight into desired behavioral changes.

> **ACCOMPLISHMENT OF T&D OBJECTIVES**—Approach to evaluating T&D programs involves determining the extent to which stated objectives have been achieved.

> **BENCHMARKING**—Process of monitoring and measuring a firm's internal processes, such as operations, and then comparing the data with information from companies that excel in those areas.

INTERNATIONAL ISO 9000 QUALITY ASSURANCE TRAINING STANDARDS
One International ISO 9000 quality assurance standard states: "Employees should receive the training and have the knowledge necessary to do their jobs." In order to comply with the standard, companies must maintain written records of their employee training to show that employees have been properly trained.

BUSINESS/GOVERNMENT/EDUCATION TRAINING PARTNERSHIPS: WORKFORCE INVESTMENT ACT
The Workforce Investment Act replaced the problem-riddled Job Training Partnership Act and consolidated more than 70 federal job-training programs. It provides states with the flexibility to develop streamlined systems in partnership with local governments. A primary focus of WIA is to meet the needs of business for skilled workers and to satisfy the training, education, and employment needs of individuals.

ORGANIZATION DEVELOPMENT
Planned and systematic attempts to change the organization, typically to a more behavioral environment. OD education and training strategies are designed to develop a more open, productive, and compatible workplace despite differences in personalities, culture, or technologies. The organizational development movement has been strongly advocated by such researchers as Chris Argyris and Warren Bennis. Organization development applies to an entire system, such as a company or a plant. Organization development is a major means of achieving change in the corporate culture.

> **SURVEY FEEDBACK**—Process of collecting data from an organizational unit through the use of questionnaires, interviews, and objective data from other sources, such as records of productivity, turnover, and absenteeism.

> **QUALITY CIRCLES**—Groups of employees who voluntarily meet regularly with their supervisors to discuss problems, investigate causes, recommend solutions, and take corrective action when authorized to do so.

> **TEAM BUILDING**—Conscious effort to develop effective workgroups and cooperative skills throughout the organization.

> **SENSITIVITY TRAINING**—Organization development technique that is designed to help individuals learn how others perceive their behavior.

LEARNING TO DEAL WITH CULTURAL DIFFERENCES

As more and more organizations move into international markets, individuals and organizations are seeing how cross-cultural differences bring both problems and opportunities. Cultural differences among nations are ingrained into the daily lives of a person and affect values and beliefs and even the way a person interacts with others.

EXERCISES

1. What do you believe would be the best method(s) of training for the following jobs?
    a. entry-level machine operator
    b. new first line supervisor
    c. new salesperson

2. Visit an HR professional in your local area. Ask the following questions:
    a. Who conducts the training in your organization?
    b. Is any of your training outsourced? If so, what?
    c. How do you evaluate the effectiveness of your training?

3. There are numerous Internet sites that pertain to information covered in this chapter. Identify two sites that apply to information contained in the chapter.

YOU AND HR
Memo One

To: (You) Human Resource Manager
From: Newly-hired Training Coordinator
Subject: Establishing a T&D Program in a Growing, High-tech Company

You were very cordial last month when I joined the company as training coordinator. You said, "Any time you need help or advice, let me know." Well, I need advice. Being fresh out of college, I feel a bit under prepared to set up the first formal T&D program for this firm. How do you suggest that I proceed? That is, what are the key steps to be taken?

Memo One Response

To: Newly-hired Training Coordinator
From: (You) Human Resource Manager
Subject: Setting Up a T&D Program

(Your memo goes here, listing what should be a proper sequence of steps.)

Memo Two

To: (You) Human Resource Manager
From: Plant Manager
Subject: Training for New Equipment

Headquarters just informed me that we are to receive some new punch press machines. My workers have never operated that equipment. What training methods do you believe would be best? I would like you to be in charge of this training.

Please give me your thoughts on how you intend to conduct this training.

Memo Two Response

To: Plant Manager
From: (You) Human Resource Manager
Subject: Training for New Equipment
(Your memo goes here in 75 to 100 words.)

DISCUSSION QUESTIONS
1. Define *training* and *development*.
2. List the primary training and development methods.
3. What are the primary training and development delivery systems?
4. What are some of the means of evaluating T&D programs? Discuss.
5. Explain the purposes of orientation to a firm.

CHAPTER STUDY QUIZZES
Fill-in
1. _____ involves learning that looks beyond today's job; it has a more long-term focus.
2. After setting the _____, management can determine the appropriate methods and the delivery system to be used.
3. _____ is an approach to advising, coaching, and nurturing, for creating a practical relationship to enhance individual career, personal, and professional growth and development.
4. In a (an) _____ exercise, the participant is asked to establish priorities for and then handle a number of business papers or e-mail messages such as memoranda, reports, and telephone messages that would typically cross a manager's desk.
5. _____ is an informal T&D method that permits employees to learn job tasks by performing them.
6. The _____ method of evaluating training and development involves monitoring and measuring a firm's internal processes, such as operations, and then comparing the data with information from companies that excel in those areas.
7. The _____ replaces the problem-riddled *Job Training Partnership Act* (JTPA) and consolidates more than 70 federal job-training programs.
8. _____ consists of all learning experiences provided by an organization resulting in an upgrading of skills and knowledge required in current and future managerial positions.
9. The initial T&D effort for new employees that inform them about the company, the job, and the workgroup is _____.
10. _____ is planned and systematic attempts to change the organization, typically to a more behavioral environment.

True/False
1. Development is designed to provide learners with the knowledge and skills needed for their present jobs.
2. Virtual reality is a unique extension of e-learning approach that permits trainees to view objects from a perspective otherwise impractical or impossible.
3. Simulators are devices or programs that replicate actual job demands.
4. In behavior modeling, participants are required to respond to specific problems they may encounter in their jobs by playing out an actual situation a person may encounter.
5. A T&D delivery system provided under the umbrella of the organization is referred to as corporate universities.
6. The vestibule delivery system takes place away from the production area on equipment that closely resembles equipment actually used on the job.
7. Benchmarking is the process of monitoring and measuring a firm's internal processes, such as operations, and then comparing the data with information from companies that excel in those areas.
8. The initial T&D effort designed for employees is orientation.
9. Organization development is a major means of achieving change in the corporate culture.
10. Sensitivity training is an OD technique designed to help individuals learn how others perceive their behavior.

Multiple Choice

1. What is the definition of *job rotation*?
    A. Approach to advising, coaching, and nurturing, for creating a practical relationship to enhance individual career, personal, and professional growth and development
    B. T&D method which permits a person to learn by copying or replicating behaviors of others to show managers how to handle various situations
    C. T&D method where participants are required to respond to specific problems they may encounter in their jobs by acting out real-world situations
    D. T&D method where employees move from one job to another to broaden their experience

2. What is the definition of *training*?
    A. Planned process of improving an organization by developing its structures, systems, and processes to enhance effectiveness and achieve desired goals
    B. Learning that goes beyond today's job and has a more long-term focus
    C. Activities designed to provide learners with the knowledge and skills needed for their present jobs
    D. Firm that recognizes the critical importance of continuous performance-related T&D and takes appropriate action

3. What is the definition of *business games*?
    A. Approach to advising, coaching, and nurturing, for creating a practical relationship to enhance individual career, personal, and professional growth and development
    B. T&D method which permits a person to learn by copying or replicating behaviors of others to show managers how to handle various situations
    C. T&D method where participants are required to respond to specific problems they may encounter in their jobs by acting out real-world situations
    D. T&D method that permits participants to assume roles such as president, controller, or marketing vice president of two or more similar hypothetical organizations and compete against each other by manipulating selected factors in a particular business situation

4. What is the definition of a *vestibule system*?
    A. Educational opportunities including degree and training programs that are delivered, either entirely or partially, via the Internet
    B. T&D delivery system provided under the umbrella of the organization
    C. T&D delivery system that takes place away from the production area on equipment that closely resembles equipment actually used on the job
    D. Unique extension of e-learning that permits trainees to view objects from a perspective otherwise impractical or impossible

5. What is the definition of *on-the-job-training (OJT)*?
    A. T&D method where employees move from one job to another to broaden their experience
    B. Training method which combines classroom instruction with on-the-job training
    C. Informal T&D method that permits an employee to learn job tasks by actually performing them
    D. T&D method allow participants to integrate theory learned in the classroom with business practices

6. In terms of T&D training, what is the definition of a *case study*?
   A. T&D method where participants are required to respond to specific problems they may encounter in their jobs by acting out real-world situations
   B. T&D method that permits participants to assume roles such as president, controller, or marketing vice president of two or more similar hypothetical organizations and compete against each other by manipulating selected factors in a particular business situation
   C. T&D method in which the participant is asked to establish priorities for and then handle a number of business papers, e-mail messages, memoranda, reports, and telephone messages that would typically cross a manager's desk
   D. T&D method in which trainees are expected to study the information provided in the case and make decisions based on it

7. In terms of T&D training, what is the definition of *behavioral modeling*?
   A. T&D method in which the participant is asked to establish priorities for and then handle a number of business papers, e-mail messages, memoranda, reports, and telephone messages that would typically cross a manager's desk
   B. T&D method that permits participants to assume roles such as president, controller, or marketing vice president of two or more similar hypothetical organizations and compete against each other by manipulating selected factors in a particular business situation
   C. T&D method that permits a person to learn by copying or replicating behaviors of others to show managers how to handle various situations
   D. T&D method where participants are required to respond to specific problems they may encounter in their jobs by acting out real-world situations

8. In terms of T&D training, what is the definition of *in-basket training*?
   A. T&D method that permits participants to assume roles such as president, controller, or marketing vice president of two or more similar hypothetical organizations and compete against each other by manipulating selected factors in a particular business situation
   B. T&D method where participants are required to respond to specific problems they may encounter in their jobs by acting out real-world situations
   C. An exercise in which the participant is asked to establish priorities for and then handle a number of business papers or e-mail messages such as memoranda, reports, and telephone messages that would typically cross a manager's desk
   D. T&D method that permits a person to learn by copying or replicating behaviors of others to show managers how to handle various situations

9. In terms of a T&D delivery system, what is the definition of a *corporate university*?
   A. T&D delivery system provided under the umbrella of the organization
   B. Publicly funded higher education establishments that deliver vocational training and associate degree programs
   C. Educational opportunities including degree and training programs that are delivered, either entirely or partially, via the Internet
   D. T&D delivery system that takes place away from the production area on equipment that closely resembles equipment actually used on the job

10. What is the definition of *training and development*?
    A. Heart of a continuous effort designed to improve employee competency and organizational performance
    B. Provides learners with the knowledge and skills needed for their present jobs
    C. Learning that goes beyond today's job and has a more long-term focus. It prepares employees to keep pace with the organization as it changes and grows
    D. Firm that recognizes the critical importance of continuous performance-related T&D and takes appropriate action

Matching Exercise

Directions: On the line provided, place the letter of the statement beside the key term.

1.	_____	Apprenticeship training	17.	_____	Online higher education
2.	_____	Behavior modeling	18.	_____	On-the-job training
3.	_____	Benchmarking	19.	_____	Organization development
4.	_____	Business games	20.	_____	Orientation
5.	_____	Case study	21.	_____	Quality circles
6.	_____	Coaching	22.	_____	Reverse mentoring
7.	_____	Corporate university	23.	_____	Role playing
8.	_____	Development	24.	_____	Sensitivity training
9.	_____	E-learning	25.	_____	Simulators
10.	_____	In-basket training	26.	_____	Survey feedback
11.	_____	Job rotation	27.	_____	Team building
12.	_____	Just-in-time training	28.	_____	Training
13.	_____	Learning organization	29.	_____	Training and development
14.	_____	Management development	30.	_____	Vestibule system
15.	_____	Mentoring	31.	_____	Virtual reality
16.	_____	Onboarding			

a. Heart of a continuous effort designed to improve employee competency and organizational performance.
b. Activities designed to provide learners with the knowledge and skill needed for their present jobs.
c. Learning that goes beyond today's job and has a more long-term focus.
d. Firm that recognizes the critical importance of continuous performance-related T&D and takes appropriate action.
e. Training provided anytime, anywhere in the world when it is needed.
f. T&D method in which trainees are expected to study the information provided in the case and make decisions based on it.
g. T&D method that permits a person to learn by copying or replicating behaviors of others to show managers how to handle various situations.
h. T&D method where participants are required to respond to specific problems they may encounter in their jobs by acting out real-world situations.
i. T&D delivery system comprised of devices or programs that replicate actual job demands.
j. T&D method that permits participants to assume roles such as president, controller, or marketing vice president of two or more similar hypothetical organizations and compete against each other by manipulating selected factors in a particular business situation.
k. T&D method in which the participant is asked to establish priorities for and then handle a number of business papers, e-mail messages, memoranda, reports, and telephone messages that would typically cross a manager's desk.
l. Informal T&D method that permits an employee to learn job tasks by actually performing them.
m. T&D method where employees move from one job to another to broaden their experience.
n. Training method that combines classroom instruction and on-the-job training.
o. T&D delivery system provided under the umbrella of the organization.
p. Educational opportunities including degree and training programs that are delivered, either entirely or partially, via the Internet.
q. T&D delivery system that takes place away from the production area on equipment that closely resembles equipment actually used on the job.
r. Unique extension of e-learning that permits trainees to view objects from a perspective otherwise impractical or impossible.
s. T&D delivery system for online instruction.
t. Consists of all learning experiences provided by an organization resulting in upgrading skills and knowledge required in current and future managerial positions.
u. Approach to advising, coaching, and nurturing, for creating a practical relationship to enhance individual career, personal, and professional growth and development.
v. Often considered a responsibility of the immediate boss who provides assistance much as a mentor.
w. Process where the older employees learn from the younger ones.
x. Initial T&D effort for new employees that informs them about the company, the job, and the workgroup.
y. Process companies use to help new executives quickly learn an organization's structure, culture and politics, as well as the ways they can start making discernible contributions to the organization as soon as possible.
z. Process of monitoring and measuring a firm's internal processes, such as operations, and then comparing the data with information from companies that excel in those areas.
aa. Planned and systematic attempts to change the organization, typically to a more behavioral environment.
bb. Process of collecting data from an organizational unit using questionnaires, interviews, and objective data from other sources such as records of productivity, turnover, and absenteeism.
cc. Groups of employees who voluntarily meet regularly with their supervisors to discuss problems, investigate causes, recommend solutions, and take corrective action when authorized to do so.
dd. Conscious effort to develop effective workgroups and cooperative skills throughout the organization.
ee. Organization development technique that is designed to help individuals learn how others perceive their behavior (also know as T-group training).

ANSWERS TO CHAPTER STUDY QUIZZES

Fill-in

1. Development
2. T&D objectives
3. Mentoring
4. In-basket
5. On-the-job training
6. Benchmarking
7. Workforce Investment Act
8. Management development
9. Orientation
10. Organization development

True/False

1. False (training)
2. True
3. True
4. False (role playing)
5. True
6. True
7. True
8. True
9. True
10. True

Multiple Choice

1. D
2. C
3. D
4. C
5. C
6. D
7. C
8. C
9. A
10. A

Matching Exercise

1. N
2. G
3. Z
4. J
5. F
6. V
7. O
8. C
9. S
10. K
11. M
12. E
13. D
14. T
15. U
16. Y
17. P
18. L
19. AA
20. X
21. CC
22. W
23. H
24. EE
25. I
26. BB
27. DD
28. B
29. A
30. Q
31. R

CHAPTER 7 Appendix

CAREER PLANNING AND DEVELOPMENT

KEY TERMS

Job security: Implies security in one job, often with one company.
Career security: Requires developing marketable skills and expertise that help ensure employment within a range of careers.
Employability doctrine: Employees owe the company their commitment while employed and the company owes its workers the opportunity to learn new skills, but that is as far as the commitment goes.
Career: General course that a person chooses to pursue throughout his or her working life.
Career planning: Ongoing process whereby an individual sets career goals and identifies the means to achieve them.
Career path: Flexible line of progression through which an employee may move during his or her employment with a company.
Career development: Formal approach used by the organization to ensure that people with the proper qualifications and experiences are available when needed.
Self-assessment: Process of learning about oneself.
Strength/weakness balance sheet: A self-evaluation procedure, developed originally by Benjamin Franklin, that assists people in becoming aware of their strengths and weaknesses
Likes and dislikes survey: Procedure that helps individuals recognize restrictions they place on themselves.
Traditional career path: Employee progresses vertically upward in the organization from one specific job to the next.
Network career path: Method of career progression that contains both a vertical sequence of jobs and a series of horizontal opportunities.
Lateral skill path: Career path that allows for lateral moves within the firm, taken to permit an employee to become revitalized and find new challenges.
Dual-career path: Career path that recognizes that technical specialists can and should be allowed to contribute their expertise to a company without having to become managers.
Free agents: People who take charge of all or part of their careers, by being their own bosses or by working for others in ways that fit their particular needs or wants.
Baby boomers: People born between just after World War II through the mid-1960s.
Generation X: Label affixed to the 40 million American workers born between the mid-1960s and late 1970.
Generation Y: People born between the late 1970s and early 1990s.
Generation I: Internet-assimilated children born after the mid-1990s.

APPENDIX STUDY OUTLINE

JOB SECURITY VERSUS CAREER SECURITY

Job security implies security in one job, often with one company. **Career security** requires developing marketable skills and expertise that help ensure employment within a range of careers. Under this so-called **employability doctrine**, employees owe the company their commitment while employed and the company owes its workers the opportunity to learn new skills, but that is as far as the commitment goes.

CAREER AND CAREER PLANNING DEFINED

CAREER—General course that a person chooses to pursue throughout his or her working life.

CAREER PLANNING—Ongoing process whereby an individual sets career goals and identifies the means to achieve them.

CAREER PLANNING
Ongoing process whereby an individual sets career goals and identifies the means to achieve them. Through career planning, a person evaluates his or her own abilities and interests, considers alternative career opportunities, establishes career goals, and plans practical developmental activities.

CAREER PLANNING—SELF-ASSESSMENT—Process of learning about oneself.

Strength/weakness balance sheet: A self-evaluation procedure, developed originally by Benjamin Franklin, that assists people in becoming aware of their strengths and weaknesses.

Likes and dislikes survey: Procedure that helps individuals recognize restrictions they place on themselves.

USING THE WEB FOR SELF-ASSESSMENT ASSISTANCE—The Internet has valuable information to assist in developing a self-assessment. Some sites are free and others charge a modest fee.

USING THE WEB FOR CAREER PLANNING ASSISTANCE—The web can often be an excellent tool for assisting you in planning your career.

CAREER PATHS AND CAREER DEVELOPMENT

CAREER PATH—Flexible line of progression through which an employee may move during his or her employment with a company.

CAREER DEVELOPMENT—Formal approach used by the organization to ensure that people with the proper qualifications and experiences are available when needed.

CAREER DEVELOPMENT METHODS
There are numerous methods for career planning and development.

MANAGER/EMPLOYEE SELF-SERVICE—Many companies are providing managers with the online ability to assist employees in planning their career paths and developing required competencies. Through online employee self-service, employees are provided with the ability to update performance goals online and to enroll in training courses.

DISCUSSIONS WITH KNOWLEDGEABLE INDIVIDUALS—In a formal discussion, the superior and subordinate may jointly agree on what career planning and development activities are best.

COMPANY MATERIAL—Some firms provide material specifically developed to assist their workers in career planning and development.

PERFORMANCE APPRAISAL SYSTEM—Noting and discussing an employee's strengths and weaknesses with his or her supervisor can uncover developmental needs.

WORKSHOPS—Some organizations conduct workshops lasting two or three days for the purpose of helping workers develop careers within the company.

CAREER PATHS
Career paths have historically focused on upward mobility within a particular occupation.

TRADITIONAL CAREER PATH—Employee progresses vertically upward in the organization from one specific job to the next.

NETWORK CAREER PATH—Method of career progression that contains both a vertical sequence of jobs and a series of horizontal opportunities.

LATERAL SKILL PATH—Career path that allows for lateral moves within the firm, taken to permit an employee to become revitalized and find new challenges.

DUAL-CAREER PATH—Career path that recognizes that technical specialists can and should be allowed to contribute their expertise to a company without having to become managers.

ADDING VALUE TO RETAIN PRESENT JOB—Regardless of the career path pursued, today's workers need to develop a plan whereby they are viewed as continually *adding value* to the organization.

DEMOTION—Demotions have long been associated with failure, but limited promotional opportunities in the future, and the fast pace of technological change, may make them more legitimate career options.

FREE AGENTS (BEING YOUR OWN BOSS)—People who take charge of all or part of their careers, by being their own bosses or by working for others in ways that fit their particular needs or wants.

DEVELOPING UNIQUE SEGMENTS OF THE WORKFORCE

Career planning and development is essential for the continual evolution of the labor force and the success of organizations, as well as individuals. Certain groups of employees are unique because of the specific characteristics of the work they do or who they are.

BABY BOOMERS—People born between just after World War II through the mid-1960s.

GENERATION X EMPLOYEES—Label affixed to the 40 million American workers born between the mid-1960s and late 1970.

GENERATION Y, AS PRESENT AND FUTURE EMPLOYEES—People born between the late 1970s and early 1990s.

GENERATION I (GOOGLE GENERATION) AS FUTURE EMPLOYEES—Internet-assimilated children born after the mid-1990s.

CHAPTER STUDY QUIZZES
Fill-in
1. Historically, a _____ was a sequence of work-related positions an individual has occupied during a lifetime, although not always with the same company.
2. _____ should not concentrate only on advancement opportunities since the present work environment has reduced many of these opportunities.
3. From a worker's perspective, following a _____ may involve weaving from company to company and from position to position as he or she obtains greater knowledge and experience.
4. Through _____, a person continuously evaluates his or her abilities and interests, considers alternative career opportunities, establishes career goals, and plans practical developmental activities.
5. Historically, it was thought that _____ was logical, linear, and indeed, planned.
6. A self-evaluation procedure, developed originally by _____ that assists people become aware of their strengths and weaknesses is the strength/weakness balance sheet.
7. The _____ career path recognizes the interchangeability of experience at certain levels and the need to broaden experience at one level before promotion to a higher level.
8. A _____ approach is often established to encourage and motivate professionals in such fields as engineering, sales, marketing, finance, and human resources.
9. The primary tie that binds a worker to the company, and vice versa, is mutual success resulting in performance that _____ to the organization.
10. _____ differ from previous generations in some significant ways including their natural affinity for technology and their entrepreneurial spirit.

True/False
1. Career planning should not concentrate only on advancement opportunities since the present work environment has reduced many of these opportunities.
2. To use a strength/weakness balance sheet, the individual lists strengths and weaknesses as they actually are.
3. Getting to know yourself is a singular event.
4. Career planning should begin with a person's job placement and initial orientation.
5. The primary responsibility for career planning rests with the individual.
6. The traditional career path is as viable a career path option as it previously was.
7. The network career path recognizes the interchangeability of experience at certain levels and the need to broaden experience at one level before promotion to a higher level.
8. Traditionally, a career path was viewed as moving upward to higher levels of management in the organization.
9. An individual's toolbox must be ever expanding and continual personal development is a necessity.
10. Generation Yers recognize that their careers cannot be founded securely on a relationship with any one employer.

Multiple Choice

1. What is the definition of a *career*?
    A. An ongoing process whereby an individual sets career goals and identifies the means to achieve them
    B. General course that a person chooses to pursue throughout his or her working life
    C. Planned succession of jobs worked out by a firm to develop its employees
    D. Flexible line of movement through which an employee may move during employment with a company

2. What is the definition of *career development*?
    A. General course that a person chooses to pursue throughout his or her working life
    B. Planned succession of jobs worked out by a firm to develop its employees
    C. An ongoing process whereby an individual sets career goals and identifies the means to achieve them
    D. Formal approach used by the organization to ensure that people with the proper qualifications and experiences are available when needed

3. Who first developed the self-evaluation procedure in which one examines his or her strengths and weaknesses?
    A. Robert Mooney
    B. George Washington
    C. Albert Einstein
    D. Benjamin Franklin

4. Who said "It takes all the running you can do, to keep in the same place."?
    A. Red Queen
    B. Mad Hatter
    C. Alice
    D. Bob Noe

5. Which of the following is an objective that can be accomplished through career development programs?
    A. effective development of available talent
    B. self-appraisal opportunities for employees considering new or nontraditional career paths
    C. development of career paths that cut across divisions and geographic locations
    D. all of the above

6. What is the definition of the *traditional career path*?
    A. Career path that contains both a vertical sequence of jobs and a series of horizontal opportunities
    B. Career path that allows for lateral moves within the firm taken to permit an employee to become revitalized and find new challenges
    C. Career path in which an employee progresses vertically upward in the organization from one specific job to the next
    D. Career path that recognizes that technical specialists can and should be allowed to contribute their expertise to a company without having to become managers

7. What is the definition of the *dual-career path*?
    A. Career path in which an employee progresses vertically upward in the organization from one specific job to the next
    B. Career path that recognizes that technical specialists can and should be allowed to contribute their expertise to a company without having to become managers
    C. Career path that contains both a vertical sequence of jobs and a series of horizontal opportunities
    D. Career path that allows for lateral moves within the firm taken to permit an employee to become revitalized and find new challenges

8. Which of the following is a career development method?
    A. discussions with knowledgeable individuals
    B. company material
    C. performance appraisal system
    D. all of the above

9. What is the definition of a *baby boomer*?
    A. Label affixed to the 41 million American workers born between the mid-1960s and late 1970
    B. People born between the late 1970s and early 1990s
    C. Internet-assimilated children born after the mid-1990s
    D. Born just after World War II through the mid-1960s

10. What unique segment of the workforce are the leading edge of a generation that promises to be the richest, smartest, and savviest ever?
    A. Baby boomers
    B. Generation X
    C. Generation Y
    D. Generation I

Matching Exercise
Directions: On the line provided, place the letter of the statement beside the key term.

1. _____ Baby boomers
2. _____ Career
3. _____ Career development
4. _____ Career path
5. _____ Career planning
6. _____ Dual-career path
7. _____ Free agents
8. _____ Generation I
9. _____ Generation X
10. _____ Generation Y
11. _____ Lateral skill path
12. _____ Likes and dislikes survey
13. _____ Network career path
14. _____ Self-assessment
15. _____ Strength/weakness balance sheet
16. _____ Traditional career path
17. _____ Job Security
18. _____ Career Security
19. _____ Employability doctrine

a. General course that a person chooses to pursue throughout his or her working life.
b. Ongoing process whereby an individual sets career goals and identifies the means to achieve them.
c. Flexible line of movement through which a person may travel during their work life.
d. Formal approach used by the organization to ensure that people with the proper qualifications and experiences are available when needed.
e. Process of learning about oneself.
f. A self-evaluation procedure, developed originally by Benjamin Franklin, that assists people in becoming aware of their strengths and weaknesses.
g. Procedure that helps individuals recognize restrictions they place on themselves.
h. Employee progresses vertically upward in the organization from one specific job to the next.
i. Method of career progression that contains both a vertical sequence of jobs and a series of horizontal opportunities.
j. Career path that allows for lateral moves within the firm taken to permit an employee to become revitalized and find new challenges.
k. Career path that recognizes that technical specialists can and should be allowed to contribute their expertise to a company without having to become managers.
l. People who take charge of all or part of their careers, by being their own bosses or by working for others in ways that fit their particular needs or wants.
m. People born between just after World War II through the mid-1960s.
n. The label affixed to the 40 million American workers born between the mid-1960s and late 1970.
o. People born between the late 1970s and early 1990s.
p. Internet-assimilated children born after the mid-1990s.
q. Implies security in one job, often with one company.
r. Requires developing marketable skills and expertise that help ensure employment within a range of careers.
s. Employees owe the company their commitment while employed and the company owes its workers the opportunity to learn new skills, but that is as far as the commitment goes.

ANSWERS TO CHAPTER STUDY QUIZZES

Fill-in
1. career
2. Career planning
3. Career path
4. Career planning
5. Career planning
6. Benjamin Franklin
7. Network
8. Dual-career
9. Adds value
10. Generation Xers

True/False
1. True
2. False (he or she perceives them)
3. False (not)
4. False (organizational career planning)
5. True
6. False (not)
7. True
8. True
9. True
10. False (Xers)

Multiple Choice
1. B
2. D
3. D
4. A
5. D
6. C
7. B
8. D
9. D
10. C

Matching Exercise
1. M
2. A
3. D
4. C
5. B
6. K
7. L
8. P
9. N
10. O
11. J
12. G
13. I
14. E
15. F
16. H
17. Q
18. R
19. S

CHAPTER 8

PERFORMANCE MANAGEMENT AND APPRAISAL

CHAPTER DESCRIPTION

This chapter begins by discussing productivity and emotional intelligence. Then performance management is defined and its relationship to performance appraisal is studied. Next, we look at the uses made of appraisal data and at how performance management, appraisal, and layoffs are interrelated. Then, the environmental factors affecting the performance appraisal process are explained. The performance appraisal process is then described and the possible criteria used in evaluating performance are discussed. Then the person(s) responsible for appraisal and the appraisal period are described, and the various performance appraisal methods are explained. The use of computer software in performance appraisal, problems associated with performance appraisal, and characteristics of an effective appraisal system are described next, followed by a discussion of the legal aspects of performance appraisal and the appraisal interview. This chapter concludes with a Global Perspective entitled "Two Cultures' Views of Performance Appraisal."

KEY TERMS

Emotional intelligence: The ability to recognize and manage emotions.
Performance management: Goal-oriented process directed toward ensuring that organizational processes are in place to maximize the productivity of employees, teams, and ultimately, the organization.
Performance appraisal: Formal system of review and evaluation of individual or team task performance.
Competencies: Broad range of knowledge, skills, traits and behaviors that may be technical in nature, relate to interpersonal skills, or be business oriented.
360-degree feedback evaluation method: Popular performance appraisal method that involves evaluation input from multiple levels within the firm as well as external sources.
Rating scales method: Performance appraisal method that rates employees according to defined factors.
Critical incident method: Performance appraisal method that requires keeping written records of highly favorable and unfavorable employee work actions.
Essay method: Performance appraisal method in which the rater writes a brief narrative describing the employee's performance.
Work standards method: Performance appraisal method that compares each employee's performance to a predetermined standard or expected level of output.
Ranking method: Performance appraisal method in which the rater places all employees from a group in order of overall performance.
Paired comparison: Variation of the ranking method in which the performance of each employee is compared with that of every other employee in the group.
Forced distribution method: Performance appraisal method in which the rater is required to assign individuals in a workgroup to a limited number of categories similar to a normal frequency distribution.
Behaviorally anchored rating scale (BARS) method: Performance appraisal method that combines elements of the traditional rating scale and critical incident methods; various performance levels are shown along a scale with each described in terms of an employee's specific job behavior.
Results-based system: Performance appraisal method in which the manager and subordinate jointly agree on objectives for the next appraisal period; in the past a form of *management by objectives.*
Halo error: Evaluation error that occurs when a manager generalizes one positive performance feature or incident to all aspects of employee performance resulting in a higher rating.
Horn error: Evaluation error that occurs when a manager generalizes one negative performance feature or incident to all aspects of employee performance resulting in a lower rating.
Leniency: Giving an undeserved high performance appraisal rating to an employee.
Strictness: Being unduly critical of an employee's work performance.
Central tendency error: Evaluation appraisal error that occurs when employees are incorrectly rated near the average or middle of a scale.

CHAPTER STUDY OUTLINE

PRODUCTIVITY AND EMOTIONAL INTELLIGENCE
Emotional intelligence is the ability to recognize and manage emotions. Some of the characteristics of individuals with high EQ include the ability to cope successfully and proactively with life's demands and pressures, and to build and make use of rewarding relationships with others, while not being afraid to make tough decisions. Research suggests that there is a positive relationship between emotionally intelligent leadership and employee engagement, client satisfaction, and the bottom line.

PERFORMANCE MANAGEMENT
Goal-oriented process directed toward ensuring that organizational processes are in place to maximize the productivity of employees, teams, and ultimately, the organization.

PERFORMANCE APPRAISAL
Formal system of review and evaluation of an individual or team's job performance.

USES OF PERFORMANCE APPRAISAL
Performance appraisal data are potentially valuable for use in numerous human resource functional areas.

HUMAN RESOURCE PLANNING—In assessing a firm's human resources, data must be available that describe the promotability and potential of all employees, especially key executives.

RECRUITMENT AND SELECTION—Performance evaluation ratings may be helpful in predicting the future performance of job applicants.

TRAINING AND DEVELOPMENT—Performance appraisal should point out an employee's specific needs for training and development.

CAREER PLANNING AND DEVELOPMENT—Career planning and development may be viewed from either an individual or organizational viewpoint.

COMPENSATION PROGRAMS—Performance appraisal results provide the basis for decisions regarding pay increases.

INTERNAL EMPLOYEE RELATIONS—Performance appraisal data are also frequently used for decisions in areas of internal employee relations including motivation, promotion, demotion, termination, layoff, and transfer.

ASSESSMENT OF EMPLOYEE POTENTIAL—Some organizations attempt to assess employee potential as they appraise job performance.

PERFORMANCE MANAGEMENT, APPRAISAL, AND LAYOFFS
Software applications are now available to assist management downsize and restructure.

PERFORMANCE APPRAISAL ENVIRONMENTAL FACTORS
Many of the external and internal environmental factors can influence the appraisal process.

PERFORMANCE APPRAISAL PROCESS

CONSIDER EXTERNAL AND INTERNAL ENVIRONMENT

IDENTIFY SPECIFIC PERFORMANCE APPRAISAL GOALS

ESTABLISH PERFORMANCE CRITERIA (STANDARDS) AND COMMUNICATE THESE PERFORMANCE EXPECTATIONS TO THOSE CONCERNED

EXAMINE WORK PERFORMED

APPRAISE PERFORMANCE

DISCUSS APPRAISAL WITH EMPLOYEE

ESTABLISH PERFORMANCE CRITERIA (STANDARDS)
Most common sets of appraisal criteria are traits, behaviors, and task outcomes.

> **TRAITS**—Many employees in organizations are evaluated on the basis of certain traits such as *attitude*, *appearance*, *initiative*, etc.
>
> **BEHAVIORS**—When an individual's task outcome is difficult to determine, it is common to evaluate the person's task-related behavior.
>
> **COMPETENCIES**—Broad range of knowledge, skills, traits and behaviors that may be technical in nature, relate to interpersonal skills, or be business oriented.
>
> **GOAL ACHIEVEMENT**—If ends are considered more important than means, goal achievement becomes the most appropriate factor to evaluate.
>
> **IMPROVEMENT POTENTIAL**—Some attention must be given to the future and the behaviors and outcomes that are needed to not only develop the employee, but also achieve the firm's goals.

RESPONSIBILITY FOR APPRAISAL
In most organizations, the human resource department is responsible for coordinating the design and implementation of performance appraisal programs.

> **IMMEDIATE SUPERVISOR**—Traditionally has been the most common choice for evaluating performance.
>
> **SUBORDINATES**—Some managers have concluded that evaluation of managers by subordinates is feasible.
>
> **PEERS AND TEAM MEMBERS**—Peer appraisal has long had proponents who believed that such an approach is reliable if the workgroup is stable over a reasonably long period of time and performs tasks that require considerable interaction.
>
> **SELF-APPRAISAL**—If individuals understand the objectives they are expected to achieve and the standards by which they are to be evaluated, they are—to a great extent—in the best position to appraise their own performance.
>
> **CUSTOMER APPRAISAL**—Behavior of customers determines the degree of success a firm achieves. Therefore, some organizations believe it is important to obtain performance input from this critical source.

APPRAISAL PERIOD
Performance evaluations are typically prepared at specific intervals. In most organizations these evaluations are made either annually or semiannually.

PERFORMANCE APPRAISAL METHODS
Type of performance appraisal system utilized depends on its purpose. If the major emphasis is on selecting people for promotion, training, and merit pay increases, a traditional method such as rating scales may be appropriate. Collaborative methods, including input from the employees themselves, may prove to be more suitable for developing employees.

360-DEGREE FEEDBACK EVALUATION METHOD—Popular performance appraisal method that involves evaluation input from multiple levels within the firm as well as external sources.

RATING SCALES METHOD—Rates employees according to defined factors. The factors chosen for evaluation are typically of two types: job-related and personal characteristics.

CRITICAL INCIDENTS METHOD—Requires written records be kept of highly favorable and unfavorable work actions.

ESSAY METHOD—Performance appraisal method in which the rater writes a brief narrative describing the employee's performance. This method tends to focus on extreme behavior in the employee's work rather than routine day-to-day performance.

WORK STANDARDS METHOD—Compares each employee's performance to a predetermined standard, or expected level of output.

RANKING METHOD—Rater places all employees in a given group in order on the basis of their overall performance. *Paired comparison* is a variation of the ranking method in which the performance of each employee is compared with that of every other employee in the group.

FORCED DISTRIBUTION METHOD—Performance appraisal method in which the rater is required to assign individuals in a workgroup to a limited number of categories similar to a normal frequency distribution.

BEHAVIORALLY ANCHORED RATING SCALES METHOD—Combines elements of the traditional rating scale and critical incident methods; various performance levels are shown along a scale with each described in terms of an employee's specific job behavior.

RESULTS-BASED SYSTEMS—Superior and subordinate jointly agree on objectives for the next appraisal period.

USE OF COMPUTER SOFTWARE
Computer software is available for recording the appraisal data. A big advantage in utilizing the computer is reduction of paperwork.

PROBLEMS IN PERFORMANCE APPRAISAL
Many of the problems commonly mentioned are not inherent in the method but, rather, reflect improper usage.

APPRAISER DISCOMFORT—Going through the procedure cuts into a manager's high-priority workload and the experience can be especially unpleasant when the employee in question has not performed well.

LACK OF OBJECTIVITY—Potential weakness of traditional methods of performance appraisal is that they lack objectivity.

HALO ERROR—Evaluation error that occurs when a manager generalizes one *positive* performance feature or incident to all aspects of employee performance resulting in a higher rating.

HORN ERROR—Evaluation error that occurs when a manager generalizes one *negative* performance feature or incident to all aspects of employee performance resulting in a lower rating.

LENIENCY/STRICTNESS—Giving of undeserved high or low ratings.

CENTRAL TENDENCY ERROR—Evaluation appraisal error that occurs when employees are incorrectly rated near the average or middle of a scale.

RECENT BEHAVIOR BIAS—Performance appraisals generally cover a specified period of time and an individual's performance should be considered for the entire period.

PERSONAL BIAS (STEREOTYPING)—Supervisors doing performance appraisals may have biases related to their employees' personal characteristics such as race, religion, gender, disability, or age group.

MANIPULATING THE EVALUATION—In some instances, supervisors control virtually every aspect of the appraisal process and are therefore in a position to manipulate the system.

EMPLOYEE ANXIETY—Evaluation process may also create anxiety for the appraised employee.

CHARACTERISTICS OF AN EFFECTIVE APPRAISAL SYSTEM
Systems that possess certain characteristics may be more legally defensible.

JOB-RELATED CRITERIA—Criteria used for appraising employee performance must be job related.

PERFORMANCE EXPECTATIONS—Managers must clearly explain their performance expectations to their subordinates in advance of the appraisal period.

STANDARDIZATION—Employees in the same job categories under a given supervisor should be appraised using the same evaluation instrument.

TRAINED APPRAISERS—In order to ensure consistency, appraisers must be well trained.

CONTINUOUS OPEN COMMUNICATION—Good appraisal system provides highly desirable feedback on a continuing basis.

CONDUCT PERFORMANCE REVIEWS—Since improved performance is a common goal of appraisal systems, withholding appraisal results is absurd.

DUE PROCESS—A formal procedure should be developed—if one does not exist—to permit employees the means for appealing appraisal results that they do not consider accurate or fair.

LEGAL IMPLICATIONS
A review of court cases makes it clear that legally defensible performance appraisal systems should be in place.

APPRAISAL INTERVIEW
Appraisal interview is the *Achilles' heel* of the entire evaluation process.

SCHEDULING THE INTERVIEW—Supervisors usually conduct a formal appraisal interview at the end of an employee's appraisal period.

INTERVIEW STRUCTURE—Successful appraisal interview should be structured in a way that allows both the supervisor and the subordinate to view it as a problem-solving rather than a faultfinding session.

USE OF PRAISE AND CRITICISM—Praise should be provided when warranted, but it can have only limited value if it is not clearly deserved; criticism, even if warranted, is especially difficult to give.

EMPLOYEES' ROLE—Two weeks or so before the review, they should go through their diaries or files and make a note of every project worked on, regardless of whether they were successful or not.

CONCLUDING THE INTERVIEW—Ideally, employees will leave the interview with positive feelings about management, the company, the job, and themselves. If the meeting results in a deflated ego, the prospects for improved performance will be bleak. While you cannot change past behavior, future performance is another matter. The interview should end with specific and mutually agreed upon plans for the employee's development. Managers should assure employees who require additional training that it will be forthcoming and that they will have the full support of their supervisor. When management does its part in employee development, it is up to the individual to perform in an acceptable manner.

TWO CULTURES' VIEW OF PERFORMANCE APPRAISAL
Performance appraisal is an area of human resource management that has special problems when translated into different cultural environments. Chinese managers often have a different idea about what performance is than do Western managers, as Chinese companies tend to focus appraisals on different criteria. Chinese managers appear to define performance in terms of personal characteristics, such as loyalty and obedience, rather than outcome measurement.

EXERCISES
1. Your performance appraisal form uses a rating form with the following characteristics: leadership, public acceptance, attitude toward people, appearance and grooming, personal conduct, outlook on life, ethical habits, resourcefulness, capacity for growth, mental alertness, and loyalty to organization. Could any of these characteristics pose a problem with regard to a legal challenge? Why? Discuss.

2. Visit an HR manager in your local area. What performance appraisal method does this firm use? Ask how well the performance appraisal method is accepted in the organization.

3. There are numerous Internet sites that pertain to information covered in this chapter. Identify two sites that apply to information contained in the chapter.

YOU AND HR
Memo One
To: (You) Human Resource Manager
From: New Assistant Hospital Administrator
Subject: Best Method to Use to Assess Performances of Health Care Workers

I've just completed a one-day seminar concerning methods of performance appraisal. Several distinctly different methods were highlighted. I'm still a bit uncertain about which PA method we should adopt to conduct PA on our health care employees. What do you suggest?

Memo One Response
To: New Assistant Hospital Administrator
From: (You) Human Resource Manager
Subject: Relative Merits of Various PA Methods

(Your memo goes here in 75 to 100 words.)

Memo Two
To: (You) Human Resource Manager
From: Maintenance Supervisor
Subject: Bad Timing for Performance Appraisals

Your memo yesterday stating the performance appraisals were due next week caught me off guard. My unit is so busy these days that I don't see how I will have time to do them. Besides, all my workers are doing what I tell them. I would probably have to rate them all outstanding. Can we put this performance appraisal bit off for a year?

Memo Two Response
To: Maintenance Supervisor
From: (You) Human Resource Manager
Subject: Performance Appraisals Delay Request

(Your memo goes here in 75 to 100 words.)

DISCUSSION QUESTIONS
1. Define *performance management* and performance *appraisal*.
2. What are the basic steps in the performance appraisal process?
3. What are the various problems associated with performance appraisal?
4. What are the characteristics of an effective appraisal system?
5. Why is the appraisal interview considered the *Achilles' heel* of the entire evaluation process?

CHAPTER STUDY QUIZZES
Fill-in
1. _____ is a formal system of review and evaluation of individual or team task performance.
2. For many organizations, the primary goal of an appraisal system is to improve individual and organizational _____.
3. Often the _____ is responsible for coordinating the design and implementation of performance appraisal programs.
4. The _____ method is a popular performance appraisal method that involves evaluation input from multiple levels within the firm as well as external sources.
5. A widely used appraisal method, which rates employees according to defined factors, is called the _____ method.
6. _____ is a variation of the ranking method in which the performance of each employee is compared with that of every other employee in the group.
7. The _____ method combines elements of the traditional rating scales and critical incidents methods.
8. _____ is a common error that occurs when employees are incorrectly rated near the average or middle of the scale.
9. _____ is perhaps the most basic criterion needed in employee performance appraisals.
10. The *Achilles' heel* of the entire evaluation process is the _____ itself.

True/False
1. Performance appraisal is a goal-oriented process directed toward ensuring that organizational processes are in place to maximize productivity of employees, teams, and ultimately, the organization.
2. If organizations consider *ends* more important than *means*, behavior outcomes become an appropriate factor to evaluate.
3. An employee's immediate supervisor has traditionally been the most common choice for evaluating performance.
4. In the paired comparison method, the rater is required to assign individuals in the workgroup to a limited number of categories similar to a normal frequency distribution.
5. Using the critical incident method requires keeping written records of highly favorable and highly unfavorable work actions.
6. Halo error is a common error that occurs when employees are incorrectly rated near the average or middle of the scale.
7. The criteria used for appraising employee performance must be job related.
8. A successful appraisal interview should be structured in a way that allows both the supervisor and the subordinate to view it as a problem-solving rather than a faultfinding session.
9. Ideally, employees will leave the interview with neutral feelings about management, the company, the job, and themselves.
10. From the employees' side, two weeks or so before the review, they should go through their diaries or files and make a note of every project worked on, regardless of whether they were successful or not.

Multiple Choice

1. What was the major conclusion of *Albermarle Paper v Moody*?
    A. Any test used in the selection process or in promotion decisions must be validated if it has an adverse impact on women and minorities
    B. Supported validation requirements for performance appraisals, as well as for selection tests
    C. Title VII does not prohibit discrimination on the basis of lack of citizenship
    D. When human resource management practices eliminate substantial numbers of minority or women applicants, the burden of proof is on the employer to show that the practice is job related

2. Which of the following is **NOT** a characteristic of an effective appraisal system?
    A. job-related criteria
    B. performance expectations
    C. standardization
    D. no employee access to results

3. What was the major conclusion of the federal district court case of *Mistretta v Sandia*?
    A. Supported validation requirements for performance appraisals, as well as for selection tests
    B. Allows seniority and promotion systems established since Title VII to stand, although they unintentionally hurt minority workers
    C. There was sufficient circumstantial evidence to indicate that age bias and age-based policies appear throughout the performance rating process to the detriment of the protected age group
    D. Court reaffirmed that race may be taken into account in admission decisions

4. Which of the following performance criteria would provide an example of traits to be evaluated?
    A. ethical behavior
    B. developing talent
    C. leadership style
    D. attitude

5. What appraisal method is used not only for conventional evaluations but also for succession planning, training, professional development, and performance management?
    A. 360-Degree Feedback Evaluation Method
    B. 720-Degree Review Method
    C. Rating Scales Method
    D. Critical Incidents Method

6. What is the definition of the *rating scale method*?
    A. Performance appraisal method that rates employees according to defined factors
    B. Performance appraisal method which requires keeping written records of highly favorable and unfavorable employee work actions
    C. Performance appraisal method in which the rater writes a brief narrative describing the employee's performance
    D. Performance appraisal method that compares each employee's performance to a predetermined standard or expected level of output

7. What is the definition of the *paired comparison* performance appraisal method?
    A. Performance appraisal method that compares each employee's performance to a predetermined standard or expected level of output
    B. Performance appraisal method that combines elements of the traditional rating scales and critical incident methods
    C. Performance appraisal method that involves comparing the performance of each employee with that of every other employee in the group
    D. Performance appraisal method that requires the rater to assign individuals in a workgroup to a limited number of categories similar to a normal frequency distribution

8. What is the definition of the *behaviorally anchored rating scale* performance appraisal method?
    A. Performance appraisal method that involves comparing the performance of each employee with that of every other employee in the group
    B. Performance appraisal method that combines elements of the traditional rating scales and critical incident methods
    C. Performance appraisal method that requires the rater to assign individuals in a workgroup to a limited number of categories similar to a normal frequency distribution
    D. Performance appraisal method that compares each employee's performance to a predetermined standard or expected level of output

9. What is the definition of *central tendency* error in performance appraisal?
    A. Occurs when a manager generalizes one *positive* performance feature or incident to all aspects of employee performance resulting in a higher rating
    B. An evaluation appraisal error that occurs when employees are incorrectly rated near the average or middle of a scale
    C. Giving undeserved high ratings
    D. Being unduly critical of an employee's work performance

10. What is the definition of the *forced distribution method* of performance appraisal?
    A. Performance appraisal method that involves comparing the performance of each employee with that of every other employee in the group
    B. Requires the rater to assign individuals in a workgroup to a limited number of categories similar to a normal frequency distribution
    C. Performance appraisal method that compares each employee's performance to a predetermined standard or expected level of output
    D. Performance appraisal method that combines elements of the traditional rating scales and critical incident methods

Matching Exercise

Directions: On the line provided, place the letter of the statement beside the key term.

1. _____ 360-degree feedback evaluation method
2. _____ Behaviorally anchored rating scale method
3. _____ Competencies
4. _____ Central tendency error
5. _____ Critical incident method
6. _____ Essay method
7. _____ Forced distribution method
8. _____ Halo error
9. _____ Horn error
10. _____ Leniency
11. _____ Performance appraisal
12. _____ Performance management
13. _____ Ranking method
14. _____ Rating scales method
15. _____ Results-based system
16. _____ Strictness
17. _____ Work standards method
18. _____ Emotional intelligence

a. Goal-oriented process directed toward ensuring that organizational processes are in place to maximize productivity of employees, teams, and ultimately, the organization.
b. Formal system of review and evaluation of individual or team task performance.
c. Broad range of knowledge, skills, traits and behaviors that may be technical in nature, relate to interpersonal skills or be business oriented.
d. Popular performance appraisal method that involves evaluation input from multiple levels within the firm as well as external sources.
e. Performance appraisal method that rates employees according to defined factors.
f. Performance appraisal method that requires a written record of highly favorable and highly unfavorable employee work actions.
g. Performance appraisal method in which the rater writes a brief narrative describing an employee's performance.
h. Performance appraisal method which compares each employee's performance to a predetermined standard or expected level of output.
i. Job evaluation method in which the rater places all employees from a group in order of overall performance.
j. Performance appraisal method in which the rater is required to assign individuals in a workgroup to a limited number of categories similar to a normal frequency distribution.
k. Performance appraisal method that combines elements of the traditional rating scale and critical incident methods; various performance levels are shown along a scale with each described in terms of an employee's specific job behavior.
l. Performance appraisal method in which the manager and subordinate jointly agree on objectives for the next appraisal period; in the past a form of *management by objectives*.
m. Evaluation error that occurs when a manager generalizes one *positive* performance feature or incident to all aspects of employee performance resulting in a higher rating.
n. Evaluation error that occurs when a manager generalizes one *negative* performance feature or incident to all aspects of employee performance resulting in a lower rating.
o. Giving an undeserved high performance appraisal rating to an employee.
p. Being unduly critical of an employee's work performance.
q. Evaluation appraisal error that occurs when employees are incorrectly rated near the average or middle of a scale.
r. Ability to recognize and manage emotions.

ANSWERS TO CHAPTER STUDY QUIZZES

Fill-in
1. Performance appraisal
2. Performance
3. Human resource department
4. 360-degree feedback evaluation
5. Rating scales
6. Paired comparison
7. Behaviorally anchored rating scale
8. Central tendency error
9. Job relatedness
10. Appraisal interview

True/False
1. False (performance management)
2. False (goal achievement)
3. True
4. False (forced distribution)
5. True
6. False (central tendency error)
7. True
8. True
9. False (positive)
10. True

Multiple Choice
1. B
2. D
3. C
4. D
5. A
6. A
7. C
8. B
9. B
10. B

Matching Exercise
1. D
2. K
3. C
4. Q
5. F
6. G
7. J
8. M
9. N
10. O
11. B
12. A
13. I
14. E
15. L
16. P
17. H
18. R

CHAPTER 9

DIRECT FINANCIAL COMPENSATION

CHAPTER DESCRIPTION

This chapter begins by considering the question of whether severance pay for executives is excessive; the various forms of compensation are described and the concept of equity in financial compensation is explained. Then the determinants of direct financial compensation are explained and how the organization influences direct financial compensation is examined. This is followed by discussions of how both the labor market and the job are factors in determining direct financial compensation. Then, topics related to job evaluation and job pricing are studied, and factors related to the employee in determining direct financial compensation are described. Team-based pay and company-wide plans are then discussed, and compensation for professionals, sales employees, contingent workers, and executives is studied. The chapter concludes with a Global Perspective entitled "China's Compensation Problems."

KEY TERMS

Compensation: Total of all rewards provided to employees in return for their services.
Direct financial compensation: Pay that a person receives in the form of wages, salary, bonuses, and commissions.
Indirect financial compensation (benefits): All financial rewards that are not included in direct financial compensation.
Nonfinancial compensation: Satisfaction that a person receives from the job itself or from the psychological and/or physical environment in which the job is performed.
Equity theory: Motivation theory that people assess their performance and attitudes by comparing both their contribution to work and the benefits they derive from it to the contributions and benefits of *comparison others* whom they select--and who in reality may or may not be like them.
Financial equity: Perception of fair pay treatment for employees.
External equity: Equity that exists when a firm's employees receive pay comparable to workers who perform similar jobs in other firms.
Internal equity: Exists when employees receive pay according to the relative value of their jobs within the same organization.
Employee equity: Equity that exists when individuals performing *similar jobs for the same firm* receive pay according to factors unique to the employee, such as performance level or seniority.
Team equity: Equity that is achieved when teams are rewarded based on their group's productivity.
Compensation policy: Policy that provide general guidelines for making compensation decisions.
Pay leaders: Organizations that pay higher wages and salaries than competing firms.
Market (going) rate: Average pay that most employers provide for the same job in a particular area or industry.
Pay followers: Companies that choose to pay below the going rate because of a poor financial condition or a belief that they do not require highly capable employees.
Labor market: Potential employees located within the geographic area from which employees are recruited.
Compensation survey: Means of obtaining data regarding what other firms are paying for specific jobs or job classes within a given labor market.
Benchmark job: Well-known job in the company and industry and one performed by a large number of employees.
Cost-of-living allowance (COLA): Escalator clause in a labor agreement that automatically increases wages as the U.S. Bureau of Labor Statistics' cost-of-living index rises.
Exempt employees: Employees categorized as executive, administrative, professional, or outside salespersons.
Job evaluation: Process that determines the relative value of one job in relation to another.
Job evaluation ranking method: Job evaluation method in which the raters examine the description of each job being evaluated and arrange the jobs in order according to their value to the company.
Classification method: Job evaluation method in which classes or grades are defined to describe a group of jobs.
Factor comparison method: Job evaluation method that assumes there are five universal factors consisting of mental requirements, skills, physical requirements, responsibilities, and working conditions; the evaluator makes decisions on these factors independently.

Point method: Job evaluation method where the raters assign numerical values to specific job factors, such as knowledge required, and the sum of these values provides a quantitative assessment of a job's relative worth.
Hay guide chart-profile method (Hay Plan): Refined version of the point method used by approximately 8,000 public and private sector organizations worldwide to evaluate clerical, trade, technical, professional, managerial and/or executive level jobs.
Job pricing: Placing a dollar value on a job's worth.
Pay grade: Grouping of similar jobs to simplify pricing jobs.
Wage curve: Fitting of plotted points on a curve to create a smooth progression between pay grades (also known as the *pay curve)*.
Pay range: Minimum and maximum pay rate with enough variance between the two to allow for a significant pay difference.
Broadbanding: Compensation technique that collapses many pay grades (salary grades) into a few wide bands in order to improve organizational effectiveness.
Merit pay: Pay increase added to employees base pay based on their level of performance.
Bonus: One-time annual financial award based on productivity that is not added to base pay.
Spot bonus: Relatively small monetary gift provided employees for outstanding work or effort during a reasonably short period of time.
Piecework: Incentive pay plan in which employees are paid for each unit they produce.
Skill-based pay: System that compensates employees for their job-related skills and knowledge, not for their job titles.
Competency-based pay: Compensation plan that rewards employees for the capabilities they attain.
Seniority: Length of time an employee has been associated with the company, division, department, or job.
Profit sharing: Compensation plans that result in the distribution of a predetermined percentage of the firm's profits to employees.
Gainsharing: Plans designed to bind employees to the firm's productivity and provide an incentive payment based on improved company performance.
Scanlon plan: Gainsharing plan that provides a financial reward to employees for savings in labor costs resulting from their suggestions.
Stock option plan: Incentive plan in which executives can buy a specified amount of stock in their company in the future at or below the current market price.
Perquisites (perks): Special benefits provided by a firm to key executives to give them something extra.
Golden parachute contract: Perquisite that protects executives in the event that another company acquires their firm or if the executive is forced to leave the firm for other reasons.

CHAPTER STUDY OUTLINE

OUTRAGEOUS SEVERANCE PAY
Today many execs are still walking away from self-made disasters with big payouts, pensions, and consulting jobs.

COMPENSATION: AN OVERVIEW

COMPENSATION—Total of all rewards provided to employees in return for their services.

DIRECT FINANCIAL COMPENSATION—Pay that a person receives in the form of wages, salary, bonuses, and commissions.

INDIRECT FINANCIAL COMPENSATION (BENEFITS)—All financial rewards that are not included in direct financial compensation.

NONFINANCIAL COMPENSATION—Satisfaction that a person receives from the job itself or from the psychological and/or physical environment in which the job is performed.

EQUITY IN FINANCIAL COMPENSATION
Organizations must strive for compensation equity.

EQUITY THEORY—Motivation theory that people assess their performance and attitudes by comparing both their contribution to work and the benefits they derive from it to the contributions and benefits of *comparison others* whom they select--and who in reality may or may not be like them.

FINANCIAL EQUITY—Perception of fair pay treatment for employees.

EXTERNAL EQUITY—Exists when a firm's employees receive pay comparable to workers who perform similar jobs in other firms.

INTERNAL EQUITY—Exists when employees receive pay according to the relative value of their jobs within the same organization.

EMPLOYEE EQUITY—Exists when individuals performing similar jobs for the same firm receive pay according to factors unique to the employee, such as performance level or seniority.

TEAM EQUITY—Achieved when teams are rewarded based on their group's productivity.

DETERMINANTS OF DIRECT FINANCIAL COMPENSATION
The organization, the labor market, the job, and the employee all have an impact on job pricing and the ultimate determination of an individual's financial compensation.

ORGANIZATION AS A DETERMINANT OF DIRECT FINANCIAL COMPENSATION

COMPENSATION POLICIES—Policies that provide general guidelines for making compensation decisions.

Pay leaders: Organizations that pay higher wages and salaries than competing firms.

Market rate, or going rate: Companies that choose to pay below the going rate because of a poor financial condition or a belief that they do not require highly capable employees.

Pay followers: Companies that choose to pay below the market rate because of poor financial condition or a belief that they do not require highly capable employees.

ORGANIZATIONAL LEVEL—Upper management often makes these decisions to ensure consistency.

ABILITY TO PAY—An organization's assessment of its ability to pay is also an important factor in determining pay levels.

LABOR MARKET AS A DETERMINANT OF DIRECT FINANCIAL COMPENSATION
Potential employees located within the geographical area from which employees are recruited.

COMPENSATION SURVEYS—Large organizations routinely conduct compensation surveys to determine prevailing pay rates within labor markets.

EXPEDIENCY—Competition for highly skilled employees may be so intense in some labor markets that managers occasionally are left to their own devices.

COST OF LIVING—Pay increase must be roughly the equivalent to the cost of living increase if a person is to maintain the previous level of real wages.

LABOR UNIONS—When a union uses comparable pay as a standard for making compensation demands, the employer must obtain accurate labor market data.

SOCIETY—Compensation paid to employees often affects a firm's pricing of its goods and/or services. Consumers may also be interested in compensation decisions.

ECONOMY—Economy's health exerts a major impact on pay decisions.

LEGISLATION—Amount of compensation a person receives can also be affected by certain federal and state legislation.

> **Davis-Bacon Act of 1931**: This act requires federal construction contractors with projects valued in excess of $2,000 to pay at least the prevailing wages in the area.
>
> **Walsh-Healy Act of 1936**: The act requires companies with federal supply contracts exceeding $10,000 to pay prevailing wages. The act also requires one and a half times the regular pay rate for hours over 8 per day or 40 per week.
>
> **Fair Labor Standards Act of 1938, as Amended**: It establishes a minimum wage, requires overtime pay, record keeping, and provides standards for child labor.

JOB AS A DETERMINANT OF DIRECT FINANCIAL COMPENSATION

Techniques used to determine a job's relative worth include job analysis, job descriptions, and job evaluation.

JOB EVALUATION—Process that determines the relative value of one job in relation to another.

> **RANKING METHOD**—Job evaluation method in which the raters examine the description of each job being evaluated and arrange the jobs in order according to their value to the company.
>
> **CLASSIFICATION METHOD**—Job evaluation method in which classes or grades are defined to describe a group of jobs.
>
> **FACTOR COMPARISON METHOD**—Job evaluation method that assumes there are five universal factors consisting of mental requirements, skills, physical requirements, responsibilities, and working conditions; the evaluator makes decisions on these factors independently.
>
> **POINT METHOD**—Job evaluation method where the raters assign numerical values to specific job factors, such as knowledge required, and the sum of these values provides a quantitative assessment of a job's relative worth.
>
> > **POINT METHOD EXAMPLE**
> >
> > **Select Job Cluster**
> >
> > **Identify Compensable Factors**
> >
> > **Determine Degrees and Define Each Compensable Factors**
> >
> > **Determine Factor Weights**
> >
> > **Determine Factor Point Values**
> >
> > **Validate Point System**
>
> **HAY GUIDE CHART-PROFILE METHOD**—Refined version of the point method used by approximately 8,000 public and private sector organizations worldwide to evaluate clerical, trade, technical, professional, managerial and/or executive level jobs.

JOB PRICING
Placing a dollar value on a job's worth.

> **PAY GRADES**—Grouping of similar jobs to simplify pricing jobs.
>
> **WAGE CURVE**—Fitting of plotted points on a curve to create a smooth progression between pay grades (also known as the *pay curve*).
>
> **PAY RANGE**—Minimum and maximum pay rate with enough variance between the two to allow for a significant pay difference.
>
> **BROADBANDING**—Compensation technique that collapses many pay grades (salary grades) into a few wide bands in order to improve organizational effectiveness.
>
> **SINGLE RATE SYSTEM**—Everyone in the same job receives the same base pay, regardless of seniority or productivity.
>
> **ADJUSTING PAY RATES**—When pay ranges have been determined and jobs assigned to pay grades, it may become obvious that some jobs are overpaid and others underpaid.

EMPLOYEE AS A DETERMINANT OF DIRECT FINANCIAL COMPENSATION
Factors related to the employee are essential in determining pay and employee equity.

> **JOB PERFORMANCE—PERFORMANCE BASED PAY**—Compensation feature generally controllable by employees is their job performance.
>
>> **Merit pay**: Pay increase added to employees base pay based on their level of performance.
>>
>> **Variable pay (bonus)**: The most common type of variable pay for performance is the bonus. The **bonus** is a one-time annual financial award based on productivity that is not added to base pay. Spot bonus is a relatively small monetary gift provided employees for outstanding work or effort during a reasonably short period of time.
>>
>> **Piecework**: Incentive pay plan in which employees are paid for each unit they produce.
>
> **SKILLS—SKILL-BASED PAY**—System that compensates employees for their job-related skills and knowledge, not for their job titles.
>
> **COMPETENCIES—COMPETENCY-BASED PAY**—Compensation plan that rewards employees for the capabilities they attain.
>
> **SENIORITY**—Length of time an employee has been associated with the company, division, department, or job.
>
> **EXPERIENCE**—Regardless of the nature of the task, experience has the potential for enhancing a person's ability to perform. Today, it is possible that experience is becoming somewhat irrelevant.
>
> **ORGANIZATION MEMBERSHIP**—Some components of individual financial compensation are given to employees without regard to the particular job they perform or their level of productivity.
>
> **POTENTIAL**—Organizations do pay some individuals based on their potential.
>
> **POLITICAL INFLUENCE**—Political influence is a factor that obviously should not be used as a determinant of financial compensation. However, to deny that it exists would be unrealistic.

LUCK—Expression has often been stated, "It certainly helps to be in the right place at the right time."

TEAM-BASED PAY
If a team is to function effectively, firms should provide a reward based on the overall team performance as well.

COMPANY-WIDE PLANS—Organizations normally base company-wide plans on the firm's productivity, cost savings, or profitability.

> **PROFIT SHARING**—Compensation plans that result in the distribution of a predetermined percentage of the firm's profits to employees.
>
> **GAINSHARING**—Plans designed to bind employees to the firm's productivity and provide an incentive payment based on improved company performance. The Scanlon plan is a gainsharing plan that provides a financial reward to employees for savings in labor costs resulting from their suggestions.

PROFESSIONAL EMPLOYEE COMPENSATION
Professionals are initially compensated primarily for the knowledge they bring to the organization.

SALES REPRESENTATIVE COMPENSATION
Designing compensation programs for sales employees involves unique considerations.

CONTINGENT WORKER COMPENSATION
In most cases, contingents earn less pay and are far less likely to receive health or retirement benefits than their permanent counterparts.

ARE TOP EXECUTIVES PAID TOO MUCH?
Over the past decade, the rise of executive compensation has truly been thought of by many as out of control. If wages overall had risen at the same pace as that of CEOs since the 1980s, the average worker today would be earning more than $184,000 a year rather than today's not quite $27,000, and the minimum wage would now be almost $45 an hour.

EXECUTIVE COMPENSATION
A company's program for compensating executives is a critical factor in attracting and retaining the best available talent.

> **BASE SALARY**—Factor in determining standard of living and also provides the basis for other forms of compensation.
>
> **SHORT-TERM INCENTIVES, OR BONUSES**—Payment of bonuses reflects a managerial belief in their incentive value.
>
> **STOCK OPTION PLANS**—Incentive plan in which executives can buy a specified amount of stock in their company in the future at or below the current market price.
>
> **PERFORMANCE-BASED PAY**—Some firms are moving toward a more performance-based compensation packages for executives.
>
> **EXECUTIVE BENEFITS (PERQUISITES OR PERKS)**—Special benefits provided by a firm to key executives to give them something extra.
>
> **GOLDEN PARACHUTES**—Perquisite that protects executives in the event that another company acquires their firm or if the executive is forced to leave the firm for other reasons.

CHINA'S COMPENSATION PROBLEMS

In a recent employee survey, 25 percent of the workers had already had three or more jobs in their career and twenty percent expected to leave their positions in the next year. Turnover in China continues to be a problem. There doesn't seem to be an end in sight. On average, employees stay with their company less than two years. Job hopping has become a culture for Chinese workers. And, the higher an individual is in the organization, the more likely he or she would leave. The same survey showed that managers felt less loyal and were less likely to continue with the firm over the next five years.

EXERCISES

1. Visit an HR manager in your local area. Ask how the organization attempts to achieve the following:
   a. external equity
   b. internal equity
   c. employee equity

2. What form of incentive compensation might be used for the following jobs to increase productivity?
   a. machine operator
   b. automobile salesperson
   c. a group of five people cooperating to get the job done

3. There are numerous Internet sites that pertain to information covered in this chapter. Identify two sites that apply to information contained in the chapter.

YOU AND HR
Memo One
To: (You) Human Resource Manager
From: Safety Director
Subject: Pay Increase for a Safety Engineer

Adria Maddox is one of my best safety engineers, and I really want to get her a pay increase. I know that you told me that she is at the top of her pay grade and that she is more than competitive in the industry but I want to give her a raise. She really does a good job. I request that you initiate the paper work to get her a pay raise.

Memo One Response
To: Safety Director
From: (You) Human Resource Manager
Subject: Request for a Pay Increase for a Safety Engineer

(Your memo goes here in 50 to 75 words.)

Memo Two
To: (You) Human Resource Manager
From: Manager of Retail Sales Clerks
Subject: Sales Contest to Try to Improve Sales within Our Store

I would like to try a sales contest to be held among our ten full-time clothing salespeople. It's the winter blahs time after Christmas, and my salespeople just don't seem to be really working to sell our merchandise.

I believe a sales contest in which the winner would get a one-week paid vacation in a sunny, warm climate would really liven up our sales effort and pay for itself in terms of added sales and new customers. Let me know what you think!

Memo Two Response
To: Manager of Retail Sales Clerks
From: (You) Human Resource Manager
Subject: Using a Contest to Try to Boost Sales

(Your memo goes here in 75 to 100 words.)

DISCUSSION QUESTIONS
1. Distinguish among external equity, internal equity, employee equity, and team equity.
2. What factors should be considered when the job is a determinant of financial compensation?
3. Distinguish between the following job evaluation methods: ranking, classification, factor comparison, and point.
4. What is the Hay guide chart-profile method of job evaluation?
5. What is the purpose of job pricing? Discuss briefly.

CHAPTER STUDY QUIZZES
Fill-in
1. _____ compensation consists of the satisfaction that a person receives from the job itself or from the psychological and/or physical environment in which the person works.
2. _____ equity exists when individuals performing similar jobs for the same firm are paid according to factors unique to the employee.
3. _____ is a primary means for determining internal equity.
4. The _____ requires companies with federal supply contracts exceeding $10,000 to pay prevailing wages.
5. The basic purpose of _____ is to eliminate internal pay inequities that exist because of illogical pay structures.
6. In the _____ method of job evaluation, raters assign numerical values to specific job components, and the sum of these values provides a quantitative assessment of a job's relative worth.
7. A refined version of the point method is the _____ method.
8. _____ is a pay increase added to employees' base pay based on their level of performance.
9. _____ pay is a system that compensates employees on the basis of job-related skills and knowledge they possess, not for their job titles.
10. _____ is a technique that collapses many pay grades (salary grades) into a few wide bands in order to improve organizational effectiveness.

True/False
1. Internal equity exists when a firm's employees are paid comparably to workers who perform similar jobs in other firms.
2. Cost of living adjustments (COLAs) in union contracts have been disappearing.
3. The most significant law affecting compensation is the Walsh-Healy Act.
4. The simplest of the four job evaluation methods is the classification method.
5. A refined version of the point method is the Hay guide chart-profile method.
6. Variable pay is a system that compensates employees on the basis of job-related skills and knowledge they possess, not for their job titles.
7. Placing a dollar value on the worth of a job is called job pricing.
8. A pay grade is the grouping of similar jobs to simplify the job pricing process.
9. A pay grade includes a minimum and maximum pay rate with enough variance between the two to allow for a significant pay difference.
10. Broadbanding is a technique that collapses many pay grades (salary grades) into a few wide bands in order to improve organizational effectiveness.

Multiple Choice

1. What is the definition of *compensation*?
    A. Pay that a person receives in the form of wages, salaries, commissions and bonuses
    B. Total of all rewards provided employees in return for their services
    C. All financial rewards that are not included in direct financial compensation
    D. Satisfaction that a person receives from the job itself or from the psychological and/or physical environment in which the person works

2. What is the definition of *external equity*?
    A. Achieved when teams are rewarded based on their group's productivity
    B. Exists when a firm's employees receive pay comparable to workers who perform similar jobs in other firms
    C. Exists when employees receive pay according to the relative value of their jobs within the same organization
    D. Exists when individuals performing similar jobs for the same firm receive pay according to factors unique to the employee, such as performance level or seniority

3. What is the purpose of the Davis-Bacon Act?
    A. First national law to deal with minimum wages and mandated a prevailing wage for all federally financed or assisted construction projects exceeding $2,000
    B. Requires companies with federal supply contracts exceeding $10,000 to pay prevailing wages
    C. Established minimum labor standards on a national basis and to eliminate low wages and long working hours
    D. Requires record keeping and provides standards for child labor

4. What is the definition of the *classification method* of job evaluation?
    A. Raters examine the description of each job being evaluated and arrange the jobs in order according to their value to the company
    B. Assumes that there are five universal factors consisting of mental requirements, skills, physical requirements, responsibilities, and working conditions and the evaluator makes decisions on these factors independently
    C. Raters assign numerical values to specific job factors and the sum of these values provides a quantitative assessment of a job's relative worth
    D. Involves defining a number of classes or grades to describe a group of jobs

5. What is the definition of the *point method* of job evaluation?
    A. Assumes that there are five universal factors consisting of mental requirements, skills, physical requirements, responsibilities, and working conditions and the evaluator makes decisions on these factors independently
    B. Raters examine the description of each job being evaluated and arrange the jobs in order according to their value to the company
    C. Involves defining a number of classes or grades to describe a group of jobs
    D. Raters assign numerical values to specific job factors and the sum of these values provides a quantitative assessment of a job's relative worth

6. What is the definition of *job pricing*?
    A. Grouping of similar jobs to simplify pricing jobs
    B. Placing a dollar value on the job's worth
    C. Fitting of plotted points to create a smooth progression between pay grades
    D. Includes a minimum and maximum pay rate with enough variance between the two to allow for a significant pay difference

7. What is the definition of a *pay grade*?
    A. Placing a dollar value on the job's worth
    B. Fitting of plotted points to create a smooth progression between pay grades
    C. Grouping of similar jobs to simplify pricing jobs
    D. Includes a minimum and maximum pay rate with enough variance between the two to allow for a significant pay difference

8. What is the definition of *merit pay*?
    A. Relatively small monetary gifts provided employees for outstanding work or effort during a reasonably short period of time
    B. One-time annual financial award based on productivity that is not added to base pay
    C. Pay increase added to employees base pay based on their level of performance
    D. Incentive pay plan where employees are paid for each unit they produce

9. What is the definition of *skill-based pay*?
    A. Incentive pay plan where employees are paid for each unit they produce
    B. System that compensates employees for their job-related *skills* and *knowledge*, not for their job titles
    C. Compensation plan that rewards employees for the capabilities they attain
    D. Relatively small monetary gifts provided employees for outstanding work or effort during a reasonably short period of time

10. What is the definition of *profit sharing*?
    A. Plans are designed to bind employees to the firm's productivity and provide an incentive payment based on improved company performance
    B. Plans that provide a financial reward to employees for savings in labor costs resulting from their suggestions
    C. Compensation plan that results in the distribution of a predetermined percentage of the firm's profits to employees
    D. Plans that embodies management/labor cooperation, collaborative problem solving, teamwork, trust, gainsharing, open-book management, and servant leadership

Matching Exercise

Directions: On the line provided, place the letter of the statement beside the key term.

1. _____ Benchmark job
2. _____ Bonus
3. _____ Broadbanding
4. _____ Classification method
5. _____ Compensation
6. _____ Compensation policy
7. _____ Compensation survey
8. _____ Competency-based pay
9. _____ Cost-of-living allowance
10. _____ Direct financial compensation
11. _____ Employee equity
12. _____ Financial equity
13. _____ Equity theory
14. _____ Exempt employees
15. _____ External equity
16. _____ Factor comparison method
17. _____ Gainsharing
18. _____ Golden parachute contract
19. _____ Hay guide chart-profile method
20. _____ Indirect financial compensation
21. _____ Internal equity
22. _____ Job evaluation
23. _____ Job evaluation ranking method
24. _____ Job pricing
25. _____ Labor market
26. _____ Market (going) rate
27. _____ Merit pay
28. _____ Nonfinancial compensation
29. _____ Pay followers
30. _____ Pay grade
31. _____ Pay leaders
32. _____ Pay range
33. _____ Perquisites (perks)
34. _____ Piecework
35. _____ Point method
36. _____ Profit sharing
37. _____ Scanlon plan
38. _____ Seniority
39. _____ Skill-based pay
40. _____ Spot bonus
41. _____ Stock option plan
42. _____ Team equity
43. _____ Wage curve

a. Total of all rewards provided employees in return for their services.
b. Pay that a person receives in the form of wages, salary, commissions, and bonuses.
c. All financial rewards that are not included in direct compensation.
d. Satisfaction that a person receives from the job itself or from the psychological and/or physical environment in which the person works.
e. Motivation theory that people assess their performance and attitudes by comparing both their contribution to work and the benefits they derive from it to the contributions and benefits of *comparison others* whom they select—and who in reality may be like or unlike them.
f. Perception of fair pay treatment for employees.
g. Equity that exists when a firm's employees receive pay comparable to workers who perform similar jobs in other firms.
h. Exists when employees receive pay according to the relative value of their jobs within the same organization.
i. Equity that exists when individuals performing similar jobs for the same firm receive pay according to factors unique to the employee, such as performance level or seniority.
j. Equity that is achieved when teams are rewarded based on their group's productivity.
k. Policy that provide general guidelines for making compensation decisions.
l. Those organizations that pay higher wages and salaries than competing firms.
m. Average pay that most employers provide for a similar job in a particular area or industry.
n. Companies that choose to pay below the going rate because of a poor financial condition or a belief that they do not require highly capable employees.
o. Potential employees located within the geographic area from which employees are recruited.
p. Means of obtaining data regarding what other firms are paying for specific jobs or job classes within a given labor market.
q. Well-known job in the company and industry and one performed by a large number of employees.
r. Escalator clause in a labor agreement that automatically increases wages as the U.S. Bureau of Labor Statistics' cost-of-living index rises.
s. Employees categorized as executive, administrative, professional, or outside salespersons.
t. Process that determines the relative value of one job in relation to another.
u. Method in which the raters examine the description of each job being evaluated and arrange the jobs in order according to their value to the company.
v. Job evaluation method in which classes or grades are defined to describe a group of jobs.
w. Job evaluation method that assumes there are five universal factors consisting of mental requirements, skills, physical requirements, responsibilities, and working conditions and the evaluator makes decisions on these factors independently.
x. Job evaluation method where the raters assign numerical values to specific job factors, such as knowledge required, and the sum of these values provides a quantitative assessment of a job's relative worth.
y. Refined version of the point method used by approximately 8,000 public and private sector organizations worldwide to evaluate clerical, trade, technical, professional, managerial and/or executive level jobs.
z. Placing a dollar value on the job's worth.
aa. Grouping of similar jobs to simplify pricing jobs.
bb. Fitting of plotted points to create a smooth progression between pay grades (also known as the *pay curve)*.
cc. Minimum and maximum pay rate for a job, with enough variance between the two to allow for a significant pay difference.
dd. Compensation technique that collapses many pay grades (salary grades) into a few wide bands in order to improve organizational effectiveness.
ee. Pay increase given to employees based on their level of performance with the increase being added to the employee's base pay.
ff. One-time annual financial award based on productivity that is not added to base pay.
gg. Relatively small monetary gift provided employees for outstanding work or effort during a reasonably short period of time.
hh. Incentive pay plan in which employees are paid for each unit they produce.
ii. System that compensates employees for their job-related skills and knowledge, not for their job titles.
jj. Compensation plan that rewards employees for the capabilities they attain.

kk. Length of time an employee has been associated with the company, division, department, or job.
ll. Compensation plans that result in the distribution of a predetermined percentage of the firm's profits to employees.
mm. Plans designed to bind employees to the firm's productivity and provide an incentive payment based on improved company performance.
nn. Gainsharing plan that provides a financial reward to employees for savings in labor costs resulting from their suggestions.
oo. Incentive plan in which executives can buy a specified amount of stock in their company in the future at or below the current market price.
pp. Any special benefits provided by a firm to a small group of key executives and designed to give the executives something extra.
qq. A perquisite that protects executives in the event that another company acquires their firm or the executive is forced to leave the firm for other reasons.

ANSWERS TO CHAPTER STUDY QUIZZES

Fill-in
1. Nonfinancial
2. Employee
3. Job evaluation
4. Walsh-Healy Act of 1936
5. Job evaluation
6. Point
7. Hay guide chart-profile
8. Merit pay
9. Skill-based
10. Broadbanding

True/False
1. False (external)
2. True
3. False (Fair Labor Standards Act of 1938)
4. False (ranking)
5. True
6. False (skill-based)
7. True
8. True
9. False (pay range)
10. True

Multiple Choice
1. B
2. B
3. A
4. D
5. D
6. B
7. C
8. C
9. B
10. C

Matching Exercise
1. Q
2. FF
3. DD
4. V
5. A
6. K
7. P
8. JJ
9. R
10. B
11. I
12. F
13. E
14. S
15. G
16. W
17. MM
18. QQ
19. Y
20. C
21. H
22. T
23. U
24. Z
25. O
26. M
27. EE
28. D
29. N
30. AA
31. L
32. CC
33. PP
34. HH
35. X
36. LL
37. NN
38. KK
39. II
40. GG
41. OO
42. J
43. BB

CHAPTER 10

BENEFITS, NONFINANCIAL COMPENSATION, AND OTHER COMPENSATION ISSUES

CHAPTER DESCRIPTION

This chapter begins by describing some unique benefits and benefits as indirect financial compensation. A discussion of mandated benefits is next presented. Voluntary benefits, including topics related to payment for time not worked, health care, on-site health care, life insurance, retirement plans, disability protection, employee stock option plans, supplemental unemployment benefits, and employee services, is discussed next. Then, customized benefit plans are presented. Premium pay, health care legislation, and communicating information about the benefit package are presented next. Factors involved in nonfinancial compensation are then described. Topics related to the job itself as a nonfinancial compensation factor, job characteristics theory, and the job environment as a total compensation factor are then presented, followed by a discussion of factors that are involved in workplace flexibility (work–life balance) and concepts regarding severance pay, comparable worth, pay secrecy, and pay compression. This chapter concludes with a Global Perspective entitled "Expat Lifestyle Is Not What It Used to Be."

KEY TERMS

Benefits: All financial rewards not included in direct financial compensation (indirect financial compensation).
Paid time off: Means of dealing with the problem of unscheduled absences by providing a certain number of days each year that employees can use for any purpose.
Sabbaticals: Temporary leaves of absence from an organization, usually at reduced pay.
Health maintenance organization: Managed-care health organization that covers all services for a fixed fee but exercise control over which doctors and health facilities a member may use.
Preferred provider organizations: Managed-care health organization in which incentives are provided to members to use services within the system; out-of-network providers may be used at greater cost.
Point-of-service: Managed-care health organization that requires a primary care physician and referrals to see specialists, as with HMOs, but permits out-of-network health care access.
Exclusive provider organization: Managed-care health organization that offers a smaller preferred provider network and usually provides few, if any, benefits when an out-of-network provider is used.
Defined contribution health care plan: System where companies give each employee a set amount of money annually with which to purchase health care coverage.
Health savings account: Tax-sheltered savings account similar to the IRA, but earmarked for medical expenses with high-deductible health plans that have annual deductibles of at least $1,050 for individuals and $2,100 for families.
Flexible spending account: Benefit plan established by employers that allows employees to deposit a certain portion of their salary into an account (before paying income taxes) to be used for eligible expenses.
Defined benefit plan: Retirement plan that provides the participant with a fixed benefit upon retirement.
Defined contribution plan: Retirement plan that requires specific contributions by an employer to a retirement or savings fund established for the employee.
401(k) plan: Defined contribution plan in which employees may defer income up to a maximum amount allowed.
Cash balance plan: Retirement plan with elements of both defined benefit plans and defined contribution plans.
Employee stock option plan (ESOP): Defined contribution plan in which a firm contributes stock shares to a trust.
Supplemental unemployment benefits: Provide additional income for employees receiving unemployment insurance benefits.
Relocation benefits: Company-paid shipment of household goods and temporary living expenses, covering all or a portion of the real estate costs associated with buying a new home and selling the previously occupied home.
Customized benefit plan: Benefit plan that permits employees to make yearly elections to largely determine their benefit package by choosing between taxable cash and numerous benefits.
Premium pay: Compensation paid to employees for working long periods of time or working under dangerous or undesirable conditions.
Hazard pay: Additional pay provided to employees who work under extremely dangerous conditions.
Shift differential: Additional money paid to reward employees for the inconvenience of working undesirable hours.

Job characteristics theory: Employees experience intrinsic compensation when their jobs rate high on five core job dimensions: skill variety, task identity, task significance, autonomy, and feedback.
Skill variety: Extent to which work requires a number of different activities for successful completion.
Task identity: Extent to which the job includes an identifiable unit of work performed from start to finish.
Task significance: Impact that the job has on other people.
Autonomy: Extent of individual freedom and discretion employees have in performing their jobs.
Feedback: Information employees receive about how well they have performed the job.
Flextime: Practice of permitting employees to choose their own working hours, within certain limitations.
Compressed workweek: Any arrangement of work hours that permits employees to fulfill their work obligation in fewer days than the typical five-day workweek.
Job sharing: Two part-time people split the duties of one job in some agreed-on manner and are paid according to their contributions.
Telecommuting: Work arrangement whereby employees, called teleworkers or telecommuters, are able to remain at home (or otherwise away from the office) and perform their work using computers and other electronic devices that connect them with their offices.
Severance pay: Compensation designed to assist laid-off employees as they search for new employment.
Comparable worth: Determination of the values of dissimilar jobs (such as company nurse and welder) by comparing them under some form of job evaluation, and the assignment of pay rates according to their evaluated worth.
Pay compression: Situation that occurs when less experienced employees are paid as much as or more than employees who have been with the organization a long time due to a gradual increase in starting salaries and limited salary adjustment for long-term employees.

CHAPTER STUDY OUTLINE

UNIQUE BENEFITS
Regardless of economic conditions, it seems organizations are continually competing for top caliber employees. Although benefits may not serve as strong motivators of performance, they are obviously important in attracting and retaining individuals. Unique benefits can take many forms, especially if the job market is very competitive and the company needs to distinguish itself in the labor force.

BENEFITS (INDIRECT FINANCIAL COMPENSATION)
All financial rewards that are not included in direct financial compensation.

MANDATED (LEGALLY REQUIRED) BENEFITS
Legally required benefits include social security, unemployment compensation, and workers' compensation.

> **SOCIAL SECURITY**—Social Security Act created a system of retirement benefits; subsequent amendments added other forms of protection, such as disability insurance, survivors benefits, and, most recently, Medicare.
>
> **UNEMPLOYMENT COMPENSATION**—Individual laid off by an organization covered by the Social Security Act may receive unemployment compensation for up to 26 weeks.
>
> **WORKERS' COMPENSATION**—Workers' compensation benefits provide a degree of financial protection for employees who incur expenses resulting from job-related accidents or illnesses.
>
> **FAMILY AND MEDICAL LEAVE ACT OF 1993**—Provides for up to 12 work weeks of unpaid leave per year for absences due to the employee's own serious health condition or the need to care for a newborn or newly-adopted child or a seriously ill child, parent, or spouse.

DISCRETIONARY (VOLUNTARY) BENEFITS
Organizations voluntarily provide numerous benefits.

PAYMENT FOR TIME NOT WORKED
In providing payment for time not worked, employers recognize that employees need time away from the job for many purposes.

PAID VACATIONS—Paid vacations provide workers with an opportunity to rest, become rejuvenated, and hopefully, become more productive.

SICK PAY AND PAID TIME OFF—Each year many firms allocate, to each employee, a certain number of days of sick leave, which they can use when ill. Paid time off is a means of dealing with the problem of unscheduled absences by providing a certain number of days each year that employees can use for any purpose.

SABBATICALS—Temporary leaves of absence from an organization, usually at reduced pay.

OTHER TYPES OF PAYMENT FOR TIME NOT WORKED—While paid vacations and sick pay comprise the largest portion of payment for time not worked, there are numerous other types that companies use.

HEALTH CARE
Specific areas include managed-care health organizations, consumer-driven health care plans, on-site health care, major medical benefits, dental and vision care, and long-term care insurance.

MANAGED-CARE HEALTH ORGANIZATIONS

Health maintenance organization: Managed-care health organization that covers all services for a fixed fee but exercise control over which doctors and health facilities a member may use.

Preferred provider organization: Managed-care health organization in which incentives are provided to members to use services within the system; out-of-network providers may be used at greater cost.

Point-of-service: Managed-care health organization that requires a primary care physician and referrals to see specialists, as with HMOs, but permits out-of-network health care access.

Exclusive provider organizations: Managed-care health organization that offers a smaller preferred provider network and usually provides few, if any, benefits when an out-of-network provider is used.

CONSUMER-DRIVEN HEALTH CARE PLANS—Companies are increasingly placing the responsibility for health care responsibility on employees.

Defined contribution health-care plan: System where companies give each employee a set amount of money annually with which to purchase health care coverage.

Health Savings Account: Tax-sheltered savings account similar to the IRA, but earmarked for medical expenses with high-deductible health plans that have annual deductibles of at least $1,000 for individuals and $2,000 for families.

Flexible spending account: Benefit plan established by employers that allows employees to deposit a certain portion of their salary into an account (before paying income taxes) to be used for eligible expenses.

ON-SITE HEALTH CARE—Way of curbing health care costs and also providing an employee benefit is the use of on-site health care.

MAJOR MEDICAL BENEFITS—Plans provide for major medical benefits to cover extraordinary expenses that result from long-term or serious health problems.

DENTAL AND VISION CARE—Dental and vision care are popular benefits in the health-care area.

LONG-TERM CARE—Long-term care involves the services and assistance provided for aging adults who need help maintaining their daily activities.

LIFE INSURANCE

Group life insurance is a benefit commonly provided to protect the employee's family in the event of his or her death.

RETIREMENT PLANS

Employers are one of our society's primary providers of retirement income.

DEFINED BENEFIT PLANS—Retirement plan that provides the participant with a fixed benefit upon retirement.

DEFINED CONTRIBUTION PLANS—Retirement plan that requires specific contributions by an employer to a retirement or savings fund established for the employee. 401(k) plan is a defined contribution plan in which employees may defer income up to a maximum amount allowed.

CASH BALANCE PLANS—Retirement plan with elements of both defined benefit plans and defined contribution plans.

DISABILITY PROTECTION

Workers' compensation protects employees from job-related accidents and illnesses. Some firms, however, provide additional protection that is more comprehensive.

EMPLOYEE STOCK OPTION PLANS

Defined contribution plan in which a firm contributes stock shares to a trust.

SUPPLEMENTAL UNEMPLOYMENT BENEFITS

Provide additional income for employees receiving unemployment insurance benefits.

EMPLOYEE SERVICES

Organizations offer a variety of benefits that can be termed employee services.

RELOCATION BENEFITS—Company-paid shipment of household goods and temporary living expenses, covering all or a portion of the real estate costs associated with buying a new home and selling the previously occupied home.

CHILD CARE—Firm may provide an on-site child care center, support an off-site center, or subsidize the costs of child care.

EDUCATIONAL ASSISTANCE—Many firms have benefits that reimburse employees for college tuition and books.

FOOD SERVICES/SUBSIDIZED CAFETERIAS—Firms that offer free or subsidized lunches feel that they get a high payback in terms of employee relations.

FINANCIAL SERVICES—Benefit that is growing in popularity permits employees to purchase different types of insurance policies through payroll deduction.

LEGAL SERVICES—Firms may have some type of legal services plan.

SCHOLARSHIPS FOR DEPENDENTS—Scholarship programs can help boost employee recruitment and retention.

CUSTOMIZED BENEFIT PLANS
Benefit plan that permits employees to make yearly elections to largely determine their benefit package by choosing between taxable cash and numerous benefits.

PREMIUM PAY
Compensation paid to employees for working long periods of time or working under dangerous or undesirable conditions.

HAZARD PAY—Additional pay provided to employees who work under extremely dangerous conditions.

SHIFT DIFFERENTIALS—Additional money paid to employees for the inconvenience of working undesirable hours.

HEALTH CARE LEGISLATION

CONSOLIDATED OMNIBUS BUDGET RECONCILIATION ACT OF 1985—Give employees the opportunity to temporarily continue their coverage they would otherwise lose because of termination, layoff, or other change in employment status.

HEALTH INSURANCE PORTABILITY AND ACCOUNTABILITY ACT OF 1996—Provides protection for approximately 25 million Americans who move from one job to another, who are self-employed, or who have pre-existing medical conditions.

EMPLOYEE RETIREMENT INCOME SECURITY ACT OF 1974—Passed to strengthen existing and future retirement programs.

OLDER WORKERS BENEFIT PROTECTION ACT of 1990—Amendment to the Age Discrimination in Employment Act, prohibits discrimination in the administration of benefits on the basis of age, but also permits early retirement incentive plans as long as they are voluntary.

PENSION PROTECTION ACT OF 2006—Contains a variety of provisions designed to strengthen the funding rules for defined benefit pension plans

COMMUNICATING INFORMATION ABOUT THE BENEFITS PACKAGE
Because employee awareness of benefits is often limited, the program information must be communicated downward.

NONFINANCIAL COMPENSATION
Consists of the satisfaction that a person receives from the job itself or from the psychological and/or physical environment in which the person works.

JOB ITSELF AS A NONFINANCIAL COMPENSATION FACTOR
The job itself is a central issue in many theories of motivation, and it is also a vital component of a total compensation program.

JOB CHARACTERISTICS THEORY
Employees experience intrinsic compensation when their jobs rate high on five core job dimensions: skill variety, task identity, task significance, autonomy, and feedback.

SKILL VARIETY—Extent to which work requires a number of different activities for successful completion.

TASK IDENTITY—Extent to which the job includes an identifiable unit of work performed from start to finish.

TASK SIGNIFICANCE—Impact that the job has on other people.

AUTONOMY—Extent of individual freedom and discretion employees have in performing their jobs.

FEEDBACK—Information employees receive about how well they have performed the job.

JOB ENVIRONMENT AS A NONFINANCIAL COMPENSATION FACTOR
Employees can draw satisfaction from their work through several non-financial factors.

SOUND POLICIES—Human resource policies and practices reflecting management's concern for its employees can serve as positive rewards.

CAPABLE MANAGERS—Anyone who has worked under a manager who does not possess the managerial skills needed to successfully lead the unit, understands the importance of having a capable individual in charge.

COMPETENT EMPLOYEES—Successful organizations emphasize continuous development and assure that competent managers and non-managers are employed.

CONGENIAL COWORKERS—Although the American culture has historically embraced individualism, most people possess, in varying degrees, a desire to be accepted by their workgroup.

APPROPRIATE STATUS SYMBOLS—Organizational rewards that take many forms such as office size and location, desk size and quality, floor covering, and title.

WORKING CONDITIONS—Definition of working conditions has been broadened considerably during the past decade. Today, an air-conditioned and reasonably safe and healthy workplace is considered necessary.

WORKPLACE FLEXIBILITY (WORK-LIFE BALANCE)
For employers, creating a work-life balanced environment can be a key strategic factor in attracting and retaining the most talented employees. By providing such an environment, employees are better able to fit family, community, and social commitments into their schedules and they appreciate that.

FLEXTIME—Practice of permitting employees to choose their own working hours, within certain limitations.

COMPRESSED WORKWEEK—Arrangement of work hours that permit employees to fulfill their work obligation in fewer days than the typical five-day workweek.

JOB SHARING—Two part-time people split the duties of one job in some agreed-on manner and are paid according to their contributions.

TWO IN A BOX—Giving two managers the same responsibilities and the same title and letting them decide how the work is to be divided (Two in a Box). Unlike job sharing, it is a full-time job for both managers.

TELECOMMUTING—Work arrangement whereby employees, called teleworkers or telecommuters, are able to remain at home (or otherwise away from the office) and perform their work using computers and other electronic devices that connect them with their offices.

PART-TIME WORK—Use of part-time workers on a regular basis has begun to gain momentum in the United States.

OTHER COMPENSATION ISSUES
Several issues that relate to compensation deserve mention.

SEVERANCE PAY—Compensation designed to assist laid-off employees as they search for new employment.

COMPARABLE WORTH—Determination of the values of dissimilar jobs (such as company nurse and welder) by comparing them under some form of job evaluation, and the assignment of pay rates according to their evaluated worth.

PAY SECRECY—Some organizations tend to keep their pay rates secret for various reasons.

PAY COMPRESSION—Situation that occurs when less experienced employees are paid as much as or more than employees who have been with the organization a long time due to a gradual increase in starting salaries and limited salary adjustment for long-term employees.

EXPAT LIFESTYLE IS NOT WHAT IT USED TO BE
For decades, being relocated to another country was a windfall for expats. They were getting paid in U.S. dollars and putting a lot of that money in the bank because dollars would go much further. Now the inverse of that is happening. Dollars don't go as far, meaning companies have to pay a lot more for U.S. citizens to go overseas.

EXERCISES
1. Visit an HR manager in your local area. Ask what voluntary benefits are provided employees. Use the following as a checklist:
   a. paid vacations
   b. sick pay/well pay
   c. health care
   d. dental and vision care
   e. retirement plans
   f. other

2. Visit an HR manager in your local area. Ask if any of the following attempts at workplace flexibility are used in his or her organization:
   a. flextime
   b. compressed work week
   c. job sharing
   d. telecommuting

3. There are numerous Internet sites that pertain to information covered in this chapter. Identify two sites that apply to information contained in the chapter.

YOU AND HR
Memo One
To: (You) Human Resource Manager
From: Long-range Planning Task Groups
Subject: Telecommuting

Our future success is tied closely to keeping costs and expenses down and employee performance as high as possible.

We're thinking about experimenting with telecommuting as a unique approach to work, but, before we do, we're seeking ideas and opinions from people throughout the managerial ranks as to the feasibility of such a thing as telecommuting.

What do you believe are the variables and/or criteria that must be considered in determining what jobs in our firm could be done through telecommuting? Please let me know.

Memo One Response
To: Long-range Planning Task Group
From: (You) Human Resource Manager
Subject: Telecommuting

(Your memo goes here in 75 to 100 words.)

Memo Two
To: (You) Human Resource Manager
From: Dock Loading Manager
Subject: Some Type of Incentive

As you know, the dock loading section is a very busy area and there is always work to do. All my workers do a good job. But, they keep complaining that their benefits are not very good. I have been told that we have some of the best benefits in our area, but I really don't know. Is there something that the company can do to let everyone know what benefits we really have?

Memo Two Response
To: Dock Loading Manager
From: (You) Human Resource Manager
Subject: Incentive Plan

(Your memo goes here in 75 to 100 words.)

DISCUSSION QUESTIONS
1. Define *benefits*.
2. What are the legally required benefits?
3. Distinguish between hazard pay and shift differential pay.
4. What factors are related to the job as a total compensation factor?
5. What compensation factors are related to the job environment?

CHAPTER STUDY QUIZZES
Fill-in
1. The _____ created a system of retirement benefits.
2. The _____ applies to private employers with 50 or more employees and to all governmental employers regardless of the number of employees.
3. In lieu of sick leave, vacation time, and a personal day or two, a growing number of companies are providing _____, a certain number of days off provided each year that employees can use for any purpose.
4. A (An) _____ is a plan in which a firm contributes stock shares to a trust.
5. A (An) _____ is paid to employees for the inconvenience of working undesirable hours.
6. The _____ Act provided new protections for approximately 25 million Americans who move from one job to another, who are self-employed, or who have preexisting medical conditions.
7. _____ is a tax-sheltered savings account similar to the IRA, but earmarked for medical expenses with high-deductible health plans that have annual deductibles of at least $1,050 for individuals and $2,100 for families.
8. _____ is the practice of permitting employees to choose their own working hours, within certain limitations.
9. The _____ is an arrangement of work hours that permits employees to fulfill their work obligation in fewer days than the typical five-day, eight hours a day, workweek.
10. _____ requires the value for dissimilar jobs, such as company nurse and welder, to be compared under some form of job evaluation, and pay rates for both jobs to be assigned according to their evaluated worth.

True/False
1. An individual laid off by an organization covered by the Social Security Act may receive unemployment compensation for up to 36 weeks.
2. The Family and Medical Leave Act apply to private employers with 20 or more employees.
3. A defined contribution plan is a retirement plan that requires specific contributions by an employer to a retirement or savings fund established for the employee.
4. The Older Workers Benefit Protection Act (OWBPA), an amendment to the Age Discrimination in Employment Act, prohibits discrimination in the administration of benefits on the basis of age, but also permits early retirement incentive plans as long as they are voluntary.
5. A cash balance plan has elements of both the defined benefit and defined contribution plans.
6. Flextime is an arrangement of work hours that permits employees to fulfill their work obligation in fewer days than the typical five-day, eight hours a day, workweek.
7. The employee's organizational level generally determines the amount of severance pay.
8. Although some firms are trimming the amount of severance pay offered, typically, one to two weeks of severance pay is given for every year of service, up to some predetermined maximum.
9. If a firm's compensation plan is illogical, secrecy may indeed be appropriate because only a well-designed system can stand careful scrutiny.
10. Comparable compression occurs when firms make pay adjustments at the lower end of the job hierarchy without commensurate adjustments at the top.

Multiple Choice

1. What law provides employees up to 12 weeks a year of unpaid leave in specified situations?
    A. Social Security Act
    B. Family and Medical Leave Act
    C. Equal Pay Act
    D. Security Administration Act

2. Which of the following is **NOT** a benefit required by law?
    A. Social Security
    B. worker compensation
    C. unemployment compensation
    D. retirement compensation

3. What is the definition of a *defined contribution health-care plan*?
    A. Companies give each employee a set amount of money annually with which to purchase health-care coverage
    B. Offers a smaller PPO provider network and usually provides little, if any, benefits when an out-of-network provider is used
    C. Tax-sheltered savings account similar to the IRA, but earmarked for medical expenses with high-deductible health plans
    D. Benefit plan established by employers that allows employees to deposit a certain portion of their salary into an account (before paying income taxes) to be used for eligible expenses

4. What is the definition of a *health savings account*?
    A. Companies give each employee a set amount of money annually with which to purchase health-care coverage
    B. Tax-sheltered savings account similar to the IRA, but earmarked for medical expenses with high-deductible health plans
    C. Benefit plan established by employers that allows employees to deposit a certain portion of their salary into an account (before paying income taxes) to be used for eligible expenses
    D. Requires a primary care physician and referrals to see specialists, as with HMOs, but permits out-of-network health care access

5. What is the definition of a *defined benefit plan*?
    A. Retirement plan that requires specific contributions by an employer to a retirement or savings fund established for the employee
    B. Formal retirement plan that provides the participant with a fixed benefit upon retirement
    C. Plan with elements of both defined benefit and defined contribution plans
    D. Plan in which employees may defer income up to a maximum amount allowed

6. What is the definition of *hazard pay*?
    A. alternative arrangement in the event the company goes out of business
    B. pay provided for the company being downsized
    C. pay for the inconvenience of working less desirable hours
    D. additional pay provided to employees who work under extremely dangerous conditions

7. What is the purpose of the Consolidated Omnibus Budget Reconciliation Act?
    A. Prohibits discrimination in the administration of benefits on the basis of age, but also permits early retirement incentive plans as long as they are voluntary
    B. Strengthens existing and future retirement programs
    C. Provides protection for Americans who move from one job to another, who are self-employed, or who have preexisting medical conditions
    D. Give employees the opportunity to temporarily continue their coverage they would otherwise lose because of termination, layoff, or other changes in employment status

8. What is the purpose of the Pension Protection Act?
   A. Prohibits discrimination in the administration of benefits on the basis of age, but also permits early retirement incentive plans as long as they are voluntary
   B. Provides protection for Americans who move from one job to another, who are self-employed, or who have preexisting medical conditions
   C. Ensure that employers make greater contributions to their pension funds, ensuring their solvency, and avoiding a potential multi-billion dollar taxpayer bailout of the Pension Benefit Guaranty Corporation
   D. Give employees the opportunity to temporarily continue their coverage they would otherwise lose because of termination, layoff, or other changes in employment status

9. According to job characteristic theory, which factor is the extent to which work requires a number of different activities for successful completion?
   A. task identity
   B. skill variety
   C. task significance
   D. autonomy

10. What is the definition of *flextime*?
    A. Arrangement of work hours that permits employees to fulfill their work obligation in fewer days than the typical five-day, eight hours a day, workweek
    B. Practice of permitting employees to choose their own working hours, within certain limitations
    C. Two part-time people split the duties of one job in some agreed-on manner and are paid according to their contributions
    D. Giving two managers the same responsibilities and the same title and letting them to decide how the work is to be divided

Matching Exercise

Directions: On the line provided, place the letter of the statement beside the key term.

1. _____ 401(k) plan
2. _____ Autonomy
3. _____ Benefits
4. _____ Cash balance plan
5. _____ Comparable worth
6. _____ Compressed workweek
7. _____ Customized benefit plans
8. _____ Defined benefit plan
9. _____ Defined contribution health care plan
10. _____ Defined contribution plan
11. _____ Employee stock option plan
12. _____ Exclusive provider organization
13. _____ Feedback
14. _____ Flexible spending account
15. _____ Flextime
16. _____ Hazard pay
17. _____ Health maintenance organization
18. _____ Health savings account
19. _____ Job characteristics theory
20. _____ Job sharing
21. _____ Paid time off
22. _____ Pay compression
23. _____ Point-of-service
24. _____ Preferred provider organizations
25. _____ Premium pay
26. _____ Relocation benefits
27. _____ Sabbaticals
28. _____ Severance pay
29. _____ Shift differential
30. _____ Skill variety
31. _____ Supplemental unemployment benefits
32. _____ Task identity
33. _____ Task significance
34. _____ Telecommuting

a. All financial rewards not included in direct financial compensation.
b. Means of dealing with the problem of unscheduled absences by providing a certain number of days each year that employees can use for any purpose.
c. Temporary leaves of absence from an organization, usually at reduced pay.
d. Managed-care health organization that covers all services for a fixed fee but control is exercised over which doctors and health facilities a member may use.
e. Managed-care health organization in which incentives are provided to members to use services within the system; out-of-network providers may be utilized at greater cost.
f. Managed-care health organization that requires a primary care physician and referrals to see specialists, as with HMOs, but permits out-of-network health care access.
g. Managed-care health organization that offers a smaller preferred provider network and usually provides few, if any, benefits when an out-of-network provider is used.
h. System where companies give each employee a set amount of money annually with which to purchase health care coverage.
i. Tax-sheltered savings account similar to the IRA, but earmarked for medical expenses with high-deductible health plans that have annual deductibles of at least $1,000 for individuals and $2,000 for families.
j. Benefit plan established by employers that allows employees to deposit a certain portion of their salary into an account before paying income taxes to be used for eligible expenses.
k. Retirement plan that provides the participant with a fixed benefit upon retirement.
l. Retirement plan that requires specific contributions by an employer to a retirement or savings fund established for the employee.
m. Defined contribution plan in which employees may defer income up to a maximum amount allowed.
n. Retirement plan with elements of both defined benefit and defined contribution plans.
o. Defined contribution plan in which a firm contributes stock shares to a trust.
p. Provide additional income for employees receiving unemployment insurance benefits.
q. Company-paid shipment of household goods and temporary living expenses, covering all or a portion of the real estate costs associated with buying a new home and selling the previously occupied home.
r. Benefit plan that permits employees to make yearly elections to largely determine their benefit package by choosing between taxable cash and numerous benefits.
s. Compensation paid to employees for working long periods of time or working under dangerous or undesirable conditions.
t. Additional pay provided to employees who work under extremely dangerous conditions.
u. Additional money paid to reward employees for the inconvenience of working undesirable hours.

v. Employees experience intrinsic compensation when their jobs rate high on five core job dimensions: skill variety, task identity, task significance, autonomy, and feedback.
w. Extent to which work requires a number of different activities for successful completion.
x. Extent to which the job includes an identifiable unit of work that is carried out from start to finish.
y. Impact that the job has on other people.
z. Extents of individual freedom and discretion employees have in performing their jobs.
aa. Information employees receive about how well they have performed the job.
bb. Practice of permitting employees to choose their own working hours, within certain limitations.
cc. Any arrangement of work hours that permits employees to fulfill their work obligation in fewer days than the typical five-day workweek.
dd. Filling of a job by two part-time people who split the duties of one full-time job in some agreed-on manner and are paid according to their contributions.
ee. Work arrangement whereby employees are able to remain at home (or otherwise away from the office) and perform their work using computers and other electronic devices that connect them with their offices.
ff. Compensation designed to assist laid-off employees as they search for new employment.
gg. Determination of the values of dissimilar jobs (such as company nurse and welder) by comparing them under some form of job evaluation, and the assignment of pay rates according to their evaluated worth.
hh. Situation that occurs when less experienced employees are paid as much as or more than employees who have been with the organization a long time due to a gradual increase in starting salaries and limited salary adjustment for long-term employees.

ANSWERS TO CHAPTER STUDY QUIZZES

Fill-in
1. Social Security Act of 1935
2. Family and Medical Leave Act
3. Paid time off (PTO)
4. Employee stock option plan
5. Shift differential
6. Health Insurance Portability and Accountability Act
7. Health savings account
8. Flextime
9. Compressed workweek
10. Comparable worth

True/False
1. False (twenty-sixth)
2. False (50)
3. True
4. True
5. True
6. False (compressed workweek)
7. True
8. True
9. True
10. False (pay)

Multiple Choice
1. B
2. D
3. A
4. B
5. B
6. D
7. D
8. C
9. B
10. B

Matching Exercise
1. M
2. Z
3. A
4. N
5. GG
6. CC
7. R
8. K
9. H
10. L
11. O
12. G
13. AA
14. J
15. BB
16. T
17. D
18. I
19. V
20. DD
21. B
22. HH
23. F
24. E
25. S
26. Q
27. C
28. FF
29. U
30. W
31. P
32. X
33. Y
34. EE

CHAPTER 11

A SAFE AND HEALTHY WORK ENVIRONMENT

CHAPTER DESCRIPTION

This chapter begins by discussing the dominant crime of the twenty-first century: identity theft. Next, the nature and role of safety and health and the role of the Occupational Safety and Health Administration are discussed. The economic impact of safety and the focus of safety programs in business operations are presented next, and the consequences of repetitive stress injuries and the purpose of ergonomics are discussed. An explanation of the effect of workplace and domestic violence on businesses follows. The nature of stress and burnout is then described. Then a section is devoted to describing why some are paid to be healthy and some have to pay because they are unhealthy. Then the sources and means of coping with stress are discussed. Following this, the purposes of wellness programs and the importance of physical fitness programs are described, and substance abuse, substance-abuse-free workplaces, the rationale for employee assistance programs, and the impact of smoking in the workplace are discussed. This chapter concludes with a Global Perspective entitled "Global Safety Programs."

KEY TERMS

Health: Employee's freedom from physical or emotional illness.
Safety: Protection of employees from injuries caused by work-related accidents.
Job hazard analysis: Multi-step process designed to study and analyze a task or job and then break down that task into steps that provide a means of eliminating associated hazards.
Repetitive stress injuries: Group of conditions caused by placing too much stress on a joint when the same action is performed repeatedly.
Carpal tunnel syndrome: Caused by pressure on the median nerve that occurs as a result of a narrowing of the passageway that houses the nerve.
Ergonomics: Study of human interaction with tasks, equipment, tools, and the physical work environment.
Workplace violence: Violent acts, including physical assaults and threats of assault, directed toward employees at work or on duty.
Negligent retention: Liability an employer may incur when a company keeps persons on the payroll whose records indicate a strong potential for wrongdoing and fails to take steps to defuse a possibly violent situation.
Stress: Body's nonspecific reaction to any demand made on it.
Burnout: Incapacitating condition in which individuals lose a sense of the basic purpose and fulfillment of their work.
Substance abuse: Use of illegal substances or the misuse of controlled substances such as alcohol and drugs.
Alcoholism: Medical disease characterized by uncontrolled and compulsive drinking that interferes with normal living patterns.
Employee assistance program (EAP): Comprehensive approach that many organizations have taken to deal with burnout, alcohol and drug abuse, and other emotional disturbances.

CHAPTER STUDY OUTLINE

DOMINANT CRIME OF THE TWENTY-FIRST CENTURY: IDENTITY THEFT
Identity theft has become a harsh reality for today's employers, especially human resources professionals, since employment records contain just about everything an identity thief could want to know about an individual. A person's identity includes many different items such as Social Security numbers, driver's license numbers, date of birth, home addresses, e-mail passwords and ATM information.

NATURE AND ROLE OF SAFETY AND HEALTH

    SAFETY—Protection of employees from injuries caused by work-related accidents.

HEALTH—Employees' freedom from physical or emotional illness.

OCCUPATIONAL SAFETY AND HEALTH ADMINISTRATION
Occupational Safety and Health Act of 1970 created the Occupational Safety and Health Administration (OSHA). OSHA aims to ensure worker safety and health in the United States by working with employers and employees to create better working environments.

SAFETY: THE ECONOMIC IMPACT
Job-related deaths and injuries of all types extract a high toll in terms of not only human misery but also economic loss.

FOCUS OF SAFETY PROGRAMS
Safety programs may be designed to accomplish their purposes in two primary ways.

UNSAFE EMPLOYEE ACTIONS—First approach in a safety program is to create a psychological environment and employee attitudes that promote safety.

UNSAFE WORKING CONDITIONS—Second approach to safety program design is to develop and maintain a safe physical working environment.

DEVELOPING SAFETY PROGRAMS—Organizational safety programs require planning for prevention of workplace accidents.

Job hazard analysis: Multi-step process designed to study and analyze a task or job and then break down that task into steps that provide a means of eliminating associated hazards.

Superfund Amendments Reauthorization Act, Title III (SARA): SARA requires businesses to communicate more openly about the hazards associated with the materials they use and produce and the wastes they generate.

Employee involvement: One way to strengthen a safety program is to include employee input, which provides workers with a sense of accomplishment.

Safety Engineer: In many companies, one staff member coordinates the overall safety program.

ACCIDENT INVESTIGATION—Safety engineer and the line manager jointly investigate accidents—why, how, and where they occur, and who is involved.

EVALUATION OF SAFETY PROGRAMS—Best indicator that a safety program is succeeding is a reduction in the frequency and severity of injuries and illnesses.

REPETITIVE STRESS INJURIES (RSI)
Group of conditions caused by placing too much stress on a joint when the same action is performed repeatedly. *Carpal tunnel syndrome* is caused by pressure on the median nerve that occurs as a result of a narrowing of the passageway that houses the nerve.

ERGONOMICS
Study of human interaction with tasks, equipment, tools, and the physical environment.

CONGRESS AND OSHA—Congress rescinded OSHA's controversial ergonomics standards in 2001. OSHA responded to this act by releasing a public notice that it would develop new guidelines addressing ergonomic hazards.

ERGONOMICS PAYOFF—Clear that there is a payoff in using ergonomics.

WORKPLACE VIOLENCE
Physical assault, threatening behavior, verbal abuse, hostility or harassment directed toward employees at work or on duty.

VULNERABLE EMPLOYEES—Employees at gas stations and liquor stores, taxi drivers and police officers working overnight shifts face the greatest danger from violence.

LEGAL CONSEQUENCES TO WORKPLACE VIOLENCE—Ever-present threat of legal action. Negligent retention is the liability an employer may incur when a company keeps persons on the payroll whose records indicate a strong potential for wrongdoing and fails to take steps to defuse a possibly violent situation.

INDIVIDUAL AND ORGANIZATIONAL CHARACTERISTICS TO MONITOR—Some firms that have had extensive experience with workplace violence are attempting to detect employees who commit minor aggressive acts and exhibit certain behaviors.

PREVENTIVE ACTION—Two parts to violence prevention. First, there must be a process in place to help with early detection of worker anger. Second, supervisors and HR staff need to be trained in how to skillfully handle difficult employment issues.

DOMESTIC VIOLENCE
Spillover from domestic violence is an unexpected threat to both women and their companies.

NATURE OF STRESS
Body's nonspecific reaction to any demand made on it.

POTENTIAL CONSEQUENCES OF STRESS—There is increasing evidence indicating that severe, prolonged stress is related to the diseases that are leading causes of death—coronary heart disease, stroke, hypertension, cancer, emphysema, diabetes, and cirrhosis; stress may even lead to suicide.

STRESSFUL JOBS—Common factor among stressful jobs is lack of employee control over work. Workers in such jobs may feel that they are trapped, treated more like machines than people.

ORGANIZATIONAL FACTORS—Factors associated with a person's employment can be potentially stressful.

Corporate Culture: Corporate culture has a lot to do with stress.

Job Itself: Some jobs are generally perceived as being more stressful than others due to the nature of the tasks involved and the degree of control the job permits.

Working Conditions: Working conditions, including the physical characteristics of the workplace and the machines and tools used, can also create stress.

PERSONAL FACTORS—Stress factors outside the job and job environment also may affect job performance.

Family: Although a frequent source of happiness and security, the family can also be a significant stressor.

Financial Problems: May place an unbearable strain on the employee.

GENERAL ENVIRONMENT—Stress is also in our general environment.

MANAGING STRESS
Experts emphasize that some stress is healthy and moderate stress is the key to survival.

BURNOUT
Incapacitating condition where individuals lose a sense of the basic purpose and fulfillment of their work. Burnout results in reduced productivity, higher turnover and generally lousy performance. Individuals in the helping professions, such as teachers and counselors, seem to be susceptible to burnout because of their jobs, whereas others may be vulnerable because of their upbringing, expectations, or personalities.

SOME ARE PAID TO BE HEALTHY; SOME HAVE TO PAY BECAUSE THEY ARE UNHEALTHY
Companies are increasingly using financial incentives to encourage employees to adopt healthier lifestyles either through a discount on premium contributions or cash. Some companies required employees to take a health risk assessment that involved blood pressure and cholesterol screening. Employees lost their health coverage if they did not cooperate.

WELLNESS PROGRAMS
Today, it is clear that optimal health is often achieved through environmental safety, organizational changes, and different lifestyles. Firms should conduct a needs assessment before implementing a wellness program in order to address appropriate employee health needs. Chronic lifestyle diseases are much more prevalent today than ever before. The good news is that people have a great deal of control over many of them.

PHYSICAL FITNESS PROGRAMS
Many U.S. business firms have exercise programs designed to help keep their workers physically fit. These programs often reduce absenteeism, accidents, and sick pay.

SUBSTANCE ABUSE
Substance abuse involves the use of illegal substances or the misuse of controlled substances such as alcohol and drugs.

ALCOHOL ABUSE—Increasingly firms are establishing alcohol abuse programs, and supervisors are now being trained to cope with this health problem.

DRUG ABUSE—Drug users are increasingly gravitating to the workplace, which is an ideal place to sell drugs.

SUBSTANCE-ABUSE-FREE WORKPLACE
The Drug-Free Workplace Act of 1988 requires some Federal contractors and all Federal grantees to agree that they will provide drug-free workplaces as a condition of receiving a contract or grant from a Federal agency.

IMPLEMENTING A DRUG-TESTING PROGRAM
The third step in establishing a substance-abuse-free workplace is to implement a drug-testing program. A drug-free workplace program should: balance the rights of employees and the rights of employers, balance the need to know and rights to privacy, balance detection and rehabilitation, and balance the respect for employees and the safety of all. The difficulty is not in formulating the policy, but rather in implementing it.

EMPLOYEE ASSISTANCE PROGRAMS
Comprehensive approach that many organizations have taken to deal with burnout, alcohol and drug abuse, and other emotional disturbances.

SMOKE FREE WORKPLACES
An important health issue facing employers today is environmental tobacco smoke. Although some smokers and advocates remain adamant that passive cigarette smoke is not harmful, the preponderance of evidence says otherwise.

GLOBAL SAFETY PROGRAMS
Global companies continue to face global safety risks. That is one of the lessons learned after the 1984 disaster in Bhopal, India, affected Union Carbide's worldwide operations. The Bhopal Disaster of 1984 was the worst industrial disaster in the history of the world.

EXERCISES
1. Through ergonomics, an attempt is made to fit the machine and work environment to the person, rather than require the person to make the adjustment. Visit a manager of an organization in your area. Ask the following questions:
    a. Have there been any attempts to implement ergonomic programs in the company?
    b. What attempts were made?
    c. How successful were these programs?

2. How stressful do you consider the following jobs? Explain your answer.
    a. college professor
    b. stockbroker on New York Stock Exchange
    c. student (yourself)
    d. executive administrative assistant for a global corporation

3. There are numerous Internet sites that pertain to information covered in this chapter. Identify two sites that apply to information contained in the chapter.

YOU AND HR
Memo One
To: (You) Human Resource Manager
From: Customer Service Department Manager
Subject: Signs of Stress

As you know, employees in my department deal with a lot of unsatisfied customers. For example, customers come to our department to get product problems resolved, and frequently they direct their outrage toward my employees. As customer dissatisfaction goes up, so do the complaints.

Lately employee performance in my department has been falling off, and I wonder if it could be the result of the stressful nature of the work in this department. Please tell me the signs or symptoms that I might observe in my employees' behaviors that would indicate that they are under undue stress.

Memo One Response
To: Customer Service Department Manager
From: (You) Human Resource Manager
Subject: Signs or Symptoms of Possible Employee Stress

(Your memo goes here in 50 to 75 words.)

Memo Two
To: (You) Human Resource Manager
From: Corporate President
Subject: Setting up a Wellness Program

I've heard a lot of positive things from other executives about wellness programs their firms have set up. Evidently, the costs of these programs are often repaid through healthier, happier employees.

Please list for me what would be the components of a wellness program for our medium-sized firm.

Memo Two Response
To: Corporate President
From: (You) Human Resource Manager
Subject: Components of a Corporate Wellness Program
(Your memo goes here in 75 to 100 words.)

DISCUSSION QUESTIONS
1. Define *safety* and *health*.
2. What are the primary ways in which safety programs are designed?
3. Describe the major sources of stress.
4. Why should a firm be concerned with employee burnout?
5. What are the steps in obtaining a substance abuse free workplace?

CHAPTER STUDY QUIZZES
Fill-in
1. The most important federal legislation in the safety and health area is the _____.
2. People developing _____ may experience pain, numbness or tingling in the hands or wrist, a weak grip, the tendency to drop objects, sensitivity to cold, and in later stages, muscle deterioration, especially in the thumb.
3. _____ is the study of human interaction with tasks, equipment, tools, and the physical environment.
4. _____ is a multi-step process designed to study and analyze a task or job and then break down that task into steps that provide a means of eliminating associated hazards.
5. _____ is the body's nonspecific reaction to any demand made on it.
6. The dangerous part of burnout is that it is _____.
7. _____ requires businesses to communicate more openly about the hazards associated with the materials they use and produce and the wastes they generate.
8. _____ is the liability an employer may occur it keeps persons on the payroll whose records indicate strong potential for wrongdoing and fails to take steps to defuse a possible violent situation.
9. Chronic lifestyle diseases are much more _____ today than ever before.
10. In developing a wellness program, firms should first conduct a (an) _____.

True/False
1. The most important federal legislation in the safety and health area is the Occupational Safety and Health Act of 1970.
2. About 30 percent of OSHA inspections have resulted from employee complaints.
3. General perceptions of OSHA have not always been positive.
4. Since its inception, OSHA has helped to cut workplace fatalities by more than 60 percent and occupational injury and illness by 40 percent.
5. Faulty management safety policies and decisions, personal factors, and environmental factors are the basic causes of accidents.
6. Burnout, while rarely fatal, is an incapacitating condition in which individuals lose a sense of the basic purpose and fulfillment of their work.
7. The common factor among stressful jobs identified by NIOSH is lack of employee feedback over work.
8. The early months of employment are often critical because work injuries increase with length of service.
9. The U.S. Bureau of Labor Statistics (BLS) reports that repetitive stress injuries account for 75 percent of cases involving days away from work.
10. One in 10 employees has personally experienced violence.

Multiple Choice

1. What is the definition of *safety*?
    A. Group of conditions caused by placing too much stress on a joint when the same action is performed repeatedly
    B. Refers to employees' freedom from physical or emotional illness
    C. Involves protecting employees from injuries caused by work-related accidents
    D. Results from pressure on the median nerve that result from a narrowing of the passageway which houses the nerve

2. What is the definition of *repetitive stress injuries*?
    A. Group of conditions caused by placing too much stress on a joint when the same action is performed repeatedly
    B. Human interaction with tasks, equipment, tools, and the physical environment
    C. Violent acts, including physical assaults and threats of assault, directed toward employees at work or on duty
    D. Liability an employer may incur when a company keeps persons on the payroll whose records indicate strong potential for wrongdoing and fails to take steps to defuse a possible violent situation

3. One of the primary task of a firm's safety engineer is to
    A. enforce company rules.
    B. prepare OSHA reports.
    C. provide safety training.
    D. operate essentially in a line capacity.

4. The early months of employment are often critical because work injuries decrease with
    A. productivity.
    B. educational background.
    C. length of service.
    D. job knowledge.

5. If the employer denies the inspector access to the work site, what must OSHA do to obtain access?
    A. file suit
    B. obtain permission from top administrator at OSHA
    C. obtain an administrative subpoena
    D. ask the local police to accompany them on the visit

6. Which of the following jobs has the most stress?
    A. doctor
    B. lawyer
    C. laborer
    D. teacher

7. What is the definition of *stress*?
    A. An incapacitating condition in which individuals lose a sense of the basic purpose and fulfillment of their work
    B. Body's nonspecific reaction to any demand made on it
    C. Causes people who have previously been highly committed to their work to become disillusioned, losing interest and motivation
    D. Associated with a midlife or mid-career crisis, but it can happen at different times to different people

8. What is the definition of *substance abuse*?
   A. Use of illegal substances or the misuse of controlled substances such as alcohol and drugs
   B. An incapacitating condition in which individuals lose a sense of the basic purpose and fulfillment of their work
   C. Group of conditions caused by placing too much stress on a joint when the same action is performed repeatedly
   D. Associated with a midlife or mid-career crisis, but it can happen at different times to different people

9. What is the definition of *negligent retention*?
   A. Liability an employer incurs when it fails to conduct a reasonable investigation of an applicant's background, and then assigns a potentially dangerous person to a position where he or she can inflict harm
   B. Liability an employer may incur when a company keeps persons on the payroll whose records indicate strong potential for wrongdoing and fails to take steps to defuse a possible violent situation
   C. Liability former employers may occur when they fail to offer a warning about a particularly severe problem with a past employee
   D. An incapacitating condition in which individuals lose a sense of the basic purpose and fulfillment of their work

10. Which of the following is a program that can be addressed by an employee assistance program?
    A. burnout
    B. alcohol and drug abuse
    C. emotional disturbance
    D. all of the above

Matching Exercise
Directions: On the line provided, place the letter of the statement beside the key term.

1. _____ Alcoholism
2. _____ Burnout
3. _____ Carpal tunnel syndrome
4. _____ Employee assistance program
5. _____ Ergonomics
6. _____ Health
7. _____ Job hazard analysis
8. _____ Negligent retention
9. _____ Repetitive stress injuries
10. _____ Safety
11. _____ Stress
12. _____ Substance abuse
13. _____ Workplace violence

a. Protection of employees from injuries caused by work-related accidents.
b. Employee's freedom from physical or emotional illness.
c. Multi-step process designed to study and analyze a task or job and then break down that task into steps that provide a means of eliminating associated hazards.
d. Group of conditions caused by placing too much stress on a joint when the same action is performed repeatedly.
e. Caused by pressure on the median nerve that occurs as a result of a narrowing of the passageway that houses the nerve.
f. Study of human interaction with tasks, equipment, tools, and the physical environment.
g. Violent acts, including physical assaults and threats of assault, directed toward employees at work or on duty.
h. Liability an employer may incur when a company keeps persons on the payroll whose records indicate strong potential for wrongdoing and fails to take steps to defuse a possible violent situation.
i. Body's nonspecific reaction to any demand made on it.
j. Incapacitating condition in which individuals lose a sense of the basic purpose and fulfillment of their work.
k. Involves the use of illegal substances or the misuse of controlled substances such as alcohol and drugs.
l. Medical disease characterized by uncontrolled and compulsive drinking that interferes with normal living patterns.
m. Comprehensive approach that many organizations have taken to deal with burnout, alcohol and drug abuse, and other emotional disturbances.

ANSWERS TO CHAPTER STUDY QUIZZES

Fill-in
1. Occupational Safety and Health Act
2. Carpal tunnel syndrome
3. Ergonomics
4. Job hazard analysis
5. Stress
6. Contagious
7. SARA
8. Negligent retention
9. Prevalent
10. Health risk assessment

True/False
1. True
2. False (70)
3. True
4. True
5. True
6. True
7. False (control)
8. False (decrease)
9. False (25)
10. True

Multiple Choice
1. C
2. A
3. C
4. C
5. C
6. C
7. B
8. A
9. B
10. D

Matching Exercise
1. L
2. J
3. E
4. M
5. F
6. B
7. C
8. H
9. D
10. A
11. I
12. K
13. G

CHAPTER 12

LABOR UNIONS AND COLLECTIVE BARGAINING

CHAPTER DESCRIPTION

This chapter begins by discussing the Change to Win Coalition; then union objectives are discussed and organized labor's strategies for a stronger movement are described. The reasons why employees join unions are explained, the basic structure of the union is described, and collective bargaining is defined. This is followed by a discussion of the steps involved in establishing the collective bargaining relationship and the two-tier wage system. Then topics related to the psychological aspects of collective bargaining, preparing for negotiations, and bargaining issues are discussed. Next, topics related to negotiating the agreement, breakdowns in negotiations, and ratifying the agreement are presented; and sections on administration of the agreement, collective bargaining in the public sector, and union decertification are provided. The chapter concludes with a section on the status of unions today and a Global Perspective entitled "The ICFTU Says Union Organizing Can Be Dangerous."

KEY TERMS

Change to Win Coalition: Union federation consisting of seven unions that broke from the AFL-CIO and formally launched a rival labor federation representing about 6 million workers in 2005.
Union salting: Process of training union organizers to apply for jobs at a company and, once hired, working to unionize employees.
Flooding the community: Process of the union inundating communities with organizers to target a particular business.
Public awareness campaigns: Labor maneuvers that do not coincide with a strike or an organizing campaign to pressure an employer for better wages, benefits, and the like.
Card check: Organizing approach by labor in which employees sign a card of support if they want unionization, and if 50 percent of the work force plus one worker sign a card, the union considers it a victory.
Right-to-work laws: Laws that prohibit management and unions from entering into agreements requiring union membership as a condition of employment.
Local union: Basic element in the structure of the U.S. labor movement.
Craft union: Bargaining unit, such as the Carpenters and Joiners union which is typically composed of members of a particular trade or skill in a specific locality.
Industrial union: Bargaining unit that generally consists of all the workers in a particular plant or group of plants.
National union: Organization composed of local unions, which it charters.
American Federation of Labor and Congress of Industrial Organizations (AFL-CIO): Central trade union federation in the United States.
Collective bargaining: Performance of the mutual obligation of the employer and the representative of the employees to meet at reasonable times and confer in good faith with respect to wages, hours, and other terms and conditions of employment, or the negotiation of an agreement, or any question arising there under, and the execution of a written contract incorporating any agreement reached if requested by either party; such obligation does not compel either party to agree to a proposal or require the making of a concession.
Bargaining unit: Group of employees, not necessarily union members, recognized by an employer or certified by an administrative agency as appropriate for representation by a labor organization for purposes of collective bargaining.
Authorization card: Document indicating that an employee wants to be represented by a labor organization in collective bargaining.
Two-tier wage system: A wage structure where newly hired workers are paid less than current employees for performing the same or similar jobs.
Mandatory bargaining issues: Bargaining issues that fall within the definition of wages, hours, and other terms and conditions of employment.
Permissive bargaining issues: Issues that may be raised, but neither side may insist that they be bargained over.
Prohibited bargaining issues: Issues that are statutorily outlawed from collective bargaining.
Closed shop: Arrangement making union membership a prerequisite for employment.

Union shop: Requirement that all employees become members of the union after a specified period of employment (the legal minimum is 30 days) or after a union shop provision has been negotiated.

Agency shop: Labor agreement provision requiring, as a condition of employment, that each nonunion member of a bargaining unit pay the union the equivalent of membership dues as a service charge in return for the union acting as the bargaining agent.

Open shop: Employment on equal terms to union members and nonmembers alike.

Checkoff of dues: Agreement by which a company agrees to withhold union dues from members' paychecks and to forward the money directly to the union.

Beachhead demands: Demands that the union does not expect management to meet when they are first made.

Mediation: Neutral third party enters the negotiations and attempts to facilitate a resolution to a labor dispute when a bargaining impasse has occurred.

Arbitration: Process in which a dispute is submitted to an impartial third party for a binding decision; an arbitrator basically acts as a judge and jury.

Rights arbitration: Arbitration involving disputes over the interpretation and application of the various provisions of an existing contract.

Interest arbitration: Arbitration that involves disputes over the terms of proposed collective bargaining agreements.

Strike: Action by union members who refuse to work in order to exert pressure on management in negotiations.

Boycott: Agreement by union members to refuse to use or buy the firm's products.

Secondary boycott: Union attempt to encourage third parties (such as suppliers and customers) to stop doing business with a firm; declared illegal by the Taft-Hartley Act.

Byline strike: Newspaper writers withhold their names from stories.

Informational picketing: Use of union members to display placards and hand out leaflets usually outside their place of business depicting information the union wants the general public to see.

Lockout: Management decision to keep union workers out of the workplace and run the operation with management personnel and/or replacement workers to encourage the union to return to the bargaining table.

Decertification: Reverse of the process that employees must follow to be recognized as an official bargaining unit.

CHAPTER STUDY OUTLINE

CHANGE TO WIN COALITION

Change to Win Coalition is a union federation consisting of seven unions that broke from the AFL-CIO and formally launched a rival labor federation representing about 6 million workers in 2005.

UNION OBJECTIVES

Although each union is a unique organization seeking its own objectives, several broad objectives characterize the labor movement as a whole:

* To secure and, if possible, improve the living standards and economic status of its members.
* To enhance and, if possible, guarantee individual security against threats and contingencies that might result from market fluctuations, technological change, or management decisions.
* To influence power relations in the social system in ways that favors and does not threaten union gains and goals.
* To advance the welfare of all who work for a living, whether union members or not.
* To create mechanisms to guard against the use of arbitrary and capricious policies and practices in the workplace.

ORGANIZED LABOR'S STRATEGIES FOR A STRONGER MOVEMENT

STRATEGICALLY LOCATED UNION MEMBERS—A few strategically located union members may exert a disproportionate amount of power.

ORGANIZING SEVERAL BIG COMPANIES AT ONCE—Service Employees International Union organized janitors at several big companies at the same time. Rather than having a campaign for each workplace, it negotiated a big industry-wide contract. This eliminates each company's fear of being undercut by competitors if it allowed higher wages.

PULLING THE UNION THROUGH—Put pressure on the end user of a company's product in order to have a successful organizing attempt.

POLITICAL INVOLVEMENT—Unions are giving money to candidates who pledge to help pass pro-labor legislation.

UNION SALTING—Process of training union organizers to apply for jobs at a company and, once hired, working to unionize employees.

FLOODING THE COMMUNITIES—Process of the union inundating communities with organizers to target a particular business.

PUBLIC AWARENESS CAMPAIGNS—Labor maneuvers that do not coincide with a strike or organizing campaign to pressure an employer for better wages, benefits, and the like.

BUILDING ORGANIZING FUNDS—AFL-CIO often asks its affiliates to increase organizing funds.

ORGANIZING THROUGH THE CARD CHECK—Organizing approach by labor in which employees sign a card of support if they want unionization, and if 50 percent of the work force plus one worker sign a card, the union considers it a victory. Card checks are expedited ways of polling workers on union representation but no secret-ballot election takes place.

WHY EMPLOYEES JOIN UNIONS
Individuals join unions for many different reasons, and these reasons tend to change over time.

DISSATISFACTION WITH MANAGEMENT—Unions look for problems in organizations and then emphasize the advantages of union membership as a means of solving them.

Compensation: If employees are dissatisfied with their wages, they may look to a union for assistance in improving their standard of living.

Job security: If the firm does not provide its employees with a sense of job security, workers may turn to a union.

Attitude of management: Employees do not like to be subjected to arbitrary and capricious actions by management.

SOCIAL OUTLET—Union-sponsored recreational and social activities, day-care centers, and other services can increase the sense of solidarity.

OPPORTUNITY FOR LEADERSHIP—Employers often promote union leaders into managerial ranks as supervisors.

FORCED UNIONIZATION—In the 28 states without right-to-work laws, it is legal for an employer to agree with the union that a new employee must join the union after a certain period of time (generally 30 days) or be terminated. Right-to-work laws prohibit management and unions from entering into agreements requiring union membership as a condition of employment.

PEER PRESSURE—Many individuals will join a union because they are urged to do so by other members of the workgroup.

UNION STRUCTURE
Labor movement has developed a multilevel organizational structure.

LOCAL UNION—Basic element in the structure of the U.S. labor movement.

> **Craft union**: Bargaining unit, such as the Carpenters and Joiners union which is typically composed of members of a particular trade or skill in a specific locality.

> **Industrial union**: Bargaining unit that generally consists of all the workers in a particular plant or group of plants.

NATIONAL UNION—Organization composed of local unions, which it charters.

AFL-CIO—Central trade union federation in the United States.

ESTABLISHING THE COLLECTIVE BARGAINING RELATIONSHIP
Bargaining unit is a group of employees, not necessarily union members, recognized by an employer or certified by an administrative agency as appropriate for representation by a labor organization for purposes of collective bargaining.

> **SIGNING AUTHORIZATION CARDS**—Document indicating that an employee wants to be represented by a labor organization in collective bargaining.

> **PETITION FOR ELECTION**—After the authorization cards have been signed, a petition for an election may be made to the appropriate regional office of the NLRB.

> **ELECTION CAMPAIGN**—When an election has been ordered, both the union and management usually promote their causes actively.

> **ELECTION AND CERTIFICATION**—After a valid election is held, the NLRB board will issue a certification of the results to the participants.

TWO-TIER WAGE SYSTEM
A wage structure where newly hired workers are paid less than current employees for performing the same or similar jobs. In 2007, the UAW and General Motors negotiated a contract which included provisions for a two-tier wage system. The negotiated wage scale for any new *non-core employees* is $14 per hour which is half of what a typical worker would earn.

COLLECTIVE BARGAINING
Collective bargaining process is fundamental to management-organized labor relations in the United States.

COLLECTIVE BARGAINING PROCESS—Both external and internal environmental factors can influence the process. The following steps are involved:

> **Preparing for Negotiation**

> **Bargaining Issues**

> **Negotiation**

> **If breakdowns, overcome breakdowns**

> **Reaching the Agreement**

> **Ratifying the Agreement**

> **Administration of the Agreement**

PSYCHOLOGICAL ASPECTS OF COLLECTIVE BARGAINING
Psychologically, the collective bargaining process is often difficult because it is an adversarial situation and must be approached as such.

PREPARING FOR NEGOTIATIONS
Bargaining issues can be divided into three categories: mandatory, permissive, and prohibited.

MANDATORY BARGAINING ISSUES—Bargaining issues that fall within the definition of wages, hours, and other terms and conditions of employment.

PERMISSIVE BARGAINING ISSUES—Issues that may be raised, but neither side may insist that they be bargained over.

PROHIBITED BARGAINING ISSUES—Issues that are statutorily outlawed from collective bargaining.

BARGAINING ISSUES
Document that results from the collective bargaining process is known as a *labor agreement* or *contract*.

RECOGNITION—Purpose is to identify the union that is recognized as the bargaining representative and to describe the bargaining unit.

MANAGEMENT RIGHTS—Section that is often, but not always, written into the labor agreement and which spells out the rights of management.

UNION SECURITY—Ensure that the union continues to exist and perform its function.

Closed shop: Arrangement making union membership a prerequisite for employment.

Union shop: Requirement that all employees become members of the union after a specified period of employment (the legal minimum is 30 days) or after a union shop provision has been negotiated.

Maintenance of membership: Employees who are members of the union at the time the labor agreement is signed or who later voluntarily joins must continue their memberships until the termination of the agreement, as a condition of employment.

Agency shop: Labor agreement provision requiring, as a condition of employment, that each nonunion member of a bargaining unit pay the union the equivalent of membership dues as a service charge in return for the union acting as the bargaining agent.

Open shop: Employment on equal terms to union members and nonmembers alike.

Dues checkoff: Agreement by which a company agrees to withhold union dues from members' paychecks and to forward the money directly to the union.

COMPENSATION—Virtually any item that can affect compensation may be included.

Wage rate schedule: The base rates to be paid each year of the contract for each job are included in this section.

Overtime and premium pay: Provisions covering hours of work, overtime pay, and premium pay, such as shift differentials, are included in this section.

Jury Pay: Some firms pay an employee's entire salary while he or she is serving jury duty.

Layoff or severance pay: The amount that employees in various jobs and/or seniority levels will be paid if they are laid off or terminated is presented in this section.

Holidays: The holidays to be recognized and the amount of pay that a worker will receive if he or she has to work on a holiday are specified.

Vacation: Spells out the amount of vacation that a person may take, based on seniority.

Family care: Benefit that has been included in recent collective bargaining agreements, with child care expected to be a hot bargaining issue in the near future.

GRIEVANCE PROCEDURE—Means by which employees can voice dissatisfaction with specific management actions; also included in this section are the procedures for disciplinary action by management and the termination procedure that must be followed.

EMPLOYEE SECURITY—Seniority and grievance handling procedures.

JOB-RELATED FACTORS—Many of the rules governing employee actions on the job are included.

NEGOTIATING THE AGREEMENT
Negotiating suggests a certain amount of give-and-take, the purpose of which is to lower the other side's expectations.

BREAKDOWNS IN NEGOTIATIONS
Several means of removing roadblocks may be used in order to get negotiations moving again.

THIRD PARTY INTERVENTION—Often a person from outside both the union and the organization can intervene to provide assistance when an agreement cannot be reached and a breakdown occurs.

Mediation: Neutral third party enters the negotiations and attempts to facilitate a resolution to a labor dispute when a bargaining impasse has occurred.

Arbitration: Process in which a dispute is submitted to an impartial third party for a binding decision; an arbitrator basically acts as a judge and jury.

Sources of mediators and arbitrators: The principle organization involved in mediation efforts, other than the available state and local agencies, is the Federal Mediation and Conciliation Service.

UNION STRATEGIES FOR OVERCOMING NEGOTIATIONS BREAKDOWNS—Strikes and boycotts are the primary means that the union may use to overcome breakdowns in negotiations.

Strikes: Action by union members who refuse to work in order to exert pressure on management in negotiations.

Virtual Strikes: It is well known that when labor calls a strike, more than labor and management are hurt. Suppliers, customers, stockholders, and possibly others are also affected. *Virtual strikes* have been proposed as a means to avoid hurting others. In a virtual strike only labor and management suffer. Here, worker wages, management salaries, and company profits go into a separate account from which neither side gets anything back unless they settle within a certain period of time. Production continues as usual, so the suffering hits only those directly involved.

Boycotts: Agreement by union members to refuse to use or buy the firm's products.

MANAGEMENT'S STRATEGY FOR OVERCOMING NEGOTIATION BREAKDOWNS—
Lockout and operating the firm by placing management and nonunion workers in the striking workers' jobs are the primary means that management may use to overcome breakdowns in negotiations.

> **Lockout**: Management decision to keep union workers out of the workplace and run the operation with management personnel and/or replacement workers to encourage the union to return to the bargaining table.

> **Continue Operations Without the Striking Workers**: Operate the firm by placing management and nonunion workers in the striking workers' jobs.

RATIFYING THE AGREEMENT
Approval process can be more difficult for the union; until it has received approval by a majority of members voting in a ratification election, the proposed agreement is not final.

ADMINISTRATION OF THE AGREEMENT
Larger and perhaps more important part of collective bargaining is the administration of the agreement, which is seldom viewed by the public.

COLLECTIVE BARGAINING IN THE PUBLIC SECTOR
Title V of the U.S. Code, the law that dictates rules for federal employees, did not allow bargaining over wage issues, except for the U.S. Postal Service.

UNION DECERTIFICATION
Decertification is essentially the reverse of the process that employees must follow to be recognized as an official bargaining unit.

> **DECERTIFICATION PROCEDURE**—Rules established by the NLRB spell out the conditions for filing a decertification petition.

> **MANAGEMENT AND DECERTIFICATION**—If management really wants the union decertified, it must learn how to be active rather than passive.

UNIONS TODAY
Overall, the fall of *Big Labor* in the private sector has been dramatic. Private-sector union membership has fallen from 39 percent of all workers in 1958 to about 7.5 percent in 2007. Even thought public sector unionization was 35.9 percent, this did little to offset the fall in private sector membership. Likewise, organized labor in the capital-goods sector saw membership fall, as businesses cut capital-investment spending, prompting manufacturers to make layoffs. Both General Motors and Ford Motor Company recently made major cuts in their labor force.

THE ICFTU SAYS UNION ORGANIZING CAN BE DANGEROUS
International Confederation of Free Trade Unions, thousands of trade unionists were arrested, jailed, tortured, fired, or intimidated, and 223 were murdered or disappeared, across the world. The ICFTU survey, which draws on data from 132 countries, concluded that over 4,000 trade unionists were arrested, 1,000 injured, and 10,000 fired.

EXERCISES
1. Visit both a company manager of a nonunion organization and a union leader. Ask the following question: "What do you believe is the future of unionism in the United States?" Contrast their responses.

2. Visit a company in your area that is nonunion. Ask management the question, "What factors to you believe permitted you to remain nonunion?" Analyze the responses.

3. There are numerous Internet sites that pertain to information covered in this chapter. Identify two sites that apply to information contained in the chapter.

YOU AND HR
Memo One
To: (You) Human Resource Manager
From: Manager of Manufacturing
Subject: Unionization Undertones in the Plant

According to the grapevine, a couple of the newly-hired employees are bad mouthing the company and trying to get other employees to sign authorization cards.

I want to counter their efforts and campaign against unionization and these employees. I would like to fire these two guys for pushing the union idea. Can I? Please advise me regarding what rights or opportunities management has to campaign against unionism. In short, what can't I do?

Memo One Response
To: Manager of Manufacturing
From: (You) Human Resource Manager
Subject: Management Rights Regarding Anti-union Campaigning

(Your memo goes here in 100 to 150 words.)

Memo Two
To: (You) Human Resource Manager
From: Newly-hired Labor Relations Administrator
Subject: New Contract

As you know I've been hired fresh from college, and my first assignment is to lay out a plan to prepare the company for negotiations with representatives of the union who represent our production employees. What steps do you suggest I follow?

Memo Two Response
To: Newly-hired Labor Relations Administrator
From: (You) Human Resource Manager
Subject: Sample Model for Company Preparation for Negotiations

(Your memo goes here in 100 to 200 words.)

DISCUSSION QUESTIONS
1. What are the primary reasons for employees joining labor unions?
2. What are the basic steps involved in the collective bargaining process?
3. Distinguish among mandatory, permissive, and prohibited bargaining issues.
4. What are the topics included in virtually all labor agreements?
5. What are the primary means through which breakdowns in negotiations may be overcome?

CHAPTER STUDY QUIZZES
Fill-in
1. The political arm of the AFL-CIO is the _____.
2. A (An) _____ union generally consists of all the workers in a particular plant or group of plants.
3. The most powerful level in the union structure is the _____ union.
4. The first step in the collective bargaining process is _____.
5. _____ bargaining issues fall within the definition of wages, hours, and other terms and conditions of employment.
6. Under a _____ arrangement employees must remain members of the union as a condition of employment.
7. Demands that the union does not expect to receive when they are first made are known as _____ demands.
8. A (An) _____ exerts economic pressure on management, and the effect often lasts much longer than that of a strike.
9. In a _____, management keeps employees out of the workplace and may run the operation with management personnel and/or temporary replacements.
10. _____ is essentially the reverse of the process that employees must follow to be recognized as an official bargaining unit.

True/False
1. Union salting involves trained union organizers applying for jobs at a company and, once hired, working to unionize employees.
2. The AFL-CIO represents the interests of labor and its member national unions at the highest level.
3. An industrial union, such as the Carpenters and Joiners union, is typically composed of members of a particular trade or skill in a specific locality.
4. The most powerful level in the union structure is the local union.
5. Evidence of union interest is expressed when at least 30 percent of the employees in a workgroup sign an authorization card.
6. Mandatory bargaining issues may be raised, but neither side may insist that they be bargained over.
7. A union shop provision does not require employees to join the union; however, the labor agreement requires, as a condition of employment, that each nonunion member of the bargaining unit pay the union the equivalent of membership dues as a kind of tax, or service charge, in return for the union acting as the bargaining agent.
8. In arbitration, a dispute is submitted to an impartial third party for a binding decision; an arbitrator basically acts as a judge and jury.
9. Contrary to many opinions, unions prefer to use the strike only as a last resort.
10. Decertification is essentially the reverse of the process that employees must follow to be recognized as an official bargaining unit.

Multiple Choice

1. Which national union joined the Change to Win coalition when it broke away from the AFL-CIO?
    A. Teamsters
    B. United Food and Commercial Workers
    C. Carpenters' Union
    D. all of the above

2. Which of the following is one of the broad objectives of the labor movement?
    A. To secure and, if possible, improve the living standards and economic status of its members
    B. To enhance and, if possible, guarantee individual security against threats and contingencies that might result from market fluctuations, technological change, or management decisions
    C. To influence power relations in the social system in ways that favors and does not threaten union gains and goals
    D. all of the above

3. Who holds membership in the national union?
    A. individual workers
    B. local union
    C. only employees with years of seniority
    D. officers of the local union

4. What is the definition of *union salting*?
    A. Process of the union inundating communities with organizers to target a particular business
    B. Involve labor maneuvers that do not coincide with a strike or an organizing campaign to pressure an employer for better wages, benefits, and the like
    C. Putting pressure on the end user of a company's product in order to have a successful organizing attempt
    D. Process of training union organizers to apply for jobs at a company and, once hired, working to unionize employees

5. The first step in becoming a bargaining unit is
    A. signing of authorization cards.
    B. petition for election.
    C. election campaign.
    D. election and certification.

6. What is involved under the checkoff of dues provision?
    A. union members pays directly to the union
    B. the company agreeing to withhold dues from members' checks for the union
    C. union dues audited annually
    D. half of union dues placed in a retirement fund for employees

7. What is the definition of *mandatory bargaining issues*?
   A. Issues that may be raised, but neither side may insist that they be bargained over
   B. Issues that are statutorily outlawed
   C. Issues that fall within the definition of wages, hours, and other terms and conditions of employment
   D. Management wanting to bargain over health benefits for retired workers

8. Management's version of a union's threat to strike is a
   A. boycott.
   B. lockout.
   C. lay-off.
   D. close-down.

9. The most effective time for a union to strike is when
   A. the firm's sales are down.
   B. the firm's inventories are high.
   C. demand for the firm's products is expanding.
   D. demand for the firm's products is low.

10. What is the definition of a *boycott*?
    A. Management keeps employees out of the workplace and runs the operation with management personnel and/or replacements
    B. When union members refuse to work in order to exert pressure on management in negotiations
    C. Agreement by union members to refuse to use or buy the firm's products
    D. Use of union members to display placards and hand out leaflets, usually outside their place of business, depicting information the union wants the general public to see

Matching Exercise

Directions: On the line provided, place the letter of the statement beside the key term.

1. _____ **AFL-CIO**
2. _____ **Agency shop**
3. _____ **Arbitration**
4. _____ **Authorization card**
5. _____ **Bargaining unit**
6. _____ **Beachhead demands**
7. _____ **Boycott**
8. _____ **Two-tier wage system**
9. _____ **Card check**
10. _____ **Change to Win Coalition**
11. _____ **Checkoff of dues**
12. _____ **Closed shop**
13. _____ **Collective bargaining**
14. _____ **Craft union**
15. _____ **Decertification**
16. _____ **Flooding the community**
17. _____ **Industrial union**
18. _____ **Committee on Political Education**
19. _____ **Interest arbitration**
20. _____ **Local union**
21. _____ **Lockout**
22. _____ **Mandatory bargaining issues**
23. _____ **Mediation**
24. _____ **National union**
25. _____ **Open shop**
26. _____ **Permissive bargaining issues**
27. _____ **Public awareness campaigns**
28. _____ **Prohibited bargaining issues**
29. _____ **Rights arbitration**
30. _____ **Right-to-work laws**
31. _____ **Secondary boycott**
32. _____ **Strike**
33. _____ **Union salting**
34. _____ **Union shop**

a. Union federation consisting of the seven unions that broke from the AFL-CIO and formally launched a rival labor federation representing about 6 million workers in 2005.
b. Laws that prohibit management and unions from entering into agreements requiring union membership as a condition of employment.
c. Process of training union organizers to apply for jobs at a company and, once hired, working to unionize employees.
d. Process of the union inundating communities with organizers to target a particular business.
e. Labor maneuvers that do not coincide with a strike or organizing campaign to pressure an employer for better wages, benefits, and the like.
f. Organizing approach by labor where employees sign a card of support if they want unionization, and if 50 percent of the work force plus one worker sign a card, the union considers it a victory.
g. Basic element in the structure of the U.S. labor movement.
h. Bargaining unit, such as the Carpenters and Joiners union which is typically composed of members of a particular trade or skill in a specific locality.
i. Bargaining unit that generally consists of all the workers in a particular plant or group of plants.
j. Organization composed of local unions, which it charters.
k. Central trade union federation in the United States.
l. Performance of the mutual obligation of the employer and the representative of the employees to meet at reasonable times and confer in good faith with respect to wages, hours, and other terms and conditions of employment, or the negotiation of an agreement, or any question arising there under, and the execution of a written contract incorporating any agreement reached if requested by either party; such obligation does not compel either party to agree to a proposal or require the making of a concession.
m. Group of employees, not necessarily union members, recognized by an employer or certified by an administrative agency as appropriate for representation by a labor organization for purposes of collective bargaining.
n. Document indicating that an employee wants to be represented by a labor organization in collective bargaining.
o. Bargaining issues that fall within the definition of wages, hours, and other terms and conditions of employment; refusal to bargain in these areas is grounds for an unfair labor practice charge.
p. Issues that may be raised by management or a union; neither side may insist that they be bargained over.
q. Issues that are statutorily outlawed from collective bargaining such as the issue of the closed shop.
r. Arrangement making union membership a prerequisite for employment.
s. Requirement that all employees become members of the union after a specified period of employment (the legal minimum is 30 days) or after a union shop provision has been negotiated.
t. Labor agreement provision requiring, as a condition of employment, that each nonunion member of a bargaining unit pay the union the equivalent of membership dues as a service charge in return for the union acting as the bargaining agent.
u. Employment on equal terms to union members and nonmembers alike.
v. Agreement by which a company agrees to withhold union dues from members' paychecks and to forward the money directly to the union.
w. Demands that the union does not expect management to meet when they are first made.
x. Process in which a neutral third party enters and attempts to resolve a labor dispute when a bargaining impasse has occurred.
y. Process in which a dispute is submitted to an impartial third party for a binding decision; an arbitrator basically acts as a judge and jury.
z. Arbitration involving disputes over the interpretation and application of the various provisions of an existing contract.
aa. Arbitration that involves disputes over the terms of proposed collective bargaining agreements.
bb. Action by union members who refuse to work in order to exert pressure on management in negotiations.
cc. Refusal by union members to use or buy their firm's products.
dd. Union attempt to encourage third parties (such as suppliers and customers) to stop doing business with a firm; declared illegal by the Taft-Hartley Act.
ee. A wage structure where newly hired workers are paid less than current employees for performing the same or similar jobs.
ff. Political arm of the AFL-CIO.
gg. Management decision to keep union workers out of the workplace and runs the operation with management personnel and/or replacement workers to encourage the union to return to the bargaining table.
hh. Reverse of the process that employees must follow to be recognized as an official bargaining unit.

ANSWERS TO CHAPTER STUDY QUIZZES

Fill-in
1. Committee on Political Education
2. Industrial
3. National
4. Preparing for negotiations
5. Mandatory
6. Union shop
7. Beachhead
8. Boycott
9. Lockout
10. Decertification

True/False
1. True
2. True
3. False (craft)
4. False (national)
5. True
6. False (permissive bargaining)
7. False (agency)
8. True
9. True
10. True

Multiple Choice
1. D
2. D
3. B
4. D
5. A
6. B
7. C
8. B
9. C
10. C

Matching Exercise
1. K
2. T
3. Y
4. N
5. M
6. W
7. CC
8. EE
9. F
10. A
11. V
12. R
13. L
14. H
15. HH
16. D
17. I
18. FF
19. AA
20. G
21. GG
22. O
23. X
24. J
25. U
26. P
27. E
28. Q
29. Z
30. B
31. DD
32. BB
33. C
34. S

CHAPTER 12 Appendix

History of Unions in the United States

Key Terms
Conspiracy: Two or more persons who band together to prejudice the rights of others or of society (such as by refusing to work or demanding higher wages).
Injunction: A prohibiting legal procedure used by employers to prevent certain union activities, such as strikes and unionization attempts.
Yellow-dog contract: A written agreement between an employee and a company made at the time of employment that prohibits a worker from joining a union or engaging in union activities.

APPENDIX STUDY OUTLINE

LABOR MOVEMENT BEFORE 1930
Development of the labor movement has been neither simple nor straightforward; prior to the 1930s, the trend definitely favored management.

CONSPIRACY—Two or more persons who band together to prejudice the rights of others or of society.

INJUNCTION—A prohibiting legal procedure used by employers to prevent certain union activities, such as strikes and unionization attempts.

YELLOW-DOG CONTRACT—Written agreement between the employee and the company made at the time of employment, prohibiting a worker from joining a union or engaging in union activities.

NOBLE ORDER OF THE KNIGHTS OF LABOR—Founded in 1869 and membership grew to more than 700,000. Nucleus of the organization that became the American Federation of Labor.

SHERMAN ANTI-TRUST ACT—Marked the entrance of the federal government into the statutory regulation of labor organizations.

LABOR MOVEMENT AFTER 1930
The pendulum began to swing away from management and toward labor.

ANTI-INJUNCTION ACT (NORRIS-LAGUARDIA ACT) OF 1932—Affirms that U.S. public policy sanctions collective bargaining and approves the formation and effective operation of labor unions.

NATIONAL LABOR RELATIONS ACT (WAGNER ACT) OF 1935—National Labor Relations Board (NLRB) was created. The NLRB was given two principal functions: (1) to establish procedures for holding bargaining-unit elections and to monitor the election procedures, and (2) to investigate complaints and prevent unlawful acts involving unfair labor practices.

LABOR MANAGEMENT RELATIONS ACT (TAFT-HARTLEY ACT) OF 1947—Extended the concept of unfair labor practices to unions; permitted states to enact right-to-work laws.

LABOR-MANAGEMENT REPORTING AND DISCLOSURE ACT (LANDRUM-GRIFFIN ACT)—1959—Requires extensive reporting on numerous internal union activities and contains severe penalties for violations.

CHAPTER STUDY QUIZZES
Fill-in
1. A _____ is two or more persons who band together to prejudice the rights of others or of society (such as by refusing to work or demanding higher wages).
2. The conspiracy doctrine was softened considerably by the decision in the landmark case _____ in 1842.
3. A _____ was a written agreement between the employee and the company made at the time of employment that prohibits a worker from joining a union or engaging in union activities.
4. The Noble Order of the Knights of Labor was founded in _____ as a secret society of the Philadelphia garment workers.
5. _____ is probably the single most important individual in American trade union history.
6. In 1890, Congress passed the _____, which marked the entrance of the federal government into the statutory regulation of labor organizations.
7. Passage of the _____ legislation marked the first time that the government declared without qualification the right of private employees to join unions and bargain collectively through representatives of their own choosing without interference from their employers.
8. According to the _____, employees shall have the right to self-organization, to form, join, or assist labor organizations, to bargain collectively through representatives of their own choosing, and to engage in other concerted activities, for the purpose of collective bargaining or other mutual aid or protection.
9. John L. Lewis, president of the _____ United Mine Workers, was elected the first president of the CIO.
10. The _____ extensively revised the National Labor Relations Act.

True/False
1. The earliest unions originated toward the end of the eighteenth century.
2. The history of the labor movement has somewhat resembled the swinging of a pendulum.
3. An important feature of the injunction doctrine is that an action by one person, though legal, may become illegal when carried out by a group.
4. Samuel Gompers of the Cigarmakers Union led some 25 labor groups representing skilled trades to found the CIO in 1886.
5. The National Labor Relations Act affirms that U.S. public policy sanctions collective bargaining and approves the formation and effective operation of labor unions.
6. The National Labor Relations Act declared legislative support, on a broad scale, for the right of employees to organize and engage in collective bargaining
7. Following passage of the Wagner Act, union membership increased from approximately 3 million to 10 million between 1935 and 1947.
8. One of the most controversial elements of the Taft-Hartley Act is its Section 14b, which permits states to enact right-to-work legislation.
9. The National Labor Relations Act spelled out a Bill of Rights for Members of Labor Organizations designed to protect certain rights of individuals in their relationships with unions.
10. The Landrum-Griffin Act added additional restrictions on picketing and secondary boycotts.

Multiple Choice

1. The earliest American unions originated
    A. after the Civil War.
    B. around the turn of the century.
    C. at the end of the 18th century.
    D. at the end of the 17th century.

2. What is the definition of a *conspiracy*?
    A. Two or more persons who band together to prejudice the rights of others or of society
    B. Prohibited legal procedure used by employers to prevent certain union activities, such as strikes and unionization attempts
    C. Written agreement between the employee and the company made at the time of employment that prohibits a worker from joining a union or engaging in union activities
    D. Prohibited activity that keep unions from organizing

3. What is the definition of the *yellow-dog contract*?
    A. Two or more persons who band together to prejudice the rights of others or of society
    B. Prohibited legal procedure used by employers to prevent certain union activities, such as strikes and unionization attempts
    C. A defensive tactic that prohibits unions from organizing
    D. Written agreement between the employee and the company made at the time of employment that prohibits a worker from joining a union or engaging in union activities

4. What was the major interpretation of *Commonwealth v Hunt*?
    A. Prohibit management and unions from entering into agreements requiring union membership as a condition of employment
    B. Established the legal right of employees to decide for themselves whether or not to join or financially support a union
    C. In order for a union to be convicted under the conspiracy doctrine, it had to be shown that the union's objectives were unlawful or the means employed to gain a legal end were unlawful
    D. Required employees covered by union-shop contracts to pay initiation fees or dues in an amount which the Board finds excessive or discriminatory under all circumstances

5. What law marked the entrance of the federal government into the statutory regulation of labor organizations?
    A. Sherman Anti-Trust Act
    B. Norris-LaGuardia Act
    C. Wagner Act
    D. Taft-Hartley Act

6. What legislation marked the first time that the government declared without qualification the right of private employees to join unions and bargain collectively through representatives of their own choosing without interference from their employers?
    A. Taft-Hartley Act
    B. Railway Labor Act
    C. Sherman Anti-Trust Act
    D. Wagner Act

7. Which law affirms that U.S. public policy sanctions collective bargaining and approves the formation and effective operation of labor unions?
    A. Taft-Hartley Act
    B. Sherman Anti-Trust Act
    C. Wagner Act
    D. Norris-LaGuardia Act

8. Which act declared legislative support, on a broad scale, for the right of employees to organize and engage in collective bargaining?
    A. Norris-LaGuardia Act
    B. Taft-Hartley Act
    C. National Labor Relations Act
    D. Sherman Anti-Trust Act

9. According to the National Labor Relations Act, which of the following is a prohibited management practices deemed to be unfair to labor?
    A. Interfering with or restraining or coercing employees in the exercise of their right to self-organization
    B. Dominating or interfering in the affairs of a union
    C. Discriminating in regard to hire or tenure or any condition of employment for the purpose of encouraging or discouraging union membership
    D. All of the above

10. What is the definition of *right-to-work laws*?
    A. Laws that require that an employer pay for services not performed
    B. Laws that prohibit management and unions from entering into agreements requiring union membership as a condition of employment
    C. Laws that require employees covered by union-shop contracts to pay initiation fees or dues in an amount which the Board finds excessive or discriminatory under all circumstances
    D. Laws that cause an employer to discriminate in any way against an employee in order to encourage or discourage union membership

Matching Exercise
Directions: On the line provided, place the letter of the statement beside the key term.
1. _____ Conspiracy
2. _____ Injunction
3. _____ Yellow-dog contract

a. Two or more persons who band together to prejudice the rights of others or of society (such as by refusing to work or demanding higher wages).
b. Prohibited legal procedure used by employers to prevent certain union activities, such as strikes and unionization attempts.
c. Written agreement between an employee and a company made at the time of employment that prohibits a worker from joining a union or engaging in union activities.

ANSWERS TO CHAPTER STUDY QUIZZES
Fill-in
1. Conspiracy
2. *Commonwealth v Hunt*
3. Yellow-dog contract
4. 1869
5. Samuel Gompers
6. Sherman Anti-Trust Act
7. Railway Labor Act
8. National Labor Relations Act
9. United Mine Workers
10. Taft-Hartley Act

True/False
1. True
2. True
3. False (conspiracy)
4. False (AFL)
5. False (Norris-LaGuardia Act)
6. True
7. False (15)
8. True
9. False (Landrum-Griffin Act)
10. True

Multiple Choice
1. C
2. A
3. D
4. C
5. A
6. B
7. D
8. C
9. D
10. B

Matching Exercise
1. A
2. B
3. C

CHAPTER 13

INTERNAL EMPLOYEE RELATIONS

CHAPTER DESCRIPTION

In this chapter, employee retention is first discussed and internal employee relations and employment at will are presented. Discipline and disciplinary action are then described, followed by a discussion of the disciplinary action process. Next, approaches to disciplinary action, problems in the administration of disciplinary action, grievance handling under a collective bargaining agreement and union-free organizations are presented. This is followed by a discussion of ombudspersons and alternative dispute resolution. Termination, outsourcing terminations, and how termination differs for various groups of workers are then discussed. We then examine demotion as an alternative to termination, and the topics of transfers, promotion, resignation, and retirement are discussed. This chapter concludes with a Global Perspective entitled "Help for Expats: A Buddy Helps Find the Way."

KEY TERMS

Internal employee relations: Those human resource management activities associated with the movement of employees within the organization.
Employment at will: Unwritten contract created when an employee agrees to work for an employer but no agreement exists as to how long the parties expect the employment to last.
Discipline: State of employee self-control and orderly conduct that indicates the extent of genuine teamwork within an organization.
Disciplinary action: Invoking a penalty against an employee who fails to meet organizational standards.
Progressive disciplinary action: Approach to disciplinary action designed to ensure that the minimum penalty appropriate to the offense is imposed.
Disciplinary action without punishment: Process in which a worker is given time off with pay to think about whether he or she wants to follow the rules and continue working for the company.
Grievance: Employee's dissatisfaction or feeling of personal injustice relating to his or her employment.
Grievance procedure: Formal, systematic process that permits employees to express complaints without jeopardizing their jobs.
Alternative dispute resolution (ADR): Procedure whereby the employee and the company agree ahead of time that any problems will be addressed by an agreed-upon means.
Ombudsperson: Complaint officer who has access to top management and who hears employee complaints, investigates, and recommends appropriate action.
Demotion: Process of moving a worker to a lower level of duties and responsibilities, which typically involves a reduction in pay.
Transfer: Lateral movement of a worker within an organization.
Promotion: Movement of a person to a higher-level position in an organization.
Exit interview: Means of revealing the real reasons employees leave their jobs; it is conducted before an employee departs the company, it provides with information on how to correct the causes of discontent, and it reduce turnover.
Postexit questionnaire: Questionnaire sent to former employees several weeks after they leave the organization to determine the real reason they left.
Attitude survey: Survey that seeks input from employees to determine their feelings about topics such as the work they perform, their supervisor, their work environment, flexibility in the workplace, opportunities for advancement, training and development opportunities, and the firm's compensation system.

CHAPTER STUDY OUTLINE

WORKER RETENTION
Most managers are keenly aware of the high cost of turnover. Therefore, organizations need to constantly give them reasons to stay. Once a quality employee has been hired, half the battle has been won. The other half consists of finding ways to retain them. Sadly, many workers do not believe that their employers are putting forth much effort to retain them. Essentially, a company must have an on-going strategy to retain these valued employees.

INTERNAL EMPLOYEE RELATIONS DEFINED
Those human resource management activities associated with the movement of employees within the organization.

EMPLOYMENT AT WILL
Unwritten contract that is created when an employee agrees to work for an employer but there is no agreement as to how long the parties expect the employment to last.

DISCIPLINE AND DISCIPLINARY ACTION
Discipline is the state of employee self-control and orderly conduct that indicates the extent of genuine teamwork within an organization. **Disciplinary action** involves invoking a penalty against an employee who fails to meet organizational standards.

DISCIPLINARY ACTION PROCESS

Consider External and Internal Environment

Set Organizational Goals

Establish Rules

Communicate Rules to Employees

Observe Performance

Compare Performance with Rules

Take Appropriate Disciplinary Action

APPROACHES TO DISCIPLINARY ACTION
Several concepts regarding the administration of disciplinary action have been developed to facilitate the disciplinary process.

HOT STOVE RULE—According to this approach, disciplinary action should have the following consequences: burns immediately, provides warning, gives consistent punishment, and burns impersonally.

PROGRESSIVE DISCIPLINARY ACTION—Approach to disciplinary action designed to ensure that the minimum penalty appropriate to the offense is imposed.

DISCIPLINARY ACTION WITHOUT PUNISHMENT—Process in which a worker is given time off with pay to think about whether he or she wants to follow the rules and continue working for the company.

PROBLEMS IN THE ADMINISTRATION OF DISCIPLINARY ACTION
The reasons managers want to avoid disciplinary action include lack of training, fear, the only one, loss of friendship, time loss, loss of temper, and rationalization.

GRIEVANCE HANDLING UNDER A COLLECTIVE BARGAINING AGREEMENT
If a union represents employees in an organization, workers who believe that they have been disciplined or dealt with unjustly can appeal through the grievance and arbitration procedures of the collective bargaining agreement.

GRIEVANCE PROCEDURE—Grievance is an employee's dissatisfaction or feeling of personal injustice relating to his or her employment. Grievance procedure is a formal, systematic process that permits employees to express complaints without jeopardizing their jobs

ARBITRATION—Process that allows the parties to submit their dispute to an impartial third party for resolution.

PROOF THAT DISCIPLINARY ACTION WAS NEEDED—Employers have learned that they must prepare records that will constitute proof of disciplinary action and the reasons for it.

GRIEVANCE HANDLING IN UNION-FREE ORGANIZATIONS
While the step-by-step procedure for handling union grievances is common practice, the means of resolving complaints in union-free firms varies.

ALTERNATIVE DISPUTE RESOLUTION
Procedure whereby the employee and the company agree ahead of time that any problems will be addressed by an agreed-upon means.

OMBUDSPERSON
Ombudsperson is a complaint officer who has access to top management and who hears employee complaints, investigates, and recommends appropriate action. Ombuds are impartial, neutral counselors who can give employees confidential advice about problems ranging from abusive managers to allegations of illegal corporate activity.

TERMINATION
The most severe penalty that an organization can impose on an employee, and therefore it should be the most carefully considered disciplinary action.

OUTSOURCING TERMINATIONS
When an outsourcing firm is used in a termination situation, the consultant typically meets with the executive wanting the termination and determines and rehearses what is to be said. At the time of the firing, the consultant is at the meeting making sure the manager adheres to the script. Most of the time managers should not defer entirely to the consultant, but it helps to have the consultant around if the manager begins to get into difficulty.

TERMINATION OF EMPLOYEES AT VARIOUS LEVELS
Regardless of the similarities in the termination of employees at various levels, distinct differences exist with regard to nonmanagerial/nonprofessional employees, executives, and middle and lower-level managers and professionals.

TERMINATION OF NONMANAGERIAL/NONPROFESSIONAL EMPLOYEES—If the firm is unionized, the termination procedure is typically well defined in the labor-management agreement.

TERMINATION OF EXECUTIVES—There is likely no formal appeals procedure for executives.

TERMINATION OF MIDDLE-AND LOWER LEVEL-MANAGERS AND PROFESSIONALS—Most vulnerable and perhaps the most neglected group of employees with regard to termination has been mid-level and lower-level managers and professionals, who are generally neither members of a union nor protected by a labor agreement.

DEMOTION AS AN ALTERNATIVE TO TERMINATION
Process of moving a worker to a lower level of duties and responsibilities which typically involves a reduction in pay.

TRANSFERS
Lateral movement of a worker within an organization.

PROMOTION
Movement of a person to a higher level position in the company.

RESIGNATION
Even when an organization is totally committed to making its environment a good place to work, workers will still resign.

ANALYZING VOLUNTARY RESIGNATIONS
When a firm wants to determine the real reasons that individuals decide to leave, it can use the exit interview and/or the postexit questionnaire.

Exit interview: Means of revealing the real reasons employees leave their jobs; it is conducted before an employee departs the company, it provides with information on how to correct the causes of discontent, and it reduce turnover.

Postexit questionnaire: Questionnaire sent to former employees several weeks after they leave the organization to determine the real reason they left.

ATTITUDE SURVEYS: A MEANS OF RETAINING QUALITY EMPLOYEES
Survey that seeks input from employees to determine their feelings about topics such as the work they perform, their supervisor, their work environment, flexibility in the workplace, opportunities for advancement, training and development opportunities, and the firm's compensation system.

ADVANCE NOTICE OF RESIGNATION
Most firms would like to have at least two weeks notice of resignation from departing workers.

RETIREMENT
Most long-term employees leave an organization through retirement.

HELP FOR EXPATS: A BUDDY HELPS FIND THE WAY
Many companies are using a formal *buddy* system when sending expatriates on assignments.

EXERCISES
1. Evaluate the following violations of standards. Using progressive discipline, how might a person be terminated for each violation?
    a. late for work
    b. unclean work area
    c. insubordination

2. Which of the following would likely be covered by employment at will? Explain why or why not.
    a. tenured college professor
    b. systems analyst
    c. company president
    d. unionized machine operator

3. There are numerous Internet sites that pertain to information covered in this chapter. Identify two sites that apply to information contained in the chapter.

YOU AND HR
Memo One
To: (You) Human Resource Manager
From: Supervisor of the Janitorial Staff
Subject: Termination of an Employee

I got mad at Jim Lax and told him to "hit the road." I fired him on the spot. The guy has really been getting on my nerves lately. Always seems to have a wisecrack when I'm seriously trying to explain something to him. He'll be stopping by to get his last check. Don't worry about him. Those union guys think they own the place.

Memo One Response
To: Supervisor of the Janitorial Staff
From: (You) Industrial Relations Manager
Subject: Handling Terminations

(Your memo goes here in 50 to 75 words.)

Memo Two
To: (You) Human Resource Manager
From: New Supervisor
Subject: Discipline Advice

Billy Bob Jordon has been coming in late a good bit lately and I am concerned. He is a good worker when he is on the job. I have not said anything to him because he does a good job. But, other workers have noticed it also. Someone said that I should use progressive disciplinary action but I did not know what that was.

Please give me directions about how to use progressive discipline.

Memo Two Response
To: New Supervisor
From: (You) Human Resource Manager
Subject: Applying Progressive Discipline to Your Employees

(Your memo goes here in 100 to 150 words.)

DISCUSSION QUESTIONS
1. Define *internal employee relations*.
2. Distinguish between discipline and disciplinary action.
3. In progressive disciplinary action, what steps are involved before employee termination?
4. Define *alternative dispute resolution (ADR)*.
5. What is meant by employment at will?

CHAPTER STUDY QUIZZES
Fill-in
1. _____ is the state of employee self-control and orderly conduct that indicates the extent of genuine teamwork within an organization.
2. _____ is intended to ensure that the minimum penalty appropriate to the offense is imposed.
3. _____ is a procedure whereby the employee and the company agree that any problems will be addressed by an agreed-upon means ahead of time.
4. Approximately two of every three U.S. workers' jobs depend almost entirely on the continued _____ of their employers.
5. Effective _____ addresses the employee's wrongful behavior, not the employee as a person.
6. Today, some organizations have abandoned warnings, reprimands, probations, demotions, unpaid disciplinary suspensions, and all other punitive responses to discipline problems in favor of _____.
7. When a firm wants to determine the _____ reasons that individuals decide to leave, it can use the exit interview and/or the postexit questionnaire.
8. Most firms would like to have at least _____ notice of resignation from departing workers.
9. A (An) _____ can be broadly defined as an employee's dissatisfaction or feeling of personal injustice relating to his or her employment.
10. In _____, the parties submit their dispute to an impartial third party for binding resolution.

True/False
1. Disciplinary action is the state of employee self-control and orderly conduct that indicates the extent of genuine teamwork within an organization.
2. The hot stove rule is intended to ensure that the minimum penalty appropriate to the offense is imposed.
3. Disciplinary action without punishment gives a worker time off with pay to think about whether he or she wants to follow the rules and continue working for the company.
4. A grievance under a collective bargaining agreement is normally not well defined.
5. The final step in most grievance procedures is arbitration.
6. When the firm is union-free, workers can generally be terminated more easily.
7. Typically, the most vulnerable and perhaps the most neglected group of employees with regard to termination have been middle and lower-level managers and professionals.
8. Approximately fifty percent of U.S. workers' jobs depend almost entirely on the continued goodwill of their employers.
9. The handling of demotions in a unionized organization is usually spelled out clearly in the labor-management agreement.
10. The two best-known ADR methods are mediation and arbitration.

Multiple Choice

1. What human resource management activities are associated with internal employee relations?
    A. promotion
    B. demotion
    C. transfer
    D. all of the above

2. What is the definition of *employment at will*?
    A. Penalty against an employee who fails to meet established standards
    B. State of employee self-control and orderly conduct that indicates the extent of genuine teamwork within an organization
    C. Unwritten contract created when an employee agrees to work for an employer but no agreement exists as to how long the parties expect the employment to last
    D. Intended to ensure that the minimum penalty appropriate to the offense is imposed

3. What is the definition of *progressive disciplinary action*?
    A. Process of giving a worker time off with pay to think about whether he or she wants to follow the rules and continue working for the company
    B. Intended to ensure that the minimum penalty appropriate to the offense is imposed
    C. Action that ensures everyone who performs the same act will be punished accordingly
    D. Action that throws out formal punitive disciplinary policies for dilemmas such as chronic tardiness or a bad attitude in favor of affirming procedures that make employees want to take personal responsibility for their actions and be models for the corporate mission and vision

4. What is the definition of *disciplinary action without punishment*?
    A. Action that ensures everyone who performs the same act will be punished accordingly
    B. Action that ensures everyone who performs the same act will be punished accordingly
    C. Action that throws out formal punitive disciplinary policies for dilemmas such as chronic tardiness or a bad attitude in favor of affirming procedures that make employees want to take personal responsibility for their actions and be models for the corporate mission and vision
    D. Process of giving a worker time off with pay to think about whether he or she wants to follow the rules and continue working for the company

5. Under a collective bargaining agreement, a grievance generally is
    A. well defined.
    B. omitted.
    C. described in broad terms.
    D. ambiguously stated.

6. What is the definition of a *grievance procedure*?
    A. Employee's dissatisfaction or feeling of personal injustice relating to his or her employment
    B. Parties submit their dispute to an impartial third party for binding resolution
    C. Formal, systematic process that permits employees to express complaints without jeopardizing their jobs
    D. Procedure whereby the employee and the company agree ahead of time that any problems will be addressed by an agreed-upon means

7. What is lateral movement of workers within the organization called?
    A. demotion
    B. promotion
    C. termination
    D. transfer

8. What is the final step in most grievance procedures?
   A. mediation
   B. conciliation
   C. arbitration
   D. agreement

9. Who are the most vulnerable and perhaps the most neglected group of employees with regard to termination?
   A. executives
   B. middle and lower-level managers and professionals
   C. staff employees
   D. union members

10. Effective disciplinary action does what?
    A. addresses the employee's wrongful behavior
    B. condemns the employee and all similar workers
    C. strikes fear into the hearts of employees
    D. management's initial response to a problem

CHAPTER 13 Matching Exercise

Directions: On the line provided, place the letter of the statement beside the key term.

1. _____ **Alternative dispute resolution**
2. _____ **Attitude survey**
3. _____ **Demotion**
4. _____ **Discipline**
5. _____ **Disciplinary action**
6. _____ **Disciplinary action without punishment**
7. _____ **Employment at will**
8. _____ **Exit interview**
9. _____ **Grievance**
10. _____ **Grievance procedure**
11. _____ **Internal employee relations**
12. _____ **Ombudsperson**
13. _____ **Progressive disciplinary action**
14. _____ **Promotion**
15. _____ **Transfer**
16. _____ **Postexit questionnaire**

a. Those human resource management activities associated with the movement of employees within the organization.
b. Unwritten contract created when an employee agrees to work for an employer but no agreement exists as to how long the parties expect the employment to last.
c. State of employee self-control and orderly conduct that indicates the extent of genuine teamwork within an organization.
d. Invoking of a penalty against an employee who fails to meet established standards.
e. Approach to disciplinary action designed to ensure that the minimum penalty appropriate to the offense is imposed.
f. Process in which a worker is given time off with pay to think about whether he or she wants to follow the rules and continue working for the company.
g. Employee's dissatisfaction or feeling of personal injustice relating to his or her employment.
h. Formal, systematic process that permits employees to express complaints without jeopardizing their jobs.
i. Procedure whereby the employee and the company agree ahead of time that any problems will be addressed by an agreed-upon means.
j. Complaint officer who has access to top management and who hears employee complaints, investigates, and recommends appropriate action.
k. Process of moving a worker to a lower level of duties and responsibilities, which typically involves a reduction in pay.
l. Lateral movement of a worker within an organization.
m. Movement of a person to a higher-level position in an organization.
n. Means of revealing the real reasons employees leave their jobs; it is conducted before an employee departs the company, it provides with information on how to correct the causes of discontent, and it reduce turnover
o. Survey that seeks input from employees to determine their feelings about topics such as the work they perform, their supervisor, their work environment, flexibility in the workplace, opportunities for advancement, training and development opportunities, and the firm's compensation system.
p. Sent to former employees several weeks after they leave the organization to determine the real reason they left.

ANSWERS TO CHAPTER STUDY QUIZZES

Fill-in

1. Discipline
2. Progressive disciplinary action
3. Alternative dispute resolution
4. Goodwill
5. Disciplinary action
6. Disciplinary action without punishment
7. Real
8. Two-weeks
9. Grievance
10. Arbitration

True/False

1. False (discipline)
2. False (progressive disciplinary action)
3. True
4. False (normally well defined)
5. True
6. True
7. True
8. False (two of every three)
9. True
10. True

Multiple Choice

1. D
2. C
3. B
4. D
5. A
6. C
7. D
8. C
9. B
10. A

Matching Exercise

1. I
2. O
3. K
4. C
5. D
6. F
7. B
8. N
9. G
10. H
11. A
12. J
13. E
14. M
15. L
16. P

CHAPTER 14
GLOBAL HUMAN RESOURCE MANAGEMENT

CHAPTER DESCRIPTION

The impact of global bribery is discussed first. Then the evolution of global business and global strategic human resource management is described. Global staffing, American companies hiring foreign-born executives and global human resource development are then explained. Global compensation, global safety and health, and global health care legislation are then examined, followed by a discussion of global employee and labor relations. This chapter concludes with a look at global legal and political factors and virtual teams.

KEY TERMS

Exporting: Selling abroad, either directly or indirectly, by retaining foreign agents and distributors.
Licensing: Arrangement whereby an organization grants a foreign firm the right to use intellectual properties such as patents, copyrights, manufacturing processes, or trade names for a specific period of time.
Franchising: Option whereby the parent company grants another firm the right to do business in a prescribed manner.
Multinational corporation: Firm that is based in one country (the parent or home country) and produces goods or provides services in one or more foreign countries (host countries).
Global corporation: Organization that has corporate units in a number of countries that are integrated to operate as one organization worldwide.
Transnational corporation: Organization that moves work to the places with the talent to handle the job and the time to do it at the right cost.
Global human resource management: Utilization of global human resources to achieve organizational objectives without regard to geographic boundaries.
Expatriate: Employee who is not a citizen of the country in which a firm's operations are located, but is a citizen of the country in which the organization is headquartered.
Host-country national: Employee who is a citizen of the country where the subsidiary is located.
Third-country national: Citizen of one country, working in a second country, and employed by an organization headquartered in a third country.
Ethnocentric staffing: Staffing approach in which companies primarily hire expatriates to staff higher-level foreign positions.
Polycentric staffing: Staffing approach in which host-country nationals are used throughout the organization, from top to bottom.
Regiocentric staffing: Staffing approach that is similar to the polycentric staffing approach, but regional groups of subsidiaries reflecting the organization's strategy and structure work as a unit.
Geocentric staffing: Staffing approach that uses a worldwide integrated business strategy.
Repatriation: Process of bringing expatriates home.
Tariffs: Taxes collected on goods that are shipped across national boundaries.
Quotas: Policies that limit the number or value of goods that can be imported across national boundaries.

CHAPTER STUDY OUTLINE

GLOBAL BRIBERY
It is getting tougher to get by with bribery in the international arena these days since more than 30 countries have passed anti-bribery laws. The U.S. is also more rigorously enforcing the Foreign Corrupt Practices Act, which prohibits U.S. firms from bribing foreign officials.

EVOLUTION OF GLOBAL BUSINESS

EXPORTING—Selling abroad, either directly or indirectly, by retaining foreign agents and distributors.

LICENSING—Arrangement whereby an organization grants a foreign firm the right to use intellectual properties such as patents, copyrights, manufacturing processes, or trade names for a specific period of time.

FRANCHISING—Option whereby the parent company grants another firm the right to do business in a prescribed manner.

MULTINATIONAL CORPORATION—Firm that is based in one country (the parent or home country) and produces goods or provides services in one or more foreign countries (host countries).

GLOBAL CORPORATION—Organization that has corporate units in a number of countries that are integrated to operate as one organization worldwide.

GLOBAL STRATEGIC HUMAN RESOURCE MANAGEMENT
Those engaged in the management of global human resources develop and work through an integrated global human resource management system similar to the one they experience domestically.

GLOBAL STAFFING
Utilization of global human resources to achieve organizational objectives without regard to geographic boundaries.

TYPE OF STAFF MEMBERS

Expatriate: Employee who is not a citizen of the country in which a firm's operations are located, but is a citizen of the country in which the organization is headquartered.

Host-country national: Employee who is a citizen of the country where the subsidiary is located.

Third-country national: Citizen of one country, working in a second country, and employed by an organization headquartered in a third country.

APPROACHES TO GLOBAL STAFFING

Ethnocentric staffing: Staffing approach in which companies primarily hire expatriates to staff higher-level foreign positions.

Polycentric staffing: Staffing approach in which host-country nationals are used throughout the organization, from top to bottom.

Regiocentric staffing: Staffing approach that is similar to the polycentric staffing approach, but regional groups of subsidiaries reflecting the organization's strategy and structure work as a unit.

Geocentric staffing: Staffing approach that uses a worldwide integrated business strategy.

SELECTING EXPATRIATES—Expatriates are often selected from those already within the organization and the process involves four distinct stages: self-selection, creating a candidate pool, technical skills assessment, and making a mutual decision.

BACKGROUND INVESTIGATION—Background investigations when working in the global environment are equally, or more, important but differences across cultures and countries often put up barriers to overcome.

HIRING TEMPS IN JAPAN—Employers in Japan have discovered a new way to find part-time workers in a hurry. They use global positioning system in cell phones to find them.

AMERICAN COMPANIES HIRING FOREIGN-BORN EXECUTIVES
A growing number of American companies are hiring foreign-born CEOs. What do PepsiCo, Coca-Cola Company, and Citigroup, have in common? They all have CEOs that were born or raised in another countries.

GLOBAL HUMAN RESOURCE DEVELOPMENT
Global training and development is needed because people, jobs, and organizations are often quite different globally.

EXPATRIATE TRAINING AND DEVELOPMENT—Training of employees going on a global assignment has often been bleak but appears to be improving. The development process should start as soon as the workforce is selected, even before beginning global operations if possible.

PRE-MOVE ORIENTATION AND TRAINING—Pre-move orientation involves training and familiarization in language, culture, history, living conditions, and local customs and peculiarities.

CONTINUAL DEVELOPMENT: ONLINE ASSISTANCE AND TRAINING—Companies are now offering Internet service in the areas of career services, cross-cultural training and employee assistance programs.

REPATRIATION ORIENTATION AND TRAINING—Orientation and training are also necessary prior to repatriation, which is the process of bringing expatriates home.

GLOBAL E-LEARNING—The costs of a training program include the instructor's salary, materials costs, travel costs, meeting room expenses, and the salaries and benefits of the people attending the program, in addition to the costs of the program. E-learning allows companies to keep the money and still receive a good training product.

GLOBAL COMPENSATION
Probably the main reason that organizations relocate to other areas of the world is because of high wage pressures that threaten their ability to compete on a global basis.

COMPENSATION FOR HOST-COUNTRY NATIONALS—Globally, the question of what constitutes a fair day's pay is not as complicated as it is in the United States; normally, it is slightly above the prevailing wage rates in the area.

EXPATRIATE COMPENSATION—International assignments for expatriates cost three to five times an assignee's host-country salary per year and more if currency exchange rates become unfavorable.

UNIQUE BENEFITS IN JAPAN—Some Japanese companies have benefits that might appear quite odd in the U.S. Because of a high demand for qualified workers, employers are constantly working to keep workers satisfied.

GLOBAL SAFETY AND HEALTH
Safety and health aspects of the job are important because employees who work in a safe environment and enjoy good health are more likely to be productive and yield long-term benefits to the organization.

GLOBAL HEALTH CARE LEGISLATION
Health care legislation is often different as a person goes from country to country.

GLOBAL EMPLOYEES AND LABOR RELATIONS
While unionism has waned in the United States, it has maintained much of its strength abroad.

GLOBAL LEGAL AND POLITICAL FACTORS—Nature and stability of legal and political systems vary throughout the globe.

> **TARIFFS**—Taxes collected on goods that are shipped across national boundaries.

> **QUOTAS**—Policies that limit the number or value of goods that can be imported across national boundaries.

VIRTUAL TEAMS IN A GLOBAL ENVIRONMENT
Virtual teams for multinational companies which operate across boundaries of time and geography have become a necessity of everyday working life.

EXERCISES

1. Other than technical competency for the job, what characteristics should a person possess for a global job in the following countries?
    a. plant manager in Great Britain
    b. engineer in Saudi Arabia
    c. plant manager in France

2. What obstacles might have to be overcome to open a global organization for the following?
    a. Coca-Cola in China
    b. Lands End in Great Britain
    c. Ford manufacturing in Thailand

3. There are numerous Internet sites that pertain to information covered in this chapter. Identify two sites that apply to information contained in the chapter.

YOU AND HR
Memo One
To: (You) Vice President—Human Resources
From: President, International Operations
Subject: Early Return to the United States

Another good manager told me today that his overseas assignment just was not what he thought it would be. He said if the company did not find a stateside assignment for him then he would find a job with another company. We are losing too many good managers. Are we preparing them right for their overseas assignments? See what other companies are doing and prepare an orientation program for my review, immediately!

Memo One Response
To: President, International Operations
From: (You) Vice President—Human Resources
Subject: Overseas Orientation Recommendations

(Your memo goes here in 75 to 100 words.)

Memo Two
To: (You) Human Resource Manager
From: Company President
Subject: Going Overseas

Bicycle transportation is big in China and there is a shortage of good quality, low priced bikes. I want you to determine the factors to be considered if we opened a bicycle plant similar to our Clarksdale, Mississippi plant in China. I know that I caught you off guard but I believe there are good opportunities in China. Make this a priority.

Memo Two Response
To: Company President
From: (You) Human Resource Manager
Subject: Factors to Consider in Opening a Plant in China

(Your memo goes here in 75 to 100 words.)

DISCUSSION QUESTIONS
1. How has the Foreign Corrupt Practices Act affected United States companies doing business in the multinational environment?
2. What is the difference between exporting, licensing, and franchising?
3. What is the difference between an expatriate, host-country national, and third-country national? Give an example of each.
4. What constitutes a fair-day's pay for host-country nationals?
5. How has globalization created a special need for e-learning?

CHAPTER STUDY QUIZZES
Fill-in
1. _____ is an arrangement whereby an organization grants a foreign firm the right to use intellectual properties such as patents, copyrights, manufacturing processes, or trade names for a specific period of time.
2. A (An) _____ has corporate units in a number of countries that are integrated to operate as one organization worldwide.
3. When host-country nationals are used throughout the organization, from top to bottom, it is referred to as _____.
4. _____ is a staffing approach that uses a worldwide integrated business strategy.
5. A (An) _____ is an employee who is a citizen of the country where the subsidiary is located.
6. _____ is the process of bringing expatriates home.
7. Certainly, in compensation-related matters, organizations should think globally but act _____.
8. Regarding tax equalization payments, under Internal Revenue Service rules, U.S. citizens living overseas can exclude from taxes up to _____ of income earned abroad.
9. With _____ staffing, companies primarily hire expatriates to staff higher-level foreign positions.
10. In Sweden, _____ percent of its employees are union members.

True/False
1. Franchising is an arrangement whereby an organization grants a foreign firm the right to use intellectual properties such as patents, copyrights, manufacturing processes, or trade names for a specific period of time.
2. A global corporation is a firm that is based in one country (the parent or home country) and produces goods or provides services in one or more foreign countries (host countries).
3. Companies primarily hire expatriates to staff higher-level foreign positions with ethnocentric staffing.
4. Regiocentric staffing is similar to the ethnocentric approach, but regional groups of subsidiaries reflecting the organizations strategy and structure work as a unit.
5. A third-country national is an employee who is a citizen of the country where the subsidiary is located.
6. Generally, expatriates are used to ensure that foreign operations are linked effectively with parent corporations.
7. Globalization has created a special need for e-learning.
8. Repatriation is the process of bringing expatriates home.
9. In compensation related matters, organizations should think globally but act locally.
10. While unionism has waned in the United States, it has maintained much of its strength abroad.

Multiple Choice

1. What is the definition of *exporting*?
    A. Arrangement whereby an organization grants a foreign firm the right to use intellectual properties such as patents, copyrights, manufacturing processes, or trade names for a specific period of time
    B. Entails selling abroad, either directly or indirectly, by retaining foreign agents and distributors
    C. Option where the parent company grants another firm the right to do business in a prescribed manner
    D. Directs manufacturing and marketing operations in several countries

2. What is the definition of *franchising*?
    A. Arrangement whereby an organization grants a foreign firm the right to use intellectual properties such as patents, copyrights, manufacturing processes, or trade names for a specific period of time
    B. Entails selling abroad, either directly or indirectly, by retaining foreign agents and distributors
    C. Option where the parent company grants another firm the right to do business in a prescribed manner
    D. Directs manufacturing and marketing operations in several countries

3. What is the definition of a *global corporation*?
    A. Firm that is based in one country (the parent or home country) and produces goods or provides services in one or more foreign countries (host countries)
    B. Organization that has corporate units in a number of countries that are integrated to operate as one organization worldwide
    C. Directs manufacturing and marketing operations in several countries
    D. Operations are coordinated by a parent company, usually based in the firm's home country

4. What is the definition of an *expatriate*?
    A. Employee who is a citizen of the country where the subsidiary is located
    B. Citizen of one country, working in a second country, and employed by an organization headquartered in a third country
    C. Employee who is not a citizen of the country in which the firm operations are located, but is a citizen of the country in which the organization is headquartered
    D. Hiring local people and operating the company like local companies whenever possible

5. What type of employees are used to ensure that foreign operations are linked effectively with parent corporations?
    A. foreigners
    B. third-country national
    C. expatriate
    D. host-country national

6. With regard to background investigation, which country prohibits criminal checks of its citizens?
    A. Mexico
    B. Japan
    C. Canada
    D. France

7. What is the process of bringing expatriates home referred to as?
    A. repatriation
    B. developmental
    C. home-country training
    D. home training

8. Approximately what percent of workers from Sweden are unionized?
   A. 26
   B. 56
   C. 76
   D. 96

9. Citizens living overseas can exclude from taxes up to how much income earned abroad with regard to tax equalization payments, under Internal Revenue Service rules?
   A. $30,000
   B. $25,000
   C. $15,000
   D. $80,000

10. What is the definition of *ethnocentric staffing*?
    A. When host-country nationals are used throughout the organization, from top to bottom
    B. Companies primarily hire expatriates to staff higher-level foreign positions
    C. Regional groups of subsidiaries reflecting the organization's strategy and structure work as a unit
    D. Staffing approach that uses a worldwide integrated business strategy

Matching Exercise
Directions: On the line provided, place the letter of the statement beside the key term.

1. _____ **Transnational corporation**
2. _____ **Ethnocentric staffing**
3. _____ **Expatriate**
4. _____ **Exporting**
5. _____ **Franchising**
6. _____ **Geocentric staffing**
7. _____ **Global corporation**
8. _____ **Global human resource management**
9. _____ **Host-country national**
10. _____ **Licensing**
11. _____ **Multinational corporation (MNC)**
12. _____ **Polycentric staffing**
13. _____ **Quotas**
14. _____ **Regiocentric staffing**
15. _____ **Repatriation**
16. _____ **Tariffs**
17. _____ **Third-country national**

a. Moves work to the places with the talent to handle the job and the time to do it at the right cost.
b. Selling abroad, either directly or indirectly, by retaining foreign agents and distributors.
c. Arrangement whereby an organization grants a foreign firm the right to use intellectual properties such as patents, copyrights, manufacturing processes, or trade names for a specific period of time.
d. Option whereby the parent company grants another firm the right to do business in a prescribed manner.
e. Firm that is based in one country (the parent or home country) and produces goods or provides services in one or more foreign countries (host countries).
f. Organization that has corporate units in a number of countries that are integrated to operate as one organization worldwide.
g. Use of global human resources to achieve organizational objectives without regard to geographic boundaries.
h. Employee who is not a citizen of the country in which the firm's operation (or subsidiary) is located but is a citizen of the country in which the organization is headquartered.
i. Employee who is a citizen of the country where the subsidiary is located.
j. Citizen of one country, working in a second country, and employed by an organization headquartered in a third country.
k. Staffing approach in which companies primarily hire expatriates to staff higher-level foreign positions.
l. Staffing approach where host-country nationals are used throughout the organization, from top to bottom.
m. Staffing approach that is similar to the polycentric staffing approach, but regional groups of subsidiaries reflecting the organization's strategy and structure work as a unit.
n. Staffing approach that uses a worldwide-integrated business strategy.
o. Process of bringing expatriates home.
p. Taxes collected on goods that are shipped across national boundaries.
q. Policies that limit the number or value of goods that can be imported across national boundaries.

ANSWERS TO CHAPTER STUDY QUIZZES

Fill-in
1. Licensing
2. Global corporation
3. Polycentric staffing
4. Geocentric staffing
5. Host-country national
6. Repatriation
7. Locally
8. $80,000
9. Ethnocentric
10. 96

True/False
1. False (licensing)
2. False (multinational corporation)
3. True
4. False (polycentric)
5. False (host-country national)
6. True
7. True
8. True
9. True
10. True

Multiple Choice
1. B
2. C
3. B
4. C
5. C
6. B
7. A
8. D
9. D
10. B

Matching Exercise
1. A
2. K
3. H
4. B
5. D
6. N
7. F
8. G
9. I
10. C
11. E
14. L
15. Q
16. M
17. O
18. P
17. J